Artificial Immune System

IEEE PRESS

About IEEE Computer Society
IEEE Computer Society is the world's leading computing membership organization and the trusted information and career-development source for a global workforce of technology leaders including: professors, researchers, software engineers, IT professionals, employers, and students. The unmatched source for technology information, inspiration, and collaboration, the IEEE Computer Society is the source that computing professionals trust to provide high-quality, state-of-the-art information on an on-demand basis. The Computer Society provides a wide range of forums for top minds to come together, including technical conferences, publications, and a comprehensive digital library, unique training webinars, professional training, and the TechLeader Training Partner Program to help organizations increase their staff's technical knowledge and expertise, as well as the personalized information tool myComputer. To find out more about the community for technology leaders, visit http://www.computer.org.

IEEE/Wiley Partnership
The IEEE Computer Society and Wiley partnership allows the CS Press authored book program to produce a number of exciting new titles in areas of computer science, computing, and networking with a special focus on software engineering. IEEE Computer Society members continue to receive a 15% discount on these titles when purchased through Wiley or at wiley.com/ieeecs.

To submit questions about the program or send proposals, please contact Mary Hatcher, Editor, Wiley-IEEE Press: Email: mhatcher@wiley.com, Telephone: 201-748-6903, John Wiley & Sons, Inc., 111 River Street, MS 8-01, Hoboken, NJ 07030-5774.

Artificial Immune System
Applications in Computer Security

Ying Tan

WILEY

Published by John Wiley & Sons, Inc., Hoboken, New Jersey.
Published simultaneously in Canada.

For general information on our other products and services or for technical support, please contact our Customer Care Department within the United States at (800) 762-2974, outside the United States at (317) 572-3993 or fax (317) 572-4002.

Wiley also publishes its books in a variety of electronic formats. Some content that appears in print may not be available in electronic formats. For more information about Wiley products, visit our web site at www.wiley.com.

Library of Congress Cataloging-in-Publication Data is available.

ISBN: 978-1-119-07628-5

Printed in the United States of America.

10 9 8 7 6 5 4 3 2 1

*This book is dedicated to my wife, Chao Deng
and my daughter, Fei Tan*

Contents

List of Figures

List of Tables

Preface

The most terrible threats to the security of computers and networking systems are the so-called computer virus and unknown intrusion. The rapid development of evasion techniques used in viruses invalidate the well-known signature-based computer virus detection techniques, so a number of novel virus detection approaches have been proposed to cope with this vital security issue. Because the natural similarities between the biological immune system (BIS) and computer security system, the artificial immune system (AIS) has been developed as a new field in the community of anti-virus researches. The various principles and mechanisms in BIS provide unique opportunities to build novel computer virus detection models with abilities of robustness and adaptiveness in detecting the known and unknown viruses.

Biological immune systems are hierarchical natural systems featuring high distribution, parallelization, and the ability to process complex information, among other useful features. It is also a dynamically adjusting system that is characterized by the abilities of learning, memory, recognition, and cognition, such that the BIS is good at recognizing and removing antigens effectively for the purpose of protection of the organism. The BIS makes full use of various intelligent ways to react to an antigen's intrusions, producing accurate immune responses by means of intrinsic and adaptive immune abilities. Through mutation, evolution, and learning to adapt to new environments, along with memory mechanisms, BIS can react much stronger and faster against foreign antigens and their likes. The BIS consists of intrinsic immune (i.e., non-specific immune) and adaptive immune (i.e., specific immune) responses that mutually cooperate to defend against foreign antigens.

An artificial immune system is an adaptive system inspired by theoretical immunology and observed immune functions, principles, and models, which are applied for problem solving. In another words, the AIS is a computational system inspired by the BIS, sometime also referred to as the second brain, made up of computational intelligence paradigms. The AIS is a dynamic, adaptive, robust, and distributed learning system. Because it has fault tolerance and noise resistance, it is very suitable for applications in time-varying unknown environments. The AIS has been applied to many complex problem fields, such as optimization, pattern recognition, fault and anomaly diagnosis, network intrusion detection, and virus detection, as well as many others.

Generally speaking, the AIS could be roughly classified into two major categories: population-based and network-based algorithms. Network-based algorithms make use of the concepts of immune network theory, while population-based algorithms use theories and models such as negative selection principle, clonal principle, danger theory, and others. During the past decades, there have been a large number of immune theories and models, such as self and nonself models, clonal selection algorithm, immune network, dendritic cell algorithms, danger theory, and so on. By mimicking BIS's mechanisms and functions, AIS has developed and is now widely used in anomaly detection, fault detection, pattern recognition, optimization, learning, and so on. Like its biological counterpart, AIS is also characterized by noise-tolerance, unsupervised learning, self-organization, memorizing, recognition, and so on.

In particular, anomaly detection techniques decide whether an unknown test sample is produced by the underlying probability distribution that corresponds to the training set of normal examples. The pioneering work of Forrest and associates led to a great deal of research and proposals of immune-inspired anomaly detection systems. For example, as for the self and nonself model, the central challenges with anomaly detection is determining the difference between normal and potentially harmful activity. Usually, only self (normal) class is available for training the system regardless of nonself (anomaly) class. Thus, the essence of the anomaly detection task is that the training set contains instances only from the self class, while the test set contains instances of both self and nonself classes. Specifically, computer security and virus detection should be regarded as the typical examples of anomaly detection in artificial immune systems whose task is protecting computers from viruses, unauthorized users, and so on. In computer security, AIS has a very strong capability of anomaly detection for defending against unknown viruses and intrusions. The adaptability is also a very important feature for AIS to learn unknown viruses and intrusions as well as quickly reacting to the learned ones. Other features of AIS like distributability, autonomy, diversity, and disposability are also required for the flexibility and stability of AIS.

Therefore, the features of the BIS are just what a computer security system needs, meanwhile the functions of BIS and computer security system are similar to each other to some extent. Therefore, the biological immune principles provide effective solutions to computer security issues. The research and development of AIS-based computer security detection are receiving increasing attention. The application of immune principles and mechanisms can better protect the computer and improve the network environment greatly.

In recent years, computer and networking technologies have developed rapidly and been used more and more widely in our daily life. At the same time, computer security issues appear frequently. The large varieties of malwares, especially new variants and unknown ones, always seriously threaten computers. What is worse is that malwares are getting more complicated and delicate, with faster speed and greater damage. Meanwhile, a huge number of spam not only occupy storage and network bandwidth, but also waste users' time to handle them, resulting in a great loss of productivity. Although many classic solutions have been proposed, there are still many limitations in dealing with the real-world computer security issues.

A computer virus is a program or a piece of code that can infect other programs by modifying them to include an evolved copy of it. Broadly, one can regard the computer virus as the malicious code designed to harm or secretly access a computer system without the owners' informed consent, such as viruses, worms, backdoors, Trojans, harmful Apps, hacker codes, and so on. All programs that are not authorized by users and that perform harmful operations in the background are referred to as viruses; they are characterized by several salient features including infectivity, destruction, concealment, latency, triggering, and so on.

Computer viruses have evolved with computer technologies and systems. Generally speaking, the development of viruses has gone through several phases, including the DOS boot phase, DOS executable phase, virus generator phase, macro virus phase, as well as virus techniques merging with hacker techniques. As computer viruses have developed and proliferated, they have become the main urgent threat to the security of computers and Internet.

The battle between viruses and anti-virus techniques is an endless warfare. Computer viruses disguise themselves by means of various kinds of evasion techniques, including metamorphic and polymorphous techniques, packer and encryption techniques, to name a few. To confront these critical situations, anti-virus techniques have to unpack the suspicious programs, decrypt them, and try to be robust to these evasion techniques. The viruses are also trying to evolve to anti-unpack, anti-decrypt, and develop to obfuscate the anti-virus techniques. The fighting between viruses and anti-virus techniques is very serious and will last forever.

Nowadays, varieties of novel viruses' techniques are continuously emergent and are often one step ahead of the anti-virus techniques. A good anti-virus technique should have to increase the difficulty of viruses' intrusion, decrease the losses caused by the viruses, and react to an outbreak of viruses as quickly as possible.

Many host-based anti-virus solutions have been proposed by researchers and companies, which could be roughly classified into three categories—static techniques, dynamic techniques, and heuristics.

Static techniques usually work on bit strings, assembly codes, and application programming interface (API) calls of a program without running the program. One of the most famous static techniques is the signature-based virus detection technique, in which a signature usually is a bit string divided from a virus sample and can identify the virus uniquely.

Dynamic techniques keep watching over the execution of every program in real time and observe the behaviors of the program. The dynamic techniques usually utilize the operating system's API sequences, system calls, and other kinds of behavior characteristics to identify the purpose of a program.

Heuristic approaches make full use of various heuristic knowledge and information in the program and its environments, by using intelligent computing techniques such as machine learning, data mining, evolutionary computing, AIS, and so on, for detecting viruses, which not only can fight the known viruses efficiently, but also can detect new variants and unseen viruses.

Because classic detection approaches of computer viruses are not able to efficiently detect new variants of viruses and unseen viruses, it is urgent to study novel virus detection approaches in depth. As for this point, the immune principle-based computer virus detection approaches have been becoming a priority choice in the community of the anti-virus researchers because it is characterized by the strong detection capability for new variants of viruses and unseen viruses. The immune-based computer virus detection approaches are able to detect new variants and unseen viruses at low false positive rates with limited overheads. These approaches have developed into a new field for computer virus detection and attracted more and more researchers and practitioners.

The computer virus has compared to a biological virus because of their similarities, such as parasitism, propagation, infection, ability to hide, and destruction. The BIS protects the body from antigens from the very beginning of life successfully, resolving the problem of defeating unseen antigens. The computer security system has functions similar to the BIS. Furthermore, the features of the AIS, such as dynamic, adaptive, robust, are also needed in the computer anti-virus system. Applying immune principles to detect viruses enables us to recognize new variants and unseen viruses by using existing knowledge. The immune principle-based virus detection approaches would own many finer features, such as being dynamic, adaptive, and robust. The AIS is considered to be able to make up for the faults of the signature-based virus detection techniques. The immune-based computer virus detection approaches have paved a new way for anti-virus research in the past decades.

Although a number of virus detection models based on immune principles have achieved great success, in particular, in detecting new variants and unseen viruses under unknown environments, there exist a few drawbacks in the AIS-based virus detection, such as a lack of rigorous theoretical analysis and very simple simulations between the AIS and the BIS. Therefore, there is still a long way to go for us to apply the immune-based virus detection approaches to the real-world computer security systems.

The objective of this book is to present our proposed major theories and models as well as their applications in malware detection in recent years, for academia, researchers, and engineering practitioners who are involved or interested in the study, use, design, and development of artificial immune systems (AIS) and AIS-based solutions to computer security issues. Furthermore, this book provides a single record of our achievements to date in computer security based on immune principles.

This book is designed for a professional audience who wishes to learn about the state of the art of artificial immune systems and AIS-based malware detection approaches. More specifically, the book offers a theoretical perspective and practical solutions to researchers, practitioners, and graduates who are working in the areas of artificial immune system-based computer security.

The organization of this book is arranged in a manner from simple to complex. In order to understand the contents of this book comprehensively, the readers should have some fundamentals of computer architecture and software, computer virus, artificial intelligence, computational intelligence, pattern recognition, and machine learning.

I hope this book will help shape the research of AIS-based malware detection appropriately and gives the state of art AIS-based malware detection methods and algorithms for interested readers who might find many algorithms in the book that are helpful for their projects, furthermore, some algorithms can also be viewed as a starting point for researchers to work with.

In addition, many newly proposed malware detection methods in didactic approach with detailed materials are presented and their excellent performance is illustrated by a number of experiments and comparisons with the state-of-the-art malware detection techniques. Furthermore, a collection of references, resources, and source codes is listed in some webpages that are available free at http://www.cil. pku.edu.cn/research/anti-malware/index.html, http://www.cil.pku.edu.cn/resources/ and http://www.cil.pku.edu.cn/publications/.

This monograph is organized into 11 chapters, which will be briefly described next.

In Chapter 1, AIS is presented after a brief introduction of BIS. Several typical AIS algorithms are presented in detail, followed by features and applications of AIS.

In Chapter 2, introductions to malware and its detection methods are described in detail. As malware has become a challenge to the security of the computer system, a number of detecting approaches have been proposed to cope with the situation. These approaches are classified into three categories: static techniques, dynamic techniques, and heuristics. The classic malware detection approaches and immune-based malware detection approaches are briefly introduced after the background knowledge of malware is given. The immune-based malware detection approaches have paved a new way for anti-malware research.

Because the detection of unknown malware is one of most important tasks in Computer Immune System (CIS) studies, by using nonself detection techniques, the diversity of anti-body (Ab) and neural networks (NN), an NN-based malware detection algorithm is proposed in Chapter 3. A number of experiments are conducted to illustrate that this algorithm has a high detection rate with a very low false-positive rate.

In Chapter 4, by using the negative selection principle in BIS, a novel generating algorithm of detector, that is, multiple-point bit mutation method, is proposed, which utilizes random multiple-point mutation to look for nonself detectors in a large range in the whole space of detectors, such that we can obtain a required detector set in a reasonable computational time.

A virus detection system (VDS) based on AIS is proposed in Chapter 5. The VDS at first generates the detector set from virus files in the dataset, negative selection and clonal selection are applied to the detector set to eliminate auto-immunity detectors and increase the diversity of the detector set in the nonself space. Two novel hybrid distances called hamming-max and shift r-bit continuous distance are proposed to calculate the affinity vectors of each file using the detector set. The VDS compares the detection rates using three classifiers, k-nearest neighbor (KNN), RBF networks, and SVM when the length of detectors is 32-bit and 64-bit, respectively. The experimental results show that the proposed VDS has a strong detection ability and good generalization performance.

As viruses become more complex, existing anti-virus methods are inefficient to detect various forms of viruses, especially new variants and unknown viruses. Inspired by the immune system, a hierarchical artificial immune system (AIS) model, which is based on matching in three layers, is proposed to detect a variety of forms of viruses in Chapter 6. Experimental results demonstrate that the proposed model can recognize obfuscated viruses efficiently with an average recognition rate of 94 percent, including new variants of viruses and unknown viruses.

In Chapter 7, a malware detection model based on the negative selection algorithm with a penalty factor was proposed to overcome the drawbacks of traditional negative selection algorithms (NSA) in defining the harmfulness of self and nonself. Unlike danger theory, the proposed model is able to detect malware through dangerous signatures extracted from programs. Instead of deleting nonself that matches self, the NSA with penalty factor (NSAPF) penalizes the nonself using penalty factor C and keeps these items in a library. In this way, the effectiveness of the proposed model is improved by the dangerous signatures that would have been discarded in the traditional NSA.

A danger feature-based negative selection algorithm (NFNSA) is presented in Chapter 8, which divides the danger feature space into four parts, and reserves the information of danger features to the utmost extent for measuring the danger of a sample efficiently. Comprehensive experimental results suggest that the DFNSA is able to reserve as much information of danger features as possible, and the DFNSA malware detection model is effective to detect unseen malware by measuring the danger of a sample precisely.

In Chapter 9, immune concentration is used to detect malwares. The local concentration-based malware detection method connects a certain number of two-element local concentration vectors as feature vector. To achieve better detection performance, particle swarm optimization (PSO) is used to optimize the parameters of local concentration. Then the hybrid concentration-based feature extraction (HCFE) approach is presented by extracting the hybrid concentration (HC) of malware in both global and local resolutions.

In Chapter 10, inspired from the immune cooperation (IC) mechanism in BIS, an IC mechanism-based learning (ICL) framework is proposed. In this framework, a sample can be expressed as an antigen-specific feature vector and an antigen-nonspecific feature vector at first, respectively, simulating the antigenic determinant and danger features in BIS. The antigen-specific and antigen-nonspecific classifiers score the two vectors and export real-valued Signal 1 and Signal 2, respectively. In collaboration with the two signals, the sample can be classified by the cooperation classifier, which resolves the signal conflict problem at the same time. The ICL framework simulates the BIS in the view of immune signals and takes full advantage of the cooperation effect of the immune signals, which improves the performance of the ICL framework dramatically.

Chapter 11 presents a new statistic named class-wise information gain (CIG). Different from information gain (IG) that only selects global features for a classification problem, the CIG is able to select the features with the highest information content for a specific class in a problem. On the basis of the CIG, a novel CIG-based malware detection method is proposed to efficiently detect malware loaders and infected executables in the wild.

Finally, a keyword index completes the book.

Due to the limited specialty knowledge and capability of mine, a few errors, typos, and inadequacies are bound to occur. The readers' critical comments and valuable suggestions are warmly welcomed at ytan@pku.edu.cn.

YING TAN
Beijing, China

Acknowledgments

I would like to thank my colleagues and students who provided strong assistance in research on such an amazing issue. I am grateful to my students who took part in the research work for this book under my guidance at Computational Intelligence Laboratory at Peking University (CIL@PKU), Institute of Intelligent Information System (IIIS) at Electronic Engineering Institute (EEI), and University of Science and Technology of China (USTC).

Almost the entire content of this book is excerpted from the research works and academic papers published by myself and my supervised PhD students and Master students, including Dr. Zhenghe GUO, Dr. Yuanchun ZHU, Dr. Wei WANG, Dr. Pengtao ZHANG, Mr. Rui CHAO, and my current graduate Mr. Weiwei HU. I would like to deliver my special thanks to all of them here. Without their hard work and unremitting efforts, it would have been impossible for me to make this book a reality.

The author owes his gratitude to all colleagues and students who have collaborated directly or indirectly with research on this issue and in writing this book.

I thank Mr. James W. Murphy and Miss Mary Hatcher, an editor at Wiley-IEEE Press, for their kind coordination and help in reviewing the manuscript of this book. I am also grateful to the editors from Wiley-IEEE Press, for their continued assistance and encouragement throughout the writing of this monograph.

While working on the topics of this book I was supported by the Natural Science Foundation of China (NSFC) under grant no. 61170057, 60673020, 60273100, 61375119, and 60875080 and Beijing Natural Science Foundation (4162029), partially supported by National Key Basic Research Development Plan (973 Plan) Project of China with grant no. 2015CB352302, and supported in part by the National High Technology Research and Development Program of China (863 Program) with Grant No. 2007AA01Z453. I would also like to thank the Natural Science Foundation of China (NSFC) and Ministry of Science and Technology of China greatly for their generous financial supports.

Finally, I am particularly grateful for the patience, support, and understanding of my family throughout many evenings and weekends devoted to this project.

About the Author

Dr. Ying Tan is a full professor and PhD advisor at the School of Electronics Engineering and Computer Science of Peking University and director of the Computational Intelligence Laboratory at Peking University (CIL@PKU: http://www.cil.pku.edu.cn). He received his BEng from Electronic Engineering Institute, MSc from Xidian University, and PhD from Southeast University, in 1985, 1988, and 1997, respectively.

His research interests include computational intelligence, swarm intelligence, data mining, machine learning, pattern recognition, intelligent information processing for information security, and fireworks algorithm. He has published more than 280 papers and authored or co-authored six books and more than ten chapters in various books. He has received three invention patents.

He serves as the editor-in-chief of the *International Journal of Computational Intelligence and Pattern Recognition* (IJCIPR), and is an associate editor of *IEEE Transactions on Cybernetics* (Cyb), and *IEEE Transactions on Neural Networks and Learning Systems* (TNNLS).

He also served as an editor of Springer's *Lecture Notes on Computer Science* (LNCS) for fifteen volumes, and has been a guest editor of several journals, including *Information Science, Softcomputing, Neurocomputing, IEEE/ACM Transactions on Computational Biology and Bioinformatics* (IEEE/ACM TCBB), *Natural Computing*, and others. He was the general chair of ICSI-CCI 2015 joint conference, was the founding general chair of the International Conference on Swarm Intelligence (ICSI 2010-2014), and was program committee co-chair of IEEE WCCI'2014. He is a senior member of IEEE.

Chapter 1

Artificial Immune System

1.1 INTRODUCTION

People have had a keen interest in the biosphere since ancient times and have gotten inspiration from the structures and functions of biological systems and their regulatory mechanisms continuously. Since the mid-twentieth century, researchers have focused on the simulation of biological systems, especially the structures and functions of human beings. For example, artificial neural network simulates the structure of the nerve system of the human brain, fuzzy control is very similar to the fuzzy thinking and inaccurate reasoning of human beings, and evolutionary computation algorithms are the direct simulations of the evolved processes of natural creatures.

In recent years, the biological immune system has become an emerging bioinformatics research area. The immune system is a complex system consisting of organs, cells, and molecules. The immune system is able to recognize the stimulation of "self" and "nonself," make a precise response, and retain the memory. It turns out from much research that the immune system consists of a variety of functions such as pattern recognition, learning, memory acquisition, diversity, fault-tolerant, distributed detection, and so on.

These attractive properties of the biological immune system have drawn extensive attention of engineering researchers who have proposed many novel algorithms and techniques based on those principles of immunology. After introducing the concept of immunity, many researchers in engineering have obtained more and more promising results, such as computer network security, intelligent robots, intelligent control, and pattern recognition and fault diagnosis. These research efforts and applications not only can help us to further understand the immune system itself, but also to re-examine and solve practical engineering problems from the perspective of information processing way in biological immune system.

Building a computer security system using the principles of the immune system opens a new research field of information security. Many structures, functions, and mechanisms of the immune system are very helpful and referential to the research into computer security, such as antibody diversity, dynamic coverage, and

Artificial Immune System: Applications in Computer Security, First Edition. Ying Tan.
© 2016 the IEEE Computer Society. Published 2016 by John Wiley & Sons, Inc.

distribution. We believe that the features of the immune system are the roots and original springs for us to build perfect computer security systems.

1.2 BIOLOGICAL IMMUNE SYSTEM

1.2.1 Overview

Biological immune system (BIS) is a highly complex, distributed, and parallel natural system with multiple levels, which can identify the self, exclude the nonself, for maintaining security and stability in the biological environment. It makes use of innate immunity and adaptive immunity to generate accurate immune response against the invading antigens. The BIS is robust to noise, distributed, self-organized, noncentral control, and has enhanced memory [1]. The original substance in an organism is called the self such as normal cells. The non-original substance in the organism is called the nonself like the invading antigens.

Biological immune systems consists of innate immunity (also known as nonspecific immune) system and adaptive immunity (also known as specific immune) system. The two systems mutually cooperate to resist the invasion of external antigens. Specifically, innate immune response starts the adaptive immune response, influences the type of adaptive immune responses, and assists adaptive immune to work. Adaptive immune response provides a more intense specific immune response [2].

Innate immune system is an inherent defense system that comes from a long-term evolutionary process. It is the first line of defense against antigens, which provides the innate immune function of the body. Usually, the innate immune system makes use of innate immune cells to recognize the common pattern formed by a variety of nonself. Therefore it can identify a variety of antigens, effectively preventing the invasion of most antigens. If an antigen breaks up the body's innate immune defense barrier, the adaptive immune system of the human body will be invoked and becomes responsible for the immune response to that specific antigen.

An adaptive immune system mainly has the following three functions:

1. Identifies specific antigens.
2. Provides the specific immune response to clear the corresponding antigen.
3. Provides a mechanism for immune memory.

Specific memory cells are able to remember the corresponding antigens. When the same antigen invades the body again, the memory cells will propagate and divide rapidly, providing a more intense immune response to it.

1.2.2 Adaptive Immune Process

Lymphocytes are the main effective immune substances in the adaptive immune system, which consists of T lymphocytes and B lymphocytes. The generation process of the lymphocytes is shown in Fig. 1.1. After negative selection, bone marrow stem

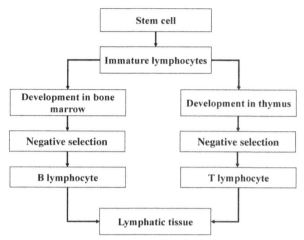

Figure 1.1   The generation and differentiation of lymphocytes.

cells grow to the B cells and T cells in the bone marrow and thymus. Other cells involved in the adaptive immune response include phagocytic cells, dendritic cells, and so on.

In the generation process of lymphocytes, they are affected by a large number of self. The lymphocytes which react with self will apoptosis, and the remaining lymphocytes will go to lymphoid organs and tissues, cycling in the organism with the lymphatic blood. This process in the biological immune system is called the negative selection process [3]. Based on the negative selection process, the biological immune system is able to successfully identify self and nonself, without the need of any nonself information.

In the first time adaptive immune response, T cells and B cells will proliferate and differentiate into effector T cells and effector B cells, respectively. The effector T cells are able to specifically recognize invading antigens and eliminate the antigens directly through cell lysis. This immune process is called cellular immunity. Different from effector T cells, the effector B cells specifically recognize and destroy the antigens by secreting antibodies, which is a kind of immunoglobulin. This process is called humoral immunity. In such a process, a few effector cells will differentiate into memory cells, achieving the immunological memory that is able to remember the antigens for a long time.

When the antigens invade the organism again, the adaptive immune system will produce the secondary immune response. In case of the secondary immune response, the memory cell is capable of proliferation and differentiation quickly, producing a large number of effector cells and providing a more intense immune response.

The proliferation and differentiation process of the lymphocytes cloning process are actually the processes of cloning and mutation of lymphocytes, respectively. Such clone and mutation processes result in the diversity of immune cells in the biological immune system. It is this kind of diversity that gives the biological immune system the ability to identify unknown antigens and new variants of known antigens.

1.3 CHARACTERISTICS OF A BIOLOGICAL IMMUNE SYSTEM

Artificial immune system (AIS) is a bionic system inspired from immunology principles of the biological immune system. The key to designing the artificial immune system is to take full advantage of the immunology principles and to replicate the effectiveness and capability of the biological immune system in computer systems. A biological immune system has a number of inspirational characteristics that artificial immune system can borrow from, including:

- Distributivity: Lymphocytes in the biological immune system are able to detect abnormity independently, with the control of a center, which means that they constitute a highly distributed system. When designing the artificial immune system, this feature is very helpful to the self protection and robustness of AIS. The architecture based on agents has been proposed to simulate the distributivity of the immune system.

- Multi-layered: The biological immune system has a multi-layer structure. A single layer of the biological immune system cannot protect the organism from all invasions, but the cooperation of multiple layers is able to achieve the security protection of the system. Although this feature is not unique to the biological immune system, it is a very important feature of the biological immune system. Studies and implementations of the multi-layered feature in the artificial immune system for computer systems can greatly enhance security of computer systems.

- Diversity: In nature, although the bodies protected by the biological immune system are the same on the whole, each body has its own differences. The diversity of different bodies is also very helpful to the protection against invasions. Diversity is from two aspects: one is the body's own diversity, the other is the diversity of the biological immune system. The combination of the two aspects increases the "diversity" greatly and is very important to the protection of our body. In the field of computer system security, the implementation of the diversity can be also achieved in two aspects—the diversity of computer operating systems and the diversity of the artificial immune system.

- Disposability: No immune cells in the biological immune system are indispensable. Every immune cell has a lifecycle. In the study of artificial immune systems, we can borrow the mechanism to achieve the lifecycle of immune antibodies.

- Autonomy: The biological immune system does not require a central control node. They can automatically recognize and destroy invading antigens and unitize the illness and death of immune cells to update themselves, achieving the immunologic function on their own.

- Adaptability: The biological immune system is able to learn newfound invading pathogens, and form the memory. The speed of response to the same pathogen invasion will be accelerated. Learning mechanisms of the biological immune system are very important to the artificial immune system. The artificial immune system should not only remember the abnormal immune information found in the past, but also dynamically learn the immune rules to handle the emerging unknown anomalies.

- No secure layer: In the biological immune system, any cell can be the invaded by pathogens, including lymphocytes. But other lymphocytes can kill the invading pathogen. The mutual help between the lymphocytes forms the basis of the security of the biological immune system.

- Dynamically changing coverage: The biological immune system can maintain a good balance between the space and time of the detector set. The biological immune system cannot form a large detector set to contain all the invasion information. At any time, the detector set flowed into the body is just a small portion of the entire detector set. The flowed detector set will update itself over time and the lifecycle. Such a mechanism has great benefits for enhancing the portability and coverage of the biological immune system.

- Identity via behavior: In the field of encryption, the encryption algorithm is used for identification. However, the biological immune system uses the representations of antibody and antigen for identification. In the field of computer systems, any representation is based on "0" and "1" at the bottom. Finding a reasonable representation will result in good recognition effect.

- Anomaly detection: The biological immune system is able to recognize the pathogen that is never seen. This phenomenon is called anomaly detection. This feature is conducive to the artificial immune system for achieving the function to detect unknown anomalies or to find new viruses in the field of computer security.

- Incomplete detection: Any match between antibodies and antigens is not a complete match. This feature can enhance the diversity and generalization of detectors. Just a few antibodies are able to detect a large number of antigens.

- Numbers game: The numbers game mainly refers to the time of the invasion and the protective response. Immune response must be faster than the speed of invasion, otherwise the immune protection will be overwhelmed by the invasion. Researchers of artificial immune system indicate that more attention should be paid to the lightweight of the system.

1.4 ARTIFICIAL IMMUNE SYSTEM

Artificial Immune System (AIS) is a computational intelligence system inspired by the working mechanism and principles of the biological immune system. Based on the concept and idea of "getting wisdom from nature," and by simulating the working mechanism of biological immune systems, artificial immune systems successfully achieve many advantages of biological immune systems, including noise patience to learn without a teacher, distributed, self-organized, no center control, and strengthening memory, and other features [4]. Artificial immune systems have developed into a hotspot research field of computational intelligence [5], and attracted many interested researchers.

There are a variety of immune algorithms and models in a artificial immune system. Among them, most algorithms try to utilize the mechanisms of learning and memory of biological immune systems for problem solving. Most algorithms and models achieved great success. In the artificial immune algorithm, the antigen corresponds to the objective function for solving problems and constraints, the antibody corresponds to candidate solution, and antigen and antibody affinity matching degree corresponds to candidate solution with objective function. The general steps of the artificial immune system algorithm 1 is shown next. In Algorithm 1, when suspended, it was the best match with the antigen-antibody, which has been optimized to the solution that solves the problem successfully.

Algorithm 1   General Steps of Artificial Immune Algorithm (AIS)

Step 1   Input antigen,
Step 2   Initialize antibody populations,
Step 3   Calculate affinity for each antibody,
Step 4   Check the lifecycle of each antibody and update the antibody,
Step 5   If the abort condition, then go to **Step 6;** otherwise steer for **Step 3**,
Step 6   Output antibodies.

Based on the negative selection mechanism of biological immune systems, Forrest and associates first proposed a negative selection algorithm [6], as shown in Algorithm 2, for anomaly detection in computer systems. This algorithm is one of the most important AIS algorithms, and is of very good robustness in identifying self and "variant," without reference to information of variant, which can be used to detect unknown antigens. It is especially suitable for unknown computer security monitoring, fault diagnosis under changing environments, computer malware detection, anomaly detection, intrusion detection, and so on.

Algorithm 2   Negative Selection Algorithm (NSA)

Step 1   Define self as a category of detector set.
Step 2   Generate a detector randomly; this detector undergoes "autologous" match. If a match occurs, then this detector is removed, otherwise it is added to the variant detector concentration.
Step 3   Abort condition judgment; if the variant does not contain a sufficient concentration detector detector, steer for **Step 2**, otherwise abort.

According to the clonal selection theory proposed by the Australian immunologist Burnet [7], Castro and Zuben proposed a clonal selection algorithm inspired by the clonal selection mechanism of the artificial immune system [8,9]. In the B cell cloning process, according to the affinity, clonal selection algorithm in the vicinity of the candidate to produce a variation of individual clones as a population of individuals for expanding the search. In such a way, the clonal selection algorithm can help prevent an evolutionary algorithm from premature, i.e., avoid falling into local minima [10], then leads to improving the optimization speed of the algorithm [11].

Application of biological diversity mechanism in the immune system helps to improve the global search ability of optimization algorithms and accelerates their convergence speeds. Negative expression mechanism of biological immune system, self-organization, and unsupervised learning may provide us useful mechanisms to cognise unknown environments by use of the known information. The mechanism of immune memory that can save the previous knowledge learned is very important and vital for many intelligent systems. Other artificial immune models and algorithms such as artificial immune network models, dendritic cells algorithms, and so on, are not introduced here due to space limitations. In the midst of the rapid development of artificial immune algorithms, many people continue to put forward a variety of novel artificial immune models and algorithms for many real-world problems.

Artificial immune systems have been successfully applied to many practical fields, including computer security, optimization, fault diagnosis, and pattern recognition, to name a few. In particular, computer malware detection based on immune principles has been developed rapidly and achieved many fruitful results and achievements, attracting more and more researchers. Nevertheless, these artificial immune systems and malware detection methods are not perfect. Most of them have some deficiencies and shortcomings, which stimulates researchers to explore more efficient models and algorithms.

1.5 ARTIFICIAL IMMUNE SYSTEM MODELS AND ALGORITHMS

1.5.1 Negative Selection Algorithm

Inspired by the generation process of T cells in immune systems, Forrest and associates [6] proposed a negative selection algorithm, which has become one of the most famous AIS algorithms. Biological immune systems have the ability to distinguish between self cells and nonself cells, which makes it able to recognize invading antigens. T cells play a key role in this process. The generation of T cells includes two stages: the initial generation stage and the negative selection stages. First, T-cell receptors are generated by a random combination of genes. In order to avoid the erroneous recognition of self, T cells are filtered in the thymus (i.e., negative selection process). The T cells that can recognize the self cells will be removed, while others that are approved by the T cells are able to participate in the immune response. Forrest and associates applied the same principle to the distinction of self and nonself in computer systems. They generated the detector set by a negative selection process to recognize the nonself that invaded the computers.

The process of negative selection algorithm is shown in Algorithm 3. The negative selection algorithm includes the detector set generation stage and the nonself detection stage. In the detector set generation process, the self gene library is constructed from the self files. Then the detector set is randomly generated. The detectors that match the self gene library are removed from the detector set according to the negative selection principle. The main role of the detector set is that it can fully cover the nonself data space. Therefore, the number of detectors tend to be more substantial. In the stage of nonself detection, the algorithm conducts the r—contiguous bits match between the sample and the detectors in the detector set one by one. Once a match occurs, the sample will be labeled as "nonself."

The key to the negative selection algorithm is to design the detector representation and matching functions. Regarding these two aspects, researchers have carried out a lot of work on negative selection algorithms [12].

Dasgupta and González [13] represented the detector as a rectangular function of the real number space, which is able to measure the degree of "abnormal."

González, Gupta, and Gómez [14] analyzed the limitations of the binary string representation and its matching process. They discussed the experimental performance of binary-type detectors and analyzed distribution of such types of detectors set in the data space. They pointed out that the binary type of detector is not able to characterize the data spatial structure well of certain issues.

Balachandran and associates [15] conducted the investigation on multiple shapes of detectors in the real value space: super rectangle, super sphericity, super spheroidicity, and so on. In addition, they gave a uniform negative selection model.

Balthrop and associates [16] proposed the r—block matching function. The matching process measures the match status of the detectors and the text character block. The matching method can reduce the vulnerabilities of detection and improve the detection range of the detector set.

Algorithm 3   Negative Selection Algorithm

Input: The self set $SELF = self_i$.
Output: The detector set $D = d_i$.
   1. $D = \phi$.
   2. **While** termination condition does not meet **do.**
   3. Randomly generate a detector set N.
   4. **For all** detector d in the detector set N.
   5. **For all** self $self_i$ in the self set $SELF$ **do**
   6. **If** $Affinity\,(d,\,self_i) < \theta$ **then**
   7. Remove d from the detector set N.
   8. Continue.
   9. **End if**
   10. **End for**
   11. **End for**
   12. $D = D \cup N$.
   13. **End while.**

Ji and Dasgupta [17] adopted the Euclidean distance as the detector matching function in the real value space, and dynamically adjusted the matching threshold value according to the length of detectors.

In the traditional negative selection algorithm, the detector set for nonself is generated randomly. This random method without wizard will consume a lot of resources. Furthermore, the traditional negative selection algorithm is more concerned about nonself characteristic of the samples, while what the biological immune system really cares about is the danger of antigens. The concern of anomaly detection in computer systems is the risk of the sample. Therefore, how to improve the negative selection algorithm's concern about the risk of the sample becomes a valuable work.

1.5.2 Clonal Selection Algorithm

In biological immune systems, each B cell produces a kind of antibody, in order to identify the corresponding antigen. When the antibody and antigen match (i.e., binding) and receive a stimulus signal emitted by the helper T cells, the corresponding B cells of antibodies are activated and cloned and differentiated into plasma cells and memory B cells. When the memory B cells encounter the same antigen again, they will generate a lot of antibodies with high affinities. Burnet [18] proposed the biological clonal selection theory to explain the process of cloning and the relationship between proliferation and differentiation of the immune cells and the affinities.

Inspired by this theory, De Castro and Von Zuben [8] proposed the clonal selection algorithm. The core idea of the algorithm is to select and clone the cells with high affinities and clear the cells with low affinities, while cloning and mutating the cells based on affinities of antigens and antibodies.

Algorithm 4 gives the pseudo-code of the clonal selection algorithm. First, the initial solution set is is regarded as the set of immune cells, and n solutions with the highest affinities are selected from the set. Then the selected n solutions are cloned. The amount of offspring is proportional to the affinity, and the degree of mutation is inversely proportional to the affinity. According to the affinity, immune cells with low affinity in the collection will be replaced with a certain probability. If an optimal solution is not found, then the algorithm goes to the next iteration. It can be seen that the algorithm gradually approaches the optimal affinity set in the iterative process, like the reinforcement learning. Furthermore, the random replacement in the algorithm is able to effectively maintain the diversity of the immune cell set.

De Castro and Von Zuben [9] further analyzed and discussed this algorithm and applied it to learning and optimization problems. They used the binary encoding for solutions.

Algorithm 4   Clonal Selection Algorithm

Input: The pattern set S.
Input: n, the number of antibodies to be cloned.
Input: d, the number of new antibodies at each iteration.

Output: The memory detector set M.

1. Randomly generate the candidate antibody set P_r.
2. Randomly generate the memory detector set M.
3. **While** termination condition does not meet **do**
4. $P = P_r \cup M$.
5. Select n antibodies with best affinities from P, denote the set as P_n.
6. $C = \phi$
7. **For all** antibody $a \in P_n$ **do**
8. Clone a to get new antibodies, denote the set as A, the size of the set A is proportional to the affinity of a.
9. $C = C \cup A$
10. **End for** $C^* = \phi$
11. **For all** antibody $a \in C$ **do**
12. Mutate the antibody a to a^*. The degree of mutation is proportional to the affinity of a.
13. $C^* = C^* \cup a^*$
14. **End for**
15. Select the best antibodies from C^*; replace M with the best set.
16. Randomly generate the candidate antibody set N_d with size d.
17. Replace the d antibodies with lowest affinities in P_r and M with antibodies in N_d.
18. **End while.**

On the basis of De Castro and Von Zuben's work, researchers have proposed a number of clonal selection algorithm variants. The clonal selection algorithm gradually becomes an important branch of artificial immune system.

Cutello and Nicosia [19] gave a new strategy to maintain diversity. For each B cell, they defined the probabilistic half-life period to control the cycle of the B cell, and updated the immune cell set according the lifecycle.

Garrett [20] added the parameters of the clonal selection algorithm to the representation of solutions, and used the real value to encode the solution. The parameters of the algorithm can be automatically adjusted in an iterative process. This method avoids the process of parameter selection, which is very useful to problems with uncertainty parameters.

Watkins and associates [21] studied the distributed nature of clonal selection algorithms and gave the parallel implementation of this algorithm. This method divided memory B cells into multiple independent groups, and each group evolves independently. At last the solutions from all of the groups are integrated to obtain the final result.

Cruz and associates [22] discussed different variants of clonal selection algorithm. The binary encoding strategy and the real value encoding strategy were compared. They also analyzed the affect of Cauchy mutation and Gaussian mutation to the performance of clonal selection algorithm.

Brownlee [23] made a comprehensive analysis of the development of the clonal selection algorithm. He pointed out that the common character of clonal selection algorithm variants in aspect of operators and the framework, and compared clonal selection algorithms with evolutionary computation algorithms.

1.5.3 Immune Network Model

Immune Network Theory [24] explains the relationship between the immune system B cells: no matter the presence or absence of the antigen, B cells in the immune system have excitation and inhibition affect with each other. The mutual excitation and inhibition of B cell-cell make the B-cell network stable. The excitation of a B cell is not only affected by the antigen, but also affected by the excitation and inhibition from other B cells in the immune network.

Inspired by the ideology of the immune network theory, Hunt and Cooke [25] proposed an artificial immune network method and applied it to the DNA sequence recognition. In this method, B cells are correlated according to the degree of affinity and inhibition. The population of B cells includes two subgroups: the initial population and the cloned population. In the training phase, the training set is divided into two parts, one for generating the initial B-cell network, and the other part is used as antigens to stimulate B-cell network. When the affinity between an antigen and a B cell exceeds a predetermined threshold, the B cell is excited and will be cloned and mutated. The generated B cells then join the network and will be dynamically adjusted by the excited state of the network.

This work found the basic features of the immune network theory. Regarding the mechanisms of the immune network and the representation method of B cells, researchers have proposed a variety of artificial immune network approaches [26].

Timmis and Neal [27] proposed the idea of artificial recognition balls. Each artificial recognition ball represent a group of similar B cells. There exist excitation and inhibition among the artificial recognition balls to maintain the stability of the immune network. This method assumes that the network resources are limited; the overall number of B cells represented by the artificial recognition balls B cells is limited.

Neal [28] proposed self-stable artificial recognition balls that are controlled distributively. Each artificial recognition ball automatically controls its own resources.

Nasaroui and associates [29] applied the fuzzy theory to the artificial immune network. The artificial recognition balls are represented as fuzzy sets in the data space. The method also proposed to merge artificial recognition balls according to affinity, which is similar to the crossover operator in evolutionary computation.

De Castro and Von Zuben [30] combined the clonal selection algorithm and the immune network theory. In the adjustment process of the network, it conducted clonal selection and suppression to the immune cells based on the affinity.

1.5.4 Danger Theory

Matzinger [31] analyzed the limitations of self and nonself theory, and proposed the immune danger theory on this basis. According to the traditional immune theory, the function of biological immune system is to distinguish between self and nonself. However, some harmless variant, such as food, embryos, and transplanted organs will not trigger an immune response. Therefore, Matzinger pointed out that the immune system's function is to detect danger, rather than detect nonself. Danger signals are generally released by injured cells before death and can synergisticly stimulate the antigen-presenting cells.

From the perspective of artificial immune system, Aickelin and Cayzer [32] analyzed the danger theory and discussed how to build the corresponding artificial immune models. They proposed the concept of the danger zone. The core of the danger theory is the cooperative stimulation of danger signals, and scope for danger signals is the local area of the injured cells (i.e., danger zone). The activation of B cells requires two conditions: one is the match of corresponding antibody and antigen, the other one is locating in a danger zone and being stimulated by the danger signal.

The key to build a danger model is to define a reasonable danger signal and the danger zone based on the original matching principle. In practical problems, danger signals can be dangerous independent mechanism and can be regarded as the information representation of a problem. For the definition of danger zones, the similarity in the space or the time can be used, and the correlation between the data can also be used. The danger theory has the potential to be used in anomaly detection and data mining.

On the basis of Aickelin and Cayzer's work, researchers have proposed a number of artificial immune models based on the danger theory [33–35].

Secker and associates [36] explored how to apply the danger theory to web mining. The definition of danger signals is based on the user's behavior and interests. The danger zone is defined according to the distance in time and space of the documents. This work mainly discussed ideas and model's framework, without giving a specific implement algorithm.

Aickelin and associates [37] analyzed the relationship between the danger-theory based artificial immune system and the intrusion detection system. They discussed how to defined the danger signals and danger zones based on the intrusion behavior in order to build a more robust intrusion detection system.

Prieto and associates [33] applied the danger theory to the control strategy of robot soccer goalkeeper. When football is located in our region, a first immune signal is generated. When an opposing player comes into the penalty area with the ball (danger zone), the dangerous signal will be generated.

Chao and associates [35] detected the anomaly in the software system based on the danger theory. In the running process of the software, the abnormal changes of the system resources will result in a danger signal, indicating the anomaly of the software.

1.5.5 Immune Concentration

Immune concentration is an immune inspired algorithm for feature extraction. In this section, I will take spam detection [38] as an example to introduce the concept of immune concentration.

The essence of the feature extraction method lies in the construction of concentration feature vectors. Tan and associates [39,40] presented global concentration

(GC) based feature extraction methods for spam filtering. Zhu and Tan [41,42] proposed local concentration (LC) based feature extraction methods. In these methods, statistical term selection methods [43] are utilized to remove uninformative terms. Then a tendency function is well designed to generate two detector sets [41,42,44,45]. The tendency of a term t_i is defined in Eq. 1.1. $T(t_i)$ measures the difference between the term's occurrence frequency in two types of messages. Terms are added to corresponding detector sets according to their tendency. Detector concentration, which corresponds to antibody concentration in BIS, are then extracted from messages by using the detector sets. In addition, a sliding window is utilized to slide over a message to extract position-correlated information from messages. By using a sliding window, a message is divided into local parts. At each movement of the window, a spam detector concentration S_i and a legitimate detector concentration L_i are calculated with respect to the two detector sets and the terms in the window according to Eqs. 1.2 and 1.3.

$$T(t_i) = P(t_i|c_l) - P(t_i|c_s) \tag{1.1}$$

where $P(t_i|c_l)$ denotes the probability of t_i's occurrence, given messages are legitimate emails, and $P(t_i|c_s)$ denotes the probability of t_i's occurrence estimated in spam.

$$S_i = \frac{\sum_{j=1}^{w_n} M(t_j, D_s)}{N_t} \tag{1.2}$$

$$L_i = \frac{\sum_{j=1}^{w_n} M(t_j, D_l)}{N_t} \tag{1.3}$$

where N_t is the number of distinct terms in the window, D_s denotes the spam detector set, D_l denotes the legitimate email detector set, and $M($ denotes the match function, which measures the number of terms in the window matched by detectors.

Each sliding window defines a specific local area in a message. To explore the effects of a sliding window, we design two strategies using a sliding window with fixed-length (FL) and using a sliding window with variable-length (VL). When a fixed-length sliding window is utilized, messages may have different number of local areas (corresponding to different number of feature dimensionality), as messages vary in length. To handle this problem, we may either expand a short message by reproduce the existing features, or reduce the dimensionality of long messages by discarding uninformative features. In VL strategy, the length of a sliding window is designed to be proportional to the length of a message, and there is no need for specific process of feature dimensionality. Preliminary experiments showed that both the two strategies are effective in extracting discriminative features. In the circumstance that the size of a window is set to infinite, a message is taken as a whole for getting concentration features, GC feature vectors are extracted. When the window size is smaller than the message length, the window divide a message into individual local parts, and LC features are extracted from each window.

1.5.6   Other Methods

Dasgupta and associates [46] made a comprehensive analysis of a variety of biological immune model, and pointed out that the biological immune system is a highly complex network composed of biological tissue, immune cells, chemical molecules, and other parts. On this basis, they proposed a multi-layer multi-resolution immune learning model, which integrated a variety of immunization strategies, including dynamical detector generation, clonal selection, and the interactions of immune cells. The method is able to make full use of the function of various immune cells; helper T cells, suppressor T cells, B cells, and antigen-presenting cells will synergistically interact information to detect anomalies.

Wang and associates [47] presented a complex immune system to simulate the representation and process of antigens. This method also used the interactions among a variety of immune cells. It comprised five immune processes, and mainly concerned the processing and representation of the antigens, and the interactions between the antigen presenting cells, T cells, and B cells. Experiments show that the system has a good memory and noise immunity.

Zhang and Hou [48] combined the niche strategy and clonal selection algorithm and proposed a hybrid immunological method. This method combined the negative selection, clonal selection, mutation, and niche strategies, which is able to effectively reduce the number of detectors.

Li and associates [49] proposed an efficient artificial immune network that combined a artificial immune network and particle swarm optimization algorithm. In the particle swarm optimization, particles' behavior can be affected by optimal particle in the population. The interacting with the optimal particle the swarm is able to speed up the convergence of the particle swarm. As far as the immune network, they introduced the interaction between immune cells and the optimal immune cell, making the immune network converging to a stable state with a faster speed.

De Castro and Von Zuben [50] proposed the Bayesian artificial immune system which replaces the basic clone and mutation operator with a probabilistic model for solving complex optimization problems.

1.6   CHARACTERISTICS OF THE ARTIFICIAL IMMUNE SYSTEM

The biological immune system has been evolving for hundreds of millions of years and plays a very important role in the protection of the body from bacterial invasion. Although the immune system may encounter problems, generally speaking, we can see its unique protective effect. The working principles of the biological immune system will have some inspiration and reference meaning on the research job of security protection technologies of computer systems, providing a brand new thinking of computer security, if the computer systems are seen as human bodies and the external intrusions as harmful viruses.

Immunity refers to the ability of the body to identify self or nonself and exclude nonself. The biological immune system is the body's natural system with functions of resistance to the disease itself and prevention of invasion from harmful bacteria. This system itself has many characteristics, some of which get certain significance on the research of computer system security.

1.6.1 Distributed Detection

The immune system works in a way of distributed detection, in which the detector to detect the bacterial invasion is very small but with high detection efficiency; centralized control center and collaboration are not required. Computer security systems are not equipped with the function of distributed detection and the use of the control center has actually reduced the factor of safety protection of the system.

1.6.2 Detection of Abnormality

The immune system is able to identify the invading bacteria that the system has never seen and take corresponding measures. The specific targets of the current computer security protection system are generally decided by the protective strategies or the protection system itself, without automatic intrusion detection of the latest way of invasion.

1.6.3 Learning and Memory

The immune system is able to automatically learn the structure of invading bacteria, and memorize this information in order to reply to this type of bacteria faster and more timely subsequently. Current computer security systems do not have the ability of self-learning.

1.6.4 Diversity

Different biological bodies have different immune systems. A certain weakness of one immune system is not the weakness of another. A virus might be able to break through one protective immune system, but the possibility of breaking through other immune systems is very small. Thus, the immune systems have strong ability to protect the overall population. While for computer systems, the security systems are always the same. Once a loophole is found, any computer system using this kind of security system will suffer the threat of invasion through this loophole.

1.6.5 Incomplete Detection

The immune system does not require making nonself test on every invading cell. It has great flexibility and may sacrifice a portion of the body functions or resources in order to ensure the normal functions of the body in general. Computer security systems generally do not have the ability of overall analysis of the system and its functions are generally specific and fixed.

1.7   APPLICATIONS OF ARTIFICIAL IMMUNE SYSTEM

1.7.1   Virus Detection

According to the ability of distinguishing self and nonself of the immune system, Forrest proposes principles and laws of BIS that AIS can take inspiration from and he has done a lot of research work to support this. By taking inspiration from the mechanism of BIS resisting and destroying unknown biological virus, T. Okamolo proposed a distributed agent-based anti-virus system. It consists of two parts: the immune system and the recovery system. The function of the immune system is identifying the nonself information (computer virus) by grasping the self information; the recovery system copies files from the non-infected computer to the computer which has been infected through the network to cover the files on it [45,51–53]. Based on the same principles, AIS is also used for hacking prevention, network security maintenance, and system maintenance.

1.7.2   Spam Filtering

Spam filtering is an important and typical pattern recognition problem because spam causes many problems to our daily communication life. In solving the problem, both classical statistical methods and AIS methods have been presented, and most of them focus on studying feature extraction methods and design of classifiers. The main function of feature extraction is to extract discriminative information from messages and transform messages into feature vectors. The statistical feature extraction methods try to collect and analyze numerical characteristics of messages, such as term frequencies, and relation between terms and email categories. Some prevalent ones are Bag-of-Words (BoW) [54], Sparse Binary Polynomial Hashing (SBPH), and Orthogonal Sparse Bigrams (OSB) [55]. Different from the statistical ones, the AIS methods [56] construct feature vectors by mimicking the process of antibody creation in BIS. In design of classifiers, classical pattern recognition methods, e.g. Naive Bayes(NB) [57,58], Support Vector Machine (SVM) [59–61], k-Nearest Neighbor (k-NN) [62,63], and Artificial Neural Network (ANN) [64,65] were proposed on the basis of statistical theory. On the contrast, AIS models were inspired by natural functions and mechanisms of BIS [56,66].

These statistical and AIS methods are quite different in terms of both origins and principles, which endow them with quite distinct properties. Combining the strength of both approaches may help achieve better performance. We will introduce and discuss several recent works of our laboratory [39–42,67–69], which applied mixed principles to feature attraction, classifier combination, and classifier updating, so as to demonstrate the rationality of combining statistical and AIS methods for

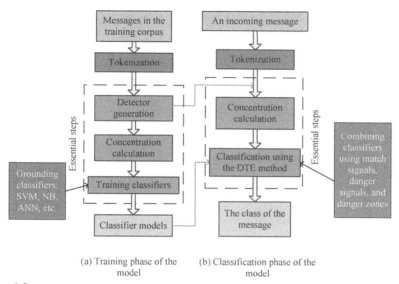

(a) Training phase of the model

(b) Classification phase of the model

Figure 1.2   Training and classification phases of the immune-based model.

spam filtering. In addition, we present a generic framework of an immune-based model for spam filtering, and online implementation strategies are given to demonstrate how to build an immune-based intelligent email server.

1.7.2.1 Concentration-Based Feature Representation

Based on these previous works, we present a generic framework of an immune-based spam filtering model, as depicted in Fig. 1.2. According to the model, concentration-based feature vectors are extracted from messages by computing match concentration of detections. Classifiers are then built on the concentration vectors of training corpus. Finally, incoming messages can be classified by using the Danger Theory-based Ensemble (DTE) method. In addition, classifiers are updated at all times based on the drift of messages and classification performance. In the following subsections, we briefly introduce and discuss the principles of these methods [70,71], and analyze the rationality of combining statistical principles with AIS ones.

Experiments were conducted on real-word corpora Ling, PU1, PU2, PU3, PUA, and Enron-Spam[1] using cross validation to investigate the performance of the concentration-based method. Meanwhile, four benchmark criteria, namely spam precision, spam recall, accuracy, and F_1 measure were adopted in analyzing the results. Among them, accuracy and F_1 were more important as they indicated the overall performance of approaches. From these experimental results, it can be seen that the combination of statistical information and immune characteristics helps achieve the

---

[1] The PU corpora and Enron-Spam are available from the web site: http://www.aueb.gr/users/ion/publications.html.

best discriminative performance. The success lies in the following aspects: (1) By using term selection methods, noise and uninformative terms can be removed, which reduce computational complexity and enhance effectiveness of detectors. (2) The concentration principle helps obtain feature vectors with lower dimensionality. (3) The sliding window strategies provide effective ways of defining local area in messages, and extracting position-correlated information.

1.7.2.2 Danger Theory Inspired Ensemble Method

Mimicking the DT theory, we defined artificial signals and danger zones, and classifiers were combined using them [67]. First, two types of artificial signals, namely, signal 1 (match signals) and danger signals, were respectively generated using two independent classifiers. Depending on the classification results, negative or positive signals would be generated. After the production of the signals, the two classifiers were interacted through the transmission of the signals. Mimicking the DT mechanism, the transmission of the signals was designed to be different. An activated signal 1 would be sent only to the specific sample, upon which the signal was arisen. However, an activated danger signal would be sent to all the test samples within the danger zone, besides the specific sample. Finally, the result was acquired based on the interaction among classifiers.

The framework of the DTE method is depicted in Fig. 1.3. A test sample gets labeled by the first two classifiers if the two signals agree with each other. Otherwise, a third classifier (self-trigger process) is utilized to solve the conflict and get the test sample classified. According to the method, three classifiers are combined in a cascade way. Similar to other cascade method, the order of classifiers can be determined according to classifier performance on training corpus. The characteristics of the DTE method lie in the interaction among classifiers by using the danger zone and the signals.

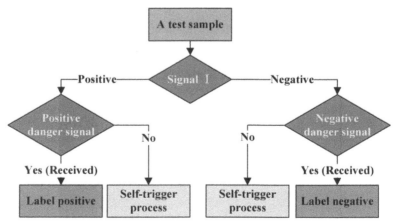

Figure 1.3   The framework of the DTE method.

The interaction between the first two classifiers is expressed as shown in Eq. 1.4.

$$E(x_i) = \sum_{x_j \in D} \delta(c_1(x_i), c_2(x_j)) K(d(x_i, x_j)) \qquad (1.4)$$

where x_i and x_j are test samples, D denotes the test set, $c_1(x)$ and $c_2(x)$ are the two classifiers, $d(x_i, x_j) = \|x_i - x_j\|$ is the distance between two samples, $K(z)$ is defined in Eq. 1.5, and $\delta(y_1, y_2) = 1$, if $y_1 = y_2$, and 0 otherwise.

$K(z)$ defines the effect of the danger zone as follows:

$$K(z) = \begin{cases} 1 & if\ z \leq \theta \\ 0 & otherwise \end{cases} \qquad (1.5)$$

where θ is the size of the danger zone.

After obtaining the weighted result $E(x_i)$, the sample x_i can get its class label using Eq. 1.6.

$$L(x_i) = \begin{cases} c_1(x_i) & if\ E(x_i) \geq 1 \\ f(x_i) & otherwise \end{cases} \qquad (1.6)$$

where $f(x)$ denotes the class label given by the third classifier.

The performance of the DTE was investigated on four real-world corpora, namely PU1, PU2, PU3, and PUA using ten-fold cross validation. In the experiments, SVM, NB, and Nearest Neighbor (NN) were utilized as three grounding classifiers. SVM was utilized to generate match signal, NB was utilized to generate danger signal, and NN was utilized in the self-trigger process. The experimental results [67] show that the danger zone provides a well defined interaction between the two types of signals, and classifier are combined through the interaction. By using the DTE method, the performance of classifiers can be effectively improved.

1.7.2.3 Immune-Based Dynamic Updating Strategies

Mimicking dynamic mechanisms of BIS, we proposed several classifier updating strategies [68,69]. The updating process of SVMs is depicted in Figs. 1.4 and 1.5. Support vectors (SVs) of a SVM are used as detectors (antibodies) and SVs are

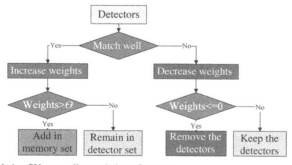

Figure 1.4 Updating SVs according to their performance.

Valid classifiers at time *t*

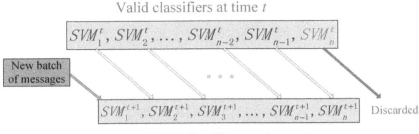

New batch
of messages

Discarded

Valid classifiers at time *t*+1

Figure 1.5 Updating SVMs with time according to their lifespan.

updated according to their performance by mimicking the dynamic mechanisms of BIS. In measuring the importance of SVs, we assign weights to SVs, and build up two sets, a Detector Set and a Memory Set. The weight is increased when a SV correctly classifies a sample (according to hamming distance), and vice versa [68,69]. When the weight of a SV is above a pre-defined threshold, the SV will be add to the memory set and the weight will be increased significantly. On the contrary, when the weight of a SV is decreased to zero, the SV will be culled from the detector set. In addition to SVs, the whole SVM is also updated with time. The updating of a SVM is in a greater magnitude as most of the SVs will be changed in this process. In the process, a sliding window strategy is adopted, and the window size controls the life-span of SVMs. When the updating moment is arrived, the oldest SVM is discarded and a new SVM will be built using the new arrival messages. The final classification decision will be made by the majority voting of the SVMs in effect.

1.7.3 Robots

D. W. Lee proposes a controlling method distributed robots based on the principle of homeostasis in the immune system. In this method, each the robot is regarded as a B cell and each environment condition as an antigen, while the behavior strategies adopted by the robots are taken as antibodies and the controlling parameters of the robots as T cells. Under different environment conditions, each robot will first select a set of behavioral strategies that are adapted to the environment conditions of itself. Then this set of behavioral strategies are individually communicated with other robots around one by one, and some behavioral strategies will be stimulated while some others are suppressed. The behavioral strategies that are stimulated more than others will finally be adopted by the robot. Based on the distributed controlling mechanism of the immune system, Lshiguro implements the gait controlling and speed measuring of a six-legged walking robot. The action strategies based on the principle of interaction between B cells in the immune system are used to control the movement of self-regulation robots. The main idea of this strategy is: several basic and different operators of the self-regulation robot are pre-designed and each operator is regarded as an agent that can make action decisions based on its surrounding environment and send controlling commands to the system, and the system will dynamically determine the robot's actions according to the collaboration and competition status between the agents.

1.7.4 Control Engineering

AIS can be readily identified as a feedback controller based on the principles of fast response and rapid determination of foreign intrusions. It has been applied to the car's rear collision prevention system by comprehensive processing signals transmitted from sensors and controlling each actuator executing corresponding operations quickly and accurately [72,73]. Takahashi designed an immune feedback controller of PID with activation item of controlling the response speed and suppression item of controlling the stabilizing effect. The validity of the controller is verified by simulating a discrete, single-input and single-output system. In addition, AIS is also used in sequence controlling, dynamic and complex controlling and other aspects.

1.7.5 Fault Diagnosis

Distributed diagnosis system combined immune network and learning vector quantization can be used to accurately detect the sensors where failure occurs in controlled object. This system has two modes: training mode and diagnosis mode. In the training mode, data of sensors working normally are trained and achieved through LVQ; in the diagnosis mode, the immune network determine the sensors with faults based on the knowledge acquired by LVQ. Experiments show that the system can automatically identify the failed sensors in the group of working sensors. While in the past, this is implemented by detecting the output of each sensor independently. The self-learning ability of the immune system is also used in the monitoring system of computer hardware, in which the system marks out the area fault occurs in and takes appropriate recovery actions one the computer hardware system goes wrong.

1.7.6 Optimized Design

For the nonlinear optimization problem with multiple local minima, the general optimization methods are difficult to find the global optimal solution, while genetic mechanism based on diversity of the immune system can be used for optimal search. It can avoid premature convergence for improving the genetic algorithm and dealing with multi-criteria problems. It has been currently used for function testing, the traveling salesman problem, VLSI layout, structure design, parameter correction of permanent magnet synchronous motor and others.

1.7.7 Data Analysis

AIS has the ability of data analysis and classification by combining the advantages of classifiers, neural networks and machine inference [74,75]. Therefore, it has been used in fields of data mining and information processing. Timmis discussed how to implement an unsupervised and self-learning AIS specifically.

1.8 SUMMARY

Biological immune system (BIS) provides a natural biological defense system for biological creatures to defend against external antigens. Artificial immune system (AIS) is a computational intelligence system inspired by the working mechanism and principle of BIS. The working mechanism simulating the BIS allows the AIS to access the many advantages of BIS. At present, AIS has been widely used in many fields such as pattern recognition, function optimization, computer security, robot control, data analysis, and so on.

REFERENCES

1. Janeway, Charles A. Jr, P.T.M.W. and Shlomchik, M.J. Immunobiology: The Immune System in Health and Disease, no. 2 June 21, 2001.
2. Zhang, X. (2010) *Viral Immunology*. vol. 1, Science Press. (in Chinese)
3. Sun, Z. and Wei, W. (2003) Artificial immune system and its application. *Computer Engineering*, **29** (15). (in Chinese)
4. Mo, H. and Jin, H. (2003) Application of artificial immune system to computer security. *Journal of Harbin Engineering University*, **24** (3), 278–282. (in Chinese)
5. Wang, J., Liu, X.Y., and Wang, X. (2006) Artificial immune system and analysis of its models. *Computer Technology and Development*, **16** (7), 105–107. (in Chinese)
6. Forrest, S., Perelson, A., Allen, L., and Cherukuri, R. (1994) Self-nonself discrimination in a computer, in Research in Security and Privacy, 1994. Proceedings. 1994 IEEE Computer Society Symposium on, IEEE, pp. 202–212.
7. Burnet, S.F.M. et al. (1959) *The Clonal Selection Theory of Acquired Immunity*, Vanderbilt University Press, Nashville.
8. De Castro, L.N. and Von Zuben, F.J. (2000) The clonal selection algorithm with engineering applications, in Proceedings of GECCO, vol. 2000, pp. 36–39.
9. De Castro, L.N. and Von Zuben, F.J. (2002) Learning and optimization using the clonal selection principle. *Evolutionary Computation, IEEE Transactions on*, **6** (3), 239–251.
10. Zhang, X. and Jiao, L. (2004) Feature selection based on immune clonal selection algorithm, *Journal of Fudan University (Natural Science)*, **43** (5), 926–929. (in Chinese)
11. Jiao, L. and Du, H. (2003) Development and prospect of the artificial immune system. *Acta Electronica Sinica*, **31** (10), 1540–1548. (in Chinese)
12. Ji, Z. and Dasgupta, D. (2007) Revisiting negative selection algorithms. *Evolutionary Computation*, **15** (2), 223–251.
13. Dasgupta, D. and González, F. (2002) An immunity-based technique to characterize intrusions in computer networks. *Evolutionary Computation, IEEE Transactions on*, **6** (3), 281–291.
14. González, F., Dasgupta, D., and Gómez, J. (2003) The effect of binary matching rules in negative selection, in *Genetic and Evolutionary Computation—GECCO 2003*, Springer, pp. 195–206.
15. Balachandran, S., Dasgupta, D., Nino, F., and Garrett, D. (2007) A framework for evolving multi-shaped detectors in negative selection, in Foundations of Computational Intelligence, 2007. FOCI 2007. IEEE Symposium on, IEEE, pp. 401–408.
16. Balthrop, J., Esponda, F., Forrest, S., and Glickman, M. (2002) Coverage and generalization in an artificial immune system, in Proceedings of the Genetic and Evolutionary Computation Conference, Citeseer, pp. 3–10.

17. Ji, Z. and Dasgupta, D. (2004) Real-valued negative selection algorithm with variable-sized detectors, in *Genetic and Evolutionary Computation–GECCO 2004*, Springer, pp. 287–298.
18. Burnet, F. (1978) Clonal selection and after. Theoretical Immunology, pp. 63–85.
19. Cutello, V. and Nicosia, G. (2002) Multiple learning using immune algorithms, in Proceedings of 4th International Conference on Recent Advances in Soft Computing, RASC, pp. 102–107.
20. Garrett, S. (2003) A paratope is not an epitope: Implications for immune network models and clonal selection. Artificial Immune Systems, pp. 217–228.
21. Watkins, A., Bi, X., and Phadke, A. (2003) Parallelizing an immune-inspired algorithm for efficient pattern recognition. *Intelligent Engineering Systems through Artificial Neural Networks: Smart Engineering System Design: Neural Networks, Fuzzy Logic, Evolutionary Programming, Complex Systems and Artificial Life*, **13**, 225–230.
22. Cruz-Cortés, N., Trejo-Pérez, D., and Coello, C. (2005) Handling constraints in global optimization using an artificial immune system. Artificial Immune Systems, pp. 234–247.
23. Brownlee, J. (2007) Clonal selection algorithms, *Tech. Rep.*, Complex Intelligent Systems Laboratory (CIS), Centre for Information Technology Research (CITR), Faculty of Information and Communication Technologies (ICT), Swinburne University of Technology, Victoria, Australia, Technical Report ID: 070209A.
24. Jerne, N. (1974) Towards a network theory of the immune system, in Annales D'Immunologie, vol. 125, pp. 373–389.
25. Hunt, J. and Cooke, D. (1996) Learning using an artificial immune system. *Journal of Network and Computer Applications*, **19** (2), 189–212.
26. Galeano, J., Veloza-Suan, A., and González, F. (2005) A comparative analysis of artificial immune network models, in Proceedings of the 2005 Conference on Genetic and Evolutionary Computation, ACM, pp. 361–368.
27. Timmis, J. and Neal, M. (2001) A resource limited artificial immune system for data analysis. *Knowledge-Based Systems*, **14** (3), 121–130.
28. Neal, M. (2002) An artificial immune system for continuous analysis of time-varying data, in Proceedings of the 1st International Conference on Artificial Immune Systems (ICARIS), vol. 1, pp. 76–85.
29. Nasaroui, O., Gonzalez, F., and Dasgupta, D. (2002) The fuzzy artificial immune system: Motivations, basic concepts, and application to clustering and web profiling, in Fuzzy Systems, 2002. FUZZ-IEEE'02. Proceedings of the 2002 IEEE International Conference on, vol. 1, IEEE, pp. 711–716.
30. de Castro, L. and Von Zuben, F. (2001) AINET: An artificial immune network for data analysis. *Data Mining: A Heuristic Approach*, **1**, 231–259.
31. Matzinger, P. (2001) Essay 1: The danger model in its historical context. *Scandinavian Journal of Immunology*, **54** (1–2), 4–9.
32. Aickelin, U. and Cayzer, S. (2002) The danger theory and its application to artificial immune systems. Artificial Immune Systems, pp. 141–148.
33. Prieto, C., Nino, F., and Quintana, G. (2008) A goalkeeper strategy in robot soccer based on danger theory, in Evolutionary Computation, 2008. CEC 2008. (IEEE World Congress on Computational Intelligence). IEEE Congress on, IEEE, pp. 3443–3447.
34. Zhang, C. and Yi, Z. (2010) A danger theory inspired artificial immune algorithm for on-line supervised two-class classification problem. *Neurocomputing*, **73** (7–9), 1244–1255.
35. Chao, Y., Yiwen, L., and Aolin, L. (2011) The danger sensed method by feature changes. *Energy Procedia*, **13**, 4429–4437.
36. Secker, A., Freitas, A., and Timmis, J. (2003) A danger theory inspired approach to web mining. Artificial Immune Systems, pp. 156–167.
37. Aickelin, U., Bentley, P., Cayzer, S., Kim, J., and McLeod, J. (2003) Danger theory: The link between AIS and IDS? Artificial Immune Systems, pp. 147–155.
38. Tan, Y. and Zhu, Y. (2010) Advances in anti-spam techniques. *CAAI Transactions on Intelligent Systems*, **5** (3), 189–201.
39. Tan, Y., Deng, C., and Ruan, G. (2009) Concentration based feature construction approach for spam detection, in *Neural Networks, 2009. IJCNN 2009. International Joint Conference on*, IEEE, pp. 3088–3093.

40. Ruan, G. and Tan, Y. (2010) A three-layer back-propagation neural network for spam detection using artificial immune concentration. *Soft Computing*, **14** (2), 139–150.

41. Zhu, Y. and Tan, Y. (2010) Extracting discriminative information from e-mail for spam detection inspired by immune system, in Evolutionary Computation (CEC), 2010 IEEE Congress on, IEEE, pp. 1–7.

42. Zhu, Y. and Tan, Y. (2011) A local concentration based feature extraction approach for spam filtering. *Information Forensics and Security, IEEE Transactions on*, **6** (2), 486–497.

43. Yang, Y. and Pedersen, J. (1997) A comparative study on feature selection in text categorization. International Conference on Machine Learning, pp. 412–420.

44. Wang, W., Zhang, P., Tan, Y., and He, X. (2011) An immune local concentration based virus detection approach. *Journal of Zhejiang University-Science C*, **12** (6), 443–454.

45. Wang, W., Zhang, P., and Tan, Y. (2010) An immune concentration based virus detection approach using particle swarm optimization, in *Advances in Swarm Intelligence*, Springer, pp. 347–354.

46. Dasgupta, D., Yu, S., and Majumdar, N. (2003) Mila multilevel immune learning algorithm, in *Genetic and Evolutionary Computation, ECCO 2003*, Springer, pp. 183–194.

47. Wang, W., Gao, S., and Tang, Z. (2008) A complex artificial immune system, in Natural Computation, 2008. ICNC'08. Fourth International Conference on, Vol. 6, IEEE, pp. 597–601.

48. Zhang, Y. and Hou, C. (2003) A clone selection algorithm with niching strategy inspiring by biological immune principles for change detection, in Intelligent Control. 2003 IEEE International Symposium on, IEEE, pp. 1000–1005.

49. Li, Z., Zhang, Y., and Tan, H. (2007) An efficient artificial immune network with elite-learning, in Natural Computation, 2007. ICNC 2007. Third International Conference on, Vol. 4, IEEE, pp. 213–217.

50. de Castro, P. and Von Zuben, F. (2009) BAIS: A bayesian artificial immune system for the effective handling of building blocks. *Information Sciences*, **179** (10), 1426–1440.

51. Chao, R. and Tan, Y. (2009) A virus detection system based on artificial immune system, in Computational Intelligence and Security, 2009. CIS'09. International Conference on, IEEE, vol. 1, pp. 6–10.

52. Guo, Z., Liu, Z., and Tan, Y. (2004) An nn-based malicious executables detection algorithm based on immune principles, in *Advances in Neural Networks-ISNN 2004*, Springer, pp. 675–680.

53. Wang, W., Zhang, P., Tan, Y., and He, X. (2009) A hierarchical artificial immune model for virus detection, in Computational Intelligence and Security, 2009. CIS'09. International Conference on, IEEE, vol. 1, pp. 1–5.

54. Androutsopoulos, I., Paliouras, G., and Michelakis, E. (2004) *Learning to filter unsolicited commercial e-mail*, "DEMOKRITOS," National Center for Scientific Research.

55. Siefkes, C., Assis, F., Chhabra, S., and Yerazunis, W.S. (2004) Combining winnow and orthogonal sparse bigrams for incremental spam filtering, in *Knowledge Discovery in Databases: PKDD 2004*, Springer, pp. 410–421.

56. Oda, T. and White, T. (2003) Developing an immunity to spam, in *Genetic and Evolutionary Computation–GECCO 2003*, Springer, pp. 231–242.

57. Sahami, M., Dumais, S., Heckerman, D., and Horvitz, E. (1998) A bayesian approach to filtering junk e-mail, in Learning for Text Categorization: Papers from the 1998 workshop, vol. 62, pp. 98–105.

58. Çıltık, A. and Gungör, T. (2008) Time-efficient spam e-mail filtering using n-gram models. *Pattern Recognition Letters*, **29** (1), 19–33.

59. Drucker, H., Wu, S., and Vapnik, V.N. (1999) Support vector machines for spam categorization. *Neural Networks, IEEE Transactions on*, **10** (5), 1048–1054.

60. Tan, Y. and Wang, J. (2004) A support vector network with hybrid kernel and minimal vapnik-chervonenkis dimension. *IEEE Trans. On Knowledge and Data Engineering*, **26** (2), 385–395.

61. Andreas, J. and Tan, Y. (2011) Swarm intelligence for non-negative matrix factorization. *International Journal of Swarm Intelligence Research*, **2** (4), 12–34.

62. Androutsopoulos, I., Paliouras, G., Karkaletsis, V., Sakkis, G., Spyropoulos, C.D., and Stamatopoulos, P. (2000) Learning to filter spam e-mail: A comparison of a naive bayesian and a memory-based approach. arXiv preprint cs/0009009.

63. Sakkis, G., Androutsopoulos, I., Paliouras, G., Karkaletsis, V., Spyropoulos, C.D., and Stamatopoulos, P. (2003) A memory-based approach to anti-spam filtering for mailing lists. *Information Retrieval*, **6** (1), 49–73.

64. Clark, J., Koprinska, I., and Poon, J. (2003) A neural network based approach to automated e-mail classification, in Web Intelligence, IEEE/WIC/ACM International Conference on, IEEE Computer Society, pp. 702–702.

65. Wu, C.H. (2009) Behavior-based spam detection using a hybrid method of rule-based techniques and neural networks. *Expert Systems with Applications*, **36** (3), 4321–4330.

66. Guzella, T.S., Mota-Santos, T.A., Uchoa, J.Q., and Caminhas, W.M. (2008) Identification of spam messages using an approach inspired on the immune system. *Biosystems*, **92** (3), 215–225.

67. Zhu, Y. and Tan, Y. (2011) A danger theory inspired learning model and its application to spam detection. Advances in Swarm Intelligence, pp. 382–389.

68. Ruan, G. and Tan, Y. (2007) Intelligent detection approaches for spam, in Natural Computation, 2007. ICNC 2007. Third International Conference on, IEEE, vol. 3, pp. 672–676.

69. Tan, Y. and Ruan, G. (2014) Uninterrupted approaches for spam detection based on svm and ais. *International Journal of Computational Intelligence*, **1** (1), 1–26.

70. Mi, G., Zhang, P., and Tan, Y. (2013) A multi-resolution-concentration based feature construction approach for spam filtering, in The International Joint Conference on Neural Networks (IJCNN 2013), IEEE, vol. 1, pp. 1–8.

71. He, W., Mi, G., and Tan, Y. (2013) Parameter optimization of local-concentration model for spam detection by using fireworks algorithm, in *The Fourth International Conference on Swarm Intelligence (ICSI 2013)*, vol. 1, Springer, pp. 439–450.

72. Huang, X., Tan, Y., and He, X. (2011) An intelligent multi-feature statistical approach for discrimination of driving conditions of hybrid electric vehicle. *IEEE Transactions on Intelligent Transportation Systems*, **12** (2), 453–465.

73. Gu, S., Tan, Y., and He, X. (2013) Recent-biased learning for time series forecast. *Information Science*, **237** (10), 29–38.

74. Gu, S., Tan, Y., and He, X. (2010) Laplacian smoothing transform for face recognition. *Science China (Information Science)*, **53** (12), 2415–2428.

75. Andreas, J. and Tan, Y. (2013) Efficient euclidean distance transform algorithm of binary images in arbitrary dimensions. *Pattern Recognition*, **46** (1), 230–242.

Chapter 2

Malware Detection

Malware has become a challenge to the security of the computer system. The rapid development of evasion techniques makes the signature-based malware detection techniques lose effectiveness. Many approaches have been proposed to cope with the situations, which are mainly classified into three categories: static techniques, dynamic techniques, and heuristics. Artificial immune systems (AIS), because of the natural similarities between the biological immune system and computer security system, have been developed into a new field for anti-malware research, attracting many researchers. The immune mechanisms provide opportunities to construct malware detection models that are robust and adaptive with the ability to detect unseen malware. In this chapter, the classic malware detection approaches and immune-based malware detection approaches are briefly introduced after the background knowledge of malware is presented. The malware detection approaches based on immune principles have paved a new way for anti-malware research.

2.1 INTRODUCTION

With the rapid development of computer technology and the Internet, the computer has been a part of daily life. Meanwhile, computer security garners more and more attention. Malwares, the new variations and unknown malwares in particular, have become the biggest threats to computer systems. Nowadays malwares are becoming more complex with faster breed speeds and stronger abilities for latency, destruction, and infection. A malware is able to spread over the globe in several minutes and may result in huge economic losses. How to protect computers from various kinds of malwares has become one of the most urgent missions.

Many companies have released anti-malware software, most of which is based on signatures. The software detects known malwares very quickly with lower false positive rates and overheads. Unfortunately, the software fails to detect new variations and unknown malwares. Based on metamorphic and polymorphous techniques, even a layman can develop new variations of known malwares easily using virus automatons. For example, Agobot has been observed to have more than 580 variations since its initial release, using polymorphism to evade detection and

Artificial Immune System: Applications in Computer Security, First Edition. Ying Tan.
© 2016 the IEEE Computer Society. Published 2016 by John Wiley & Sons, Inc.

disassembly [1]. Thus, traditional malware detection approaches based on signatures are no longer fit for the new environments; as well, dynamic techniques and heuristics have started to emerge.

Dynamic techniques (such as virtual machine) mostly monitor the behaviors of a program with the help of application programming interface (API) call sequences generated at runtime. However, because of the huge overheads of monitoring API calls, it is very hard to deploy the dynamic techniques on personal computers.

Data mining approaches, one of the most popular heuristics, try to mine frequent patterns or association rules to detect malwares using classic classifiers. These have led to some success. However, data mining loses the semantic information of the code and cannot easily recognize unknown malwares.

As we know, malware is similar to biological virus in many aspects, such as parasitism, breed, and infection. In nature, the biological immune system (BIS) protects the body from antigens, resolving the problem of unknown antigens [2], so applying immune mechanisms to anti-malware has developed into a new field for the past few years, attracting many researchers. Forrest applied the immune theory to computer anomaly detection for the first time in 1994 [3]. Since then, many researchers have proposed various kinds of malware detection models and achieved some success; most of them are mainly derived from ARTificial Immune System (ARTIS) [4–6].

Over time, more and more immune mechanisms have become clear. Immune-based malware detection approaches make use of more immune theories and the study deepens continuously. The simulations to BIS keep going ahead. Now the malware detection objects have included raw bit strings, process calls, and process call arguments.

2.2 MALWARE

2.2.1 Definition and Features

In a broad sense, malware includes viruses, worms, backdoors, Trojans, and so on [7]. With the development of malware, the lines between different types of malwares are no longer clear. Now all the software that is not authorized by users and performs harmful operations in the background is referred to as malware [8–11].

The features of malware are given as below:

- Infectivity: Infectivity is the fundamental and essential feature of malware, which is the foundation to classify a malware. When a malware intrudes in a computer system, it starts to scan the programs and computers on the Internet that can be infected. Then through self-duplicating, it spreads to the other programs and computers.

- Destruction: Based on the extent of destruction, malware is divided into benign malware and malignant malware. Benign malware merely occupies system resources, such as GENP, W-BOOT. Malignant malware usually has clear purposes, for example, destroying data, deleting files, and formating disks.

- Concealment: Malwares often attach themselves to benign programs and start up with the host programs. They perform harmful operations in the background hiding from users.
- Latency: After intruding in a computer system, malwares hide themselves from users instead of attacking the system immediately. This feature makes malwares have longer lives. They spread themselves and infect other programs in this period.
- Trigger: Most malwares have one or more trigger conditions. When these conditions are satisfied, the malwares begin to destroy the system.

Other features of the malwares include illegality, expressiveness, and unpredictability.

2.2.2 The Development Phases of Malware

Malwares are evolved with computer technology all the time. The development of malwares generally goes through several phases including:

- DOS boot phase: Figs. 2.1 and 2.2 illustrate the boot procedures of DOS without and with boot sector virus, respectively. Before the system obtains right of control, the malware starts up, modifies interrupt vector, and copies itself to infect the disk. These are the original infection procedures of malwares. Similar infection procedures can be found in malwares now.
- DOS executable phase: In this phase, the malwares exist in a computer system in the term of executable files. They control the system when users run applications infected by the malwares. Most malwares now are executable files.
- Malware generator phase: Malware generators, called malware automatons, can generate new variations of known malwares with different signatures.

Figure 2.1 Normal boot procedure of DOS.

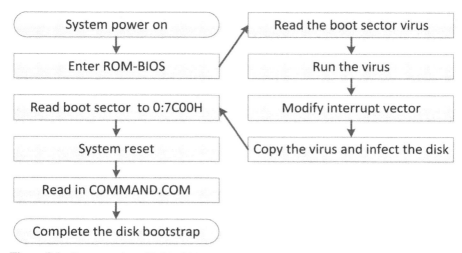

Figure 2.2   Boot procedure of DOS with boot sector virus.

Metamorphic techniques are used here to obfuscate scanners based on signatures, including instruction reordering, register renaming, code expansion, code shrinking, and garbage code insertion [12].

- Macro malware phase: Before the emerging of macro malwares, all the malwares merely infected executable files because this almost is the only way for the malwares to obtain the right of execution. When users run a host of a malware, the malware starts up and controls the system. Infecting data files cannot help the malware to run itself. The emerging of macro malwares changed this situation and their punching bags are data files, mainly Microsoft Office files.

- Malware techniques merging with hacker techniques: Merging of malware techniques and hacker techniques has been a tendency. It makes the malwares have much stronger concealment, latency, and much faster breed speed than ever before.

2.3 CLASSIC MALWARE DETECTION APPROACHES

Malware has become a major threat to the security of the computer and the Internet. A wide range of host-based solutions have been proposed by many researchers and companies [13–37]. These techniques are broadly classified into three types: static techniques, dynamic techniques, and heuristics [9–11,13–22].

The fight between malwares and the anti-malware techniques is more violent now than ever before. The malwares disguise themselves using various evasion techniques such as metamorphic and polymorphous techniques, packer, and encryption techniques. Coping with the new environments, the anti-malware techniques unpack the suspicious programs, decrypt them, and try to be robust to those evasion techniques. Nevertheless, the malwares evolve to anti-unpack, anti-decrypt, and develop obfuscate the anti-malware techniques again. The fight will never stop and the malware techniques will always be ahead of the anti-malware techniques. What we can do is to increase the difficulty of intrusion, decrease the losses caused by the malwares, and react to them as quickly as possible.

2.3.1   Static Techniques

Static techniques mostly operate on program bit strings and disassembled instructions. One of the most famous static techniques is the signatures-based detection technique.

The signatures-based detection technique is the mainstream anti-malware method and most software now is based on signatures. A signature is a bit string split from a virus sample and it can identify a virus uniquely. The software based on signatures is referred to as scanner.

In order to extract a signature from a malware, the experts first disassemble the virus sample to assembly code. Then they analyze it in the semantic level to figure out the mechanisms and workflow of the malware. Finally, a signature is extracted out representing the malware sample uniquely.

This technique is able to detect known viruses very quickly with lower false positive and high true positive rates. It is the simplest method with minimal overheads. Nevertheless, since a signature of a new malware can be only extracted by experts after the outbreak of this virus, it takes a long time and the losses caused by the virus cannot recover easily. Furthermore, with the development of malware techniques, there are many techniques to help the virus evade from the scanners based on signatures, such as metamorphic and polymorphous techniques, packer, and encryption techniques. Signatures-based techniques are easily defeated by these techniques. For example, simple program entry point modifications consisting of two extra jump instructions effectively defeat most scanners based on signatures [23].

To conclude, signatures-based techniques are vulnerable to evasion techniques. As a result, dynamic and heuristic approaches are developed to cope with these situations.

2.3.2   Dynamic Techniques

Malware should show some special behaviors when they infect other applications. For example, writing operations to executable files, dangerous operations such as formatting a disk and switching between malware and its host. These behaviors give us an opportunity to recognize the malwares. Dynamic techniques decide whether a code is infected by running the code and observing its behaviors. Usually dynamic techniques utilize the operating system's API sequences, system calls, and other kinds of behavior characteristics to identify the purpose of a program [24].

There are two main types of dynamic techniques: behavior monitoring approach and virtual machine approach.

Based on the assumption that the malwares have some special behaviors that can identify themselves and never emerge in benign programs, the behavior monitors keep watch on any behavior of malware and wish to prevent destruction from the dangerous operations.

This approach has the ability to detect known malwares, new variations, and unknown malwares. However, letting malwares run in a real machine is very dangerous. If the behavior monitor fails to kill a malware, the malware takes control of the computer. Moreover, the overheads brought by a monitor are huge and unacceptable to ordinary computers. The false positive rate is high inevitably. And the approach cannot recognize the type and name of a malware; thus, it cannot eliminate the malware from a computer. Furthermore, it is very hard to implement a relative perfect behavior monitor.

Virtual machine approach creates a virtual machine (VM) and lets the programs run in it. The execution environment of a program here is the VM which is software instead of the physical machine, so the computer is safe even if the VM is crashed by a malware. It is very easy to collect all the information when a program runs in a VM. If the VM finds some dangerous operations, it would give the users a tip. If it confirms that the running program is a malware, then it kills the malware.

Virtual machine is very safe and can recognize almost all the malwares, including encrypted and packed viruses. The VM approach has become one of the most effective malware detection approaches. Whereas the virtual machine brings comparable overheads to the host computers. How to implement a relative perfect virtual machine is a new field to study. In addition, the virtual machine only simulates parts of the computer's functions and it provides opportunities for anti-virtual machine techniques.

Anti-virtual machine techniques have been used in many malwares recently. For example, inserting some special instructions into a malware may cause the crash of the virtual machine. Entry point obscuring is also involved by the malwares to evade from the virtual machine approach.

A number of researchers [16–18,25–27] proposed some models based on dynamic techniques to detect the malwares. Although these techniques have produced promising results, they can produce high rates of false positive errors, an issue which has yet to be resolved [28].

2.3.3 Heuristics

Sulaiman and associates proposed a static analysis framework for detecting variations of malwares that was called disassembled code analyzer for malware (DCAM) [29]. Different from traditional static code analysis, the authors extracted signatures from disassembled codes generated by PE explorer instead of raw program bit strings. Each signature was a key/value pair where the key represented the label and the value represented the set of instructions associated with the label. The number of the instructions in a signature had to exceed a threshold in order to contain enough information. The files that got through three steps of matching were considered benign programs; otherwise DCAM classified the files as malwares. The

DCAM worked very well in the authors' experiments and could prevent breakouts of previous identified malwares.

Henchiri and Japkowicz adopted a data-mining approach to extract frequent patterns (FPs) for detecting malware [30]. Based on intra-family support and inter-family support, they filtered FPs twice, trying to obtain more general FPs. From the final set of FPs, traditional machine learning algorithms were involved to train the model and make classification, such as ID3, J48. They verified the effectiveness of their model using five-fold cross validation, showing some good results. Nevertheless, FPs are merely fixed-length bit strings with no definite meaning and cannot represent real signatures of the malwares.

Karnik and associates proposed a malware detection model using cosine similarity analysis to detecting obfuscated viruses [31]. Their work was based on the premise that given a variant of a malware, they can detect any obfuscated version of the malware with high probability. Actually, their model was only worked on code transposition. The biggest issue in this model was that how to extract functions within a program cannot be completed in real time.

Ye and associates used associative classification and post-processing techniques for malware detection based on the analysis of API execution sequences called by portable executable (PE) files [14]. First, they extracted the API calls from Windows PE files as the features of the samples and stored them in a signature database. Then they extended a modified FP-growth algorithm to generate the association rules [10,15]. Finally, by adopting post-processing techniques of the associative classification, the authors reduced the number of rules and got a concise classifier. Promising results demonstrated that the efficiency and ability of the model outperformed popular anti-malware software, as well as previous data-mining based malware detection systems.

Tabish and associates proposed a malware detection model using statistical analysis of the byte-level file content [11]. This model was not based on signatures. It neither memorized specific strings appearing in the file contents nor depended on prior knowledge of file types. As a result, the model was robust to the most commonly used evasion techniques. Although better results could be obtained in this way, there were high false positive rates, because this approach only used statistics from the training set.

Many researchers have proposed various kinds of heuristics to detect the malwares with some success [19–22,32–36].

2.4 IMMUNE-BASED MALWARE DETECTION APPROACHES

2.4.1 An Overview of Artificial Immune System

2.4.1.1 Artificial Immune System

AIS is a computational system inspired by the biological immune system (BIS), which is referred to as the second brain. AIS as a dynamic, adaptive, robust, distributed learning system have the ability of fault tolerant and noise resistant, and is fit for the applications under various unknown environments.

AIS have been applied to many complex problem domains, such as optimization, pattern recognition, fault and anomaly diagnosis, network intrusion detection, and virus detection.

The steps of the general artificial immune algorithm are shown in Algorithm 5.

Algorithm 5   General Artificial Immune Algorithm

---

1. Input antigens.
2. Initialize antibody population.
3. Calculate the affinities of the antibodies.
4. Lifecycle event and update the antibodies—creation and destruction.
5. If the terminate criteria are satisfied, go to 6; otherwise, go to 3.
6. Output the antibodies.

There are three typical algorithms in AIS: negative selection algorithm (NSA), clonal selection algorithm, and immune network model.

2.4.1.2 Motivations of Applying Immune Mechanisms to Malware Detection

As discussed, malware is similar to biological virus in many aspects, such as parasitism, breed, infection, and destruction. The biological immune system (BIS) protected body from antigens from the beginning of life, resolving the problem of unknown antigens [2]. The computer system is designed from the prototype of human beings and the computer security system has the similar functions with BIS. Furthermore, the futures of AIS, such as dynamic, adaptive, robust, are needed in the computer anti-malware system (CAMS). To sum up, applying immune mechanisms to computer security systems, especially the CAMS, is reasonable and has developed into a new field, attracting many researchers. The relationship of BIS and CAMS is given in Table 2.1.

Applying immune mechanisms to malware detection helps the CAMS recognize new variations and unknown malwares, using existing knowledge. The CAMS with immune mechanisms would be more robust to make up the fault

Table 2.1   The Relationship of BIS and CAMS

BIS	CAMS
Antigens	Malwares
Antibodies	Detectors for the malwares
Binding of an antigen and an antibody	Pattern matching of the malwares and detectors

of the signatures-based malware detection techniques. The immune-based malware detection approaches have paved a new way for anti-malware research [9,37–41].

2.4.2   An Overview of Artificial Immune System for Malware Detection

With the development of immunology, immune mechanisms have begun to be applied in the field of computer security. Forrest and associates first proposed a negative selection algorithm to detect anomaly modification on protected data in 1994 [3] and later applied it to UNIX process detection [42]. It is the beginning of applying immune theory to the computer security system.

Kephart and associates described a blueprint of a computer immune system in [5]. They set forth some criteria that must be met to provide real world, functional protection from rapidly spreading viruses, including innate immunity, adaptive immunity, delivery and dissemination, high speed, scalability, safety and reliability, as well as customer control. In fact, these criteria have become the standards for other computer immune systems from then on.

Based on the clonal selection theory of Burnet, the clone selection algorithm was presented by Kim and Bentley [43].

Matzinger proposed the "danger theory" in 2002 [44]. The danger theory believes the immune system is more concerned with entities that do damage than with those are foreign, which corrects the fault of the traditional self and nonself model in defining of harmfulness of self and nonself.

Since then, more and more researchers have devoted themselves to the study of computer immune systems based on immune mechanisms and various kinds of immune-based malware detection models have been proposed [12,40,41,45–57].

Kenneth and associates introduced a new artificial immune system based on REtrovirus ALGOrithm (REALGO) which was inspired by reverse transcription RNA as found in the biological systems [46]. In the learning phase, positive selection generated new antibodies using genetic algorithm based on known malware signatures and negative selection ensured that these antibodies did not trigger on self. The REALGO provided a memory for each antibody in the genetic algorithm so that an antibody could remember its best situation. With the help of the memory, the REALGO was able to revert back to the previous generation and mutate in a different "direction" to escape local extremum.

Li Zhou and associates presented an immunity based malware detection approach with process call arguments and user feedback [47]. It collected arguments of process calls instead of the sequences of process, and utilized these arguments to train detectors with real-valued negative selection algorithm [48]. In the testing phase, they adjusted the threshold between benign programs and viruses through user feedback. The detection rate achieved was 0.7, which proved the approach could cope with unknown malwares. However, letting users distinguish a virus from normal files and give feedback was very difficult.

Li Tao proposed a dynamic detection model for malwares based on an immune system [50]. Through dynamic evolution of self, an antibody gene library, and detectors, this model reduced the size of the self set, raised the generating efficiency of detectors, and resolved the problem of detector training time being exponential with respect to the size of self.

Immune-based malware detection techniques have the ability to detect new variations and unknown malwares and paved a new way for anti-malware research. These techniques developed into a new field for malware detection and attracted more and more researchers. However, there is a lack of application of rigorous theoretical principles of mathematics. In addition, the simulations to BIS are still very simple. Combining the characteristics of malware detection with the studies of immune algorithms is needed. There is still a long way to go to apply immune-based malware detection techniques in the real world.

2.4.3 An Immune-Based Virus Detection System Using Affinity Vectors

2.4.3.1 Overview

Aiming at building a light-weight, limited computer resources and early virus warning system, an immune-based virus detection system using affinity vectors (IVDS) was proposed [38]. At first, the IVDS generates a detector set from viruses in the train set, using negative selection and clonal selection. Negative selection eliminates autoimmunity detectors and ensures that any detector in the detector set does not match self; clonal selection increases the diversity of the detector set, which helps the model obtain a stronger ability to recognize new variations and unknown viruses. Then two novel hybrid distances called hamming-max and shift r- bit-continuous distance are presented to calculate the affinity vectors of each file. Finally, based on the affinity vectors, three classic classifiers—SVM, RBF network, and k-nearest neighbor (KNN)—are involved to verify the performance of the model.

2.4.3.2 Experiments and Analysis

The dataset used here is CILPKU08 [58]. Three test datasets are obtained by randomly dividing CILPKU08 dataset as shown in Table 2.2.

Table 2.2 The Test Data Sets in The Experiments

Datasets	Training set		Test set		Percentage of Training set
	Benign programs	Viruses	Benign programs	Viruses	
Dataset 1	71	885	213	2662	0.25
Dataset 2	142	1773	142	1773	0.5
Dataset 3	213	2662	71	885	0.75

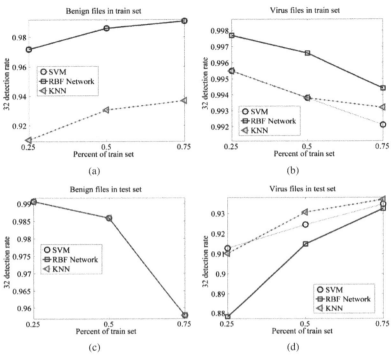

Figure 2.3   The detection accuracy of SVM, RBF network, and KNN.

Here, the percentage of training set $= NTS/(NTS + NDS)$. (NTS and NDS denote the number of programs in the training set and test set, respectively.) The experimental results are shown in Fig. 2.3.

As shown in Fig. 2.3, IVDS achieves high accuracy in detecting unknown viruses when the percentage of the training set is 25 percent. RBF network has better performance than SVM and KNN for the training set and worse accuracy for the test set. We can conclude from this phenomenon that the RBF network has weaker generalization ability here. Whereas the SVM and KNN have stable performances for the training set and test set with different percentages of the training set.

2.4.4   A Hierarchical Artificial Immune Model for Virus Detection

2.4.4.1   Overview

A hierarchical artificial immune model for virus detection (HAIM) has been presented [37]. The motivation of the HAIM is to make full use of the relativity between viruses' signatures. Generally speaking, a virus usually contains several heuristic signatures and a heuristic signature may appear in various viruses. We believe there is some relativity between these heuristic signatures and that an orderly

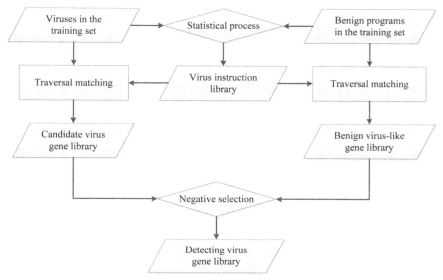

Figure 2.4   Virus gene library generating process.

combination of some signatures makes up a virus. The HAIM, taking a virus as an unit, detects viruses based on the simple relativity between signatures in a virus sample. The HAIM is composed of two modules: the virus gene library generating module and self-nonself classification module. The first module is used to generate the detecting gene library to accomplish the training of given data. The second module is assigned as the detecting phase in terms of the results from the first module for detecting the suspicious programs. The processes of the two modules are given in Figs. 2.4 and 2.5.

The virus gene library generating module extracts a virus instruction library based on the statistics from the training set. Here, an instruction is a bit string with two bytes. Then a candidate virus gene library and a benign virus-like gene library are obtained by traversing all the viruses and benign programs in the training set using a sliding window, respectively. Finally, according to the negative selection mechanism, the candidate virus library is upgraded as the detecting virus gene library.

In the self-nonself classification module, suspicious virus-like genes are extracted from a suspicious program, and they will be used for the classification. The method to calculate the affinity of a suspicious program is illustrated in Fig. 2.6. Getting through the matching processes with three levels, a wise decision is made to classify the program.

2.4.4.2   Experiments and Analysis

The experiments are made using the CILPKU08 dataset [58]. By randomly dividing the dataset into the training set and test set nine times, nine tests have been done. The experimental results are shown in Table 2.3.

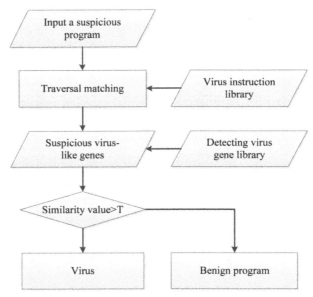

Figure 2.5 Self-nonself classification process.

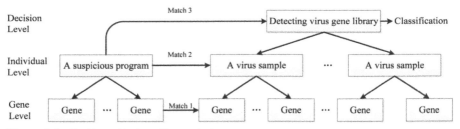

Figure 2.6 The hierarchical matching method.

It is easy to ascertain from Table 2.3 that the HAIM is a very stable model with good performance. It achieves high true negative rates for the unseen benign programs in the test sets with all the false positive rates lower than 2 percent. The average true positive rate achieves 93.27 percent for unknown viruses in the test sets which is comparably high.

2.4.5 A Malware Detection Model Based on a Negative Selection Algorithm with a Penalty Factor

2.4.5.1 Overview

The negative selection algorithm is one of the most important algorithms in artificial immune systems. After deleting detectors that match self, the NSA obtains a

Table 2.3 Experimental Results Obtained by HAIM

	Overall accuracy	False positive rate	True positive rate
Test 1	95.40%	1.80%	92.20%
Test 2	96.30%	1.40%	93.70%
Test 3	97.00%	1.30%	95.10%
Test 4	98.30%	1.10%	97.60%
Test 5	97.40%	1.40%	96.10%
Test 6	96.90%	1.60%	95.30%
Test 7	94.70%	0.70%	90.00%
Test 8	93.60%	1.70%	88.90%
Test 9	94.50%	1.50%	90.50%

detector set, in which none of the items matches self, and which is then used to detect viruses [9]. A traditional NSA assumes that all self is harmless and all nonself is harmful. However, in organisms this is not always the case. Taking cancer cells as an example, not all self is harmless; and similarly, not all nonself is harmful, for example, food. A computer security system, therefore, only has to identify dangerous virus instead of reacting to all nonself.

Take formatting a disk as an example. This operation is dangerous; programs implementing this operation are considered "dangerous." If a program implementing this operation neither reads any command line parameters nor asks the user to confirm, it could be malware. This type of dangerous signature provides some useful information. In fact, the operation of formatting a disk can be included in both malware and benign programs. Deleting such dangerous code snippets, as is done by the traditional NSA, destroys useful information, which is obviously a disadvantage for the malware detection model. Theoretically, every program, regardless of whether it is a benign program or malware, can use almost any of the instructions and functions in a computer system. Moreover, almost all the functions used in malware are also used by specific benign programs, for example, formatting a disk, modifying the registry. If a "perfect" self set is given, the traditional NSA would be ineffective because it would delete too many detectors. Based on the analysis, a malware detection model based on a negative selection algorithm with penalty factor (MDM-NSAPF) was proposed to overcome the drawback of traditional negative selection algorithms in defining the harmfulness of self and nonself [13]. The MDM-NSAPF consists of a malware signature extraction module (MSEM) and a suspicious program detection module (SPDM). A flowchart for the MSEM is shown in Fig. 2.7.

In the MSEM, a malware candidate signature library (MCSL) and a benign program malware-like signature library (BPMSL) are extracted, respectively, from the malware and benign programs of the training set after generating the malware instruction library (MIL). Taking the MCSL as "nonself" and the BPMSL as self, a NSAPF is introduced to extract the malware detection signature library (MDSL) consisting of MDSL1 and MDSL2. Signatures in the MDSL1 are characteristic

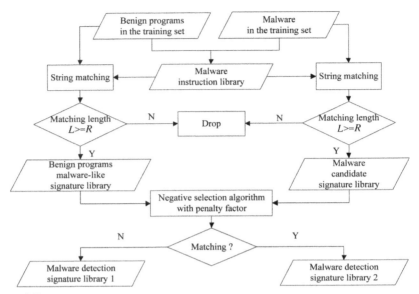

Figure 2.7   Flowchart for MSEM.

signatures of nonself, whereas signatures in the MDSL2 are dangerous ones belonging to both self and nonself, and which should be penalized by penalty factor C after ascertaining, through probabilistic methods, to what extent they represent malware. In the SPDM, signatures of suspicious programs are extracted using the MIL. Then r-contiguous bit matching is computed between the signatures of the suspicious program and the MDSL. If the matching value exceeds the given program classification threshold, we classify the program as malware; otherwise it is considered a benign program.

2.4.5.2 Experiments and Analysis

Experiments were conducted using the three datasets: Henchiri dataset, CILPKU08 dataset, and VX Heavens dataset [59]. The results on the Henchiri dataset and CILPKU08 dataset are shown in Figs. 2.8 and 2.9.

From Fig. 2.8, the optimal overall accuracy of the MDM-NSAPF achieves 96 percent on the test set with penalty factor C = 0.90. With a decrease in penalty factor C, the penalty to signatures in MDSL2 decreases. As a result, the MDSL2 provide helpful information with more and more false information. The overall accuracy increases at first and drops at last. The results confirm that the MDSL2 plays a positive role to improve the effectiveness of the MDM-NSAPF. As illustrated in Fig. 2.9, the overall accuracy of MDM-NSAPF is about 1 percent to 3 percent higher than that of HAIM. The area under the receiver operating characteristic curve (AUC) was set as the measure of the effectiveness of MDM-NSAPF on the VX Heavens dataset. The results are shown in Fig. 2.10. Compared with the

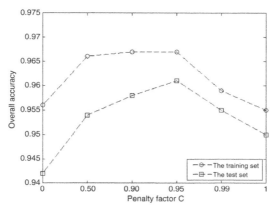

Figure 2.8 Results for Henchiri dataset.

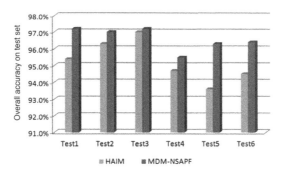

Figure 2.9 Results for CILPKU08 dataset.

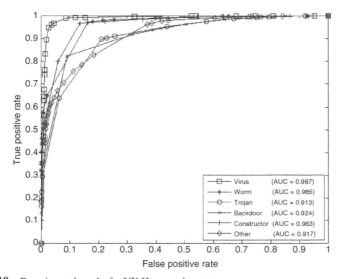

Figure 2.10 Experimental results for VX Heavens dataset.

results of Tabish [11], the optimal AUC of the MDM-NSAPF is on average 0.04 higher.

The MDM-NSAPF focuses on the harmfulness of the code and extracts dangerous signatures, which are included in the MDSL. By adjusting the penalty factor C, the model achieves a tradeoff between the true positive and false positive rates to satisfy the requirements of various users. Comprehensive experimental results confirm that the proposed model is effective in detecting unknown malware with lower false positive rates.

2.5 SUMMARY

The classic malware detection approaches cannot detect new variations and unknown malwares effectively. New malware detection methods are needed urgently. Immune-based computer malware detection approaches, because of the ability to detect unseen malwares, have developed into a new field for anti-malware research. Researchers have proposed a number of malware detection models based on immune mechanisms and achieved some success. However, there is a lack of application of rigorous theoretical principles of mathematics. The simulations of AIS to BIS are very simple. There is still a long way to go to apply immune-based malware detection approaches in the real world.

REFERENCES

1. Bailey, M., Oberheide, J., Andersen, J., Mao, Z.M., Jahanian, F., and Nazario, J. (2007) Automated classification and analysis of internet malware, in *Recent Advances in Intrusion Detection*, Springer, pp. 178–197.
2. Perelson, A.S. and Weisbuch, G. (1997) Immunology for physicists. *Reviews of Modern Physics*, **69** (4), 1219.
3. Forrest, S., Perelson, A., Allen, L., and Cherukuri, R. (1994) Self-nonself discrimination in a computer, in Research in Security and Privacy, 1994. Proceedings., 1994 IEEE Computer Society Symposium on, IEEE, pp. 202–212.
4. Kephart, J.O. and Arnold, W.C. (1994) Automatic extraction of computer virus signatures, in 4th virus bulletin international conference, pp. 178–184.
5. Kephart, J., Sorkin, G., Swimmer, M., and White, S. (1999) *Blueprint for a Computer Immune System*∗, Springer.
6. Okamoto, T. and Ishida, Y. (2000) A distributed approach against computer viruses inspired by the immune system. *IEICE Transactions on Communications*, **83** (5), 908–915.
7. Fu J.M., Peng G.J., Z.H.G. (2009) *Computer Virus Analysis and Confronting*, Wuhan University Press, China.
8. Wikipedia . URL http://en.wikipedia.org/wiki/Malware.
9. Zhang, P., Wang, W., and Tan, Y. (2010) A malware detection model based on a negative selection algorithm with penalty factor. *Science China Information Sciences*, **53** (12), 2461–2471.
10. Ye, Y., Wang, D., Li, T., and Ye, D. (2007) Imds: Intelligent malware detection system, in Proceedings of the 13th ACM SIGKDD International Conference on Knowledge Discovery and Data Mining, ACM, pp. 1043–1047.
11. Tabish, S.M., Shafiq, M.Z., and Farooq, M. (2009) Malware detection using statistical analysis of byte-level file content, in Proceedings of the ACM SIGKDD Workshop on CyberSecurity and Intelligence Informatics, ACM, pp. 23–31.

12. Al Daoud, E. (2009) Metamorphic viruses detection using artificial immune system, in Communication Software and Networks, 2009. ICCSN'09. International Conference on, IEEE, pp. 168–172.

13. Zhang, P., Wang, W., and Tan, Y. (2010) A malware detection model based on a negative selection algorithm with penalty factor. *SCIENCE CHINA Information Sciences*, **53** (12), 2461–2471.

14. Ye, Y., Jiang, Q., and Zhuang, W. (2008) Associative classification and post-processing techniques used for malware detection, in Anti-Counterfeiting, Security and Identification, 2008. ASID 2008. 2nd International Conference on, IEEE, pp. 276–279.

15. Ye, Y., Wang, D., Li, T., Ye, D., and Jiang, Q. (2008) An intelligent pe-malware detection system based on association mining. *Journal in Computer Virology*, **4** (4), 323–334.

16. Christodorescu, M., Jha, S., Seshia, S.A., Song, D., and Bryant, R.E. (2005) Semantics-aware malware detection, in Security and Privacy, 2005 IEEE Symposium on, IEEE, pp. 32–46.

17. Xiaosong, Z., Xiaohui, P., and Xiaoshu, L. (2009) Analysis of virtual machine applied to malware detection system, in Information Engineering and Electronic Commerce, 2009. IEEC'09. International Symposium on, IEEE, pp. 290–294.

18. Wang, C., Pang, J., Zhao, R., Fu, W., and Liu, X. (2009) Malware detection based on suspicious behavior identification, in Education Technology and Computer Science, 2009. ETCS'09. First International Workshop on, IEEE, vol. 2, pp. 198–202.

19. Han, Q.L., Hao, Y.J., Zhang, Y., Lu, Z.P., and Zhang, R. (2008) A new malware detection method based on raw information, in Apperceiving Computing and Intelligence Analysis, 2008. ICACIA 2008. International Conference on, pp. 307–310, doi: 10.1109/ICACIA.2008.4770030

20. Gavrilut, D., Cimpoesu, M., Anton, D., and Ciortuz, L. (2009) Malware detection using machine learning, in Computer Science and Information Technology, 2009. IMCSIT'09. International Multiconference on, IEEE, pp. 735–741.

21. Zolkipli, M.F. and Jantan, A. (2010) A framework for malware detection using combination technique and signature generation, in Computer Research and Development, 2010 Second International Conference on, IEEE, pp. 196–199.

22. Komashinskiy, D. and Kotenko, I. (2010) Malware detection by data mining techniques based on positionally dependent features, in Parallel, Distributed and Network-Based Processing (PDP), 2010 18th Euromicro International Conference on, IEEE, pp. 617–623.

23. Xu, J., Sung, A.H., Mukkamala, S., and Liu, Q. (2007) Obfuscated malicious executable scanner. *Journal of Research & Practice in Information Technology*, **39** (3).

24. Kerchen, P., Lo, R., Crossley, J., Elkinbard, G., and Olsson, R. (1990) Static analysis virus detection tools for unix systems, in Proceedings of the 13th National Computer Security Conference, pp. 350–365.

25. LISTON, T. (2007) Hiding virtualization from attackers and malware.

26. Willems, C., Holz, T., and Freiling, F. (2007) Toward automated dynamic malware analysis using cwsandbox. *IEEE Security and Privacy*, **5** (2), 32–39.

27. Yan, W., Zhang, Z., and Ansari, N. (2008) Revealing packed malware. *Security & Privacy, IEEE*, **6** (5), 65–69.

28. Hofmeyr, S.A., Forrest, S., and Somayaji, A. (1998) Intrusion detection using sequences of system calls. *Journal of Computer Security*, **6** (3), 151–180.

29. Sulaiman, A., Ramamoorthy, K., Mukkamala, S., and Sung, A.H. (2005) Disassembled code analyzer for malware (dcam), in Information Reuse and Integration, Conf, 2005. IRI-2005 IEEE International Conference on, IEEE, pp. 398–403.

30. Henchiri, O. and Japkowicz, N. (2006) A feature selection and evaluation scheme for computer virus detection, in Data Mining, 2006. ICDM'06. Sixth International Conference on, IEEE, pp. 891–895.

31. Karnik, A., Goswami, S., and Guha, R. (2007) Detecting obfuscated viruses using cosine similarity analysis, in Modelling & Simulation, 2007. AMS'07. First Asia International Conference on, IEEE, pp. 165–170.

32. Bruschi, D., Martignoni, L., and Monga, M. (2007) Code normalization for self-mutating malware. *IEEE Security and Privacy*, **5** (2), 46–54.

33. Li, J., Mao, J., Wei, T., and Zou, W. (2009) A static method for detection of information theft malware, in Electronic Commerce and Security, 2009. ISECS'09. Second International Symposium on, IEEE, vol. 1, pp. 236–240.

34. Treadwell, S. and Zhou, M. (2009) A heuristic approach for detection of obfuscated malware, in Intelligence and Security Informatics, 2009. ISI'09. IEEE International Conference on, IEEE, pp. 291–299.

35. Ye, Y., Li, T., Jiang, Q., and Wang, Y. (2010) CIMDS: adapting postprocessing techniques of associative classification for malware detection. *Systems, Man, and Cybernetics, Part C: Applications and Reviews, IEEE Transactions on*, **40** (3), 298–307.

36. Shaorong, F. and Zhixue, H. (2010) An incremental associative classification algorithm used for malware detection, in Future Computer and Communication (ICFCC), 2010 2nd International Conference on, IEEE, vol. 1, pp. V1–757.

37. Wang, W., Zhang, P., Tan, Y., and He, X. (2009) A hierarchical artificial immune model for virus detection, in Computational Intelligence and Security, 2009. CIS'09. International Conference on, IEEE, vol. 1, pp. 1–5.

38. Chao, R. and Tan, Y. (2009) A virus detection system based on artificial immune system, in Computational Intelligence and Security, 2009. CIS'09. International Conference on, IEEE, vol. 1, pp. 6–10.

39. Wang, W., Zhang, P., and Tan, Y. (2010) An immune concentration based virus detection approach using particle swarm optimization, in *Advances in Swarm Intelligence*, Springer, pp. 347–354.

40. Guo, Z., Liu, Z., and Tan, Y. (2004) An nn-based malicious executables detection algorithm based on immune principles, in *Advances in Neural Networks-ISNN 2004*, Springer, pp. 675–680.

41. Tan, Y. and Guo, Z. (2005) Algorithms of non-self detector by negative selection principle in artificial immune system, in *Advances in Natural Computation*, Springer, pp. 867–875.

42. Forrest, S., Hofmeyr, S., Somayaji, A., and Longstaff, T. (1996) A sense of self for unix processes, in Security and Privacy, 1996. Proceedings., 1996 IEEE Symposium on, IEEE, pp. 120–128.

43. Kim, J. and Bentley, P.J. (2001) Towards an artificial immune system for network intrusion detection: An investigation of clonal selection with a negative selection operator, in Evolutionary Computation, 2001. Proceedings of the 2001 Congress on, IEEE, vol. 2, pp. 1244–1252.

44. Matzinger, P. (2002) The danger model: a renewed sense of self. *Science's STKE*, **296** (5566), 301.

45. Lee, H., Kim, W., and Hong, M. (2004) Artificial immune system against viral attack, in *Computational Science-ICCS 2004*, Springer, pp. 499–506.

46. Edge, K.S., Lamont, G.B., and Raines, R.A. (2006) A retrovirus inspired algorithm for virus detection & optimization, in Proceedings of the 8th Annual Conference on Genetic and Evolutionary Computation, ACM, pp. 103–110.

47. Li, Z., Liang, Y., Wu, Z., and Tan, C. (2007) Immunity based virus detection with process call arguments and user feedback, in Bio-Inspired Models of Network, Information and Computing Systems, 2007. Bionetics 2007. 2nd, IEEE, pp. 57–64.

48. Gonzalez, F.A. and Dasgupta, D. (2003) Anomaly detection using real-valued negative selection. *Genetic Programming and Evolvable Machines*, **4** (4), 383–403.

49. Balachandran, S., Dasgupta, D., Nino, F., and Garrett, D. (2007) A framework for evolving multi-shaped detectors in negative selection, in Foundations of Computational Intelligence, 2007. FOCI 2007. IEEE Symposium on, IEEE, pp. 401–408.

50. Li, T. (2008) Dynamic detection for computer virus based on immune system. *Science in China Series F: Information Sciences*, **51** (10), 1475–1486.

51. Harmer, P.K., Williams, P.D., Gunsch, G.H., and Lamont, G.B. (2002) An artificial immune system architecture for computer security applications. *Evolutionary Computation, IEEE Transactions on*, **6** (3), 252–280.

52. Marhusin, M.F., Cornforth, D., and Larkin, H. (2008) Malicious code detection architecture inspired by human immune system, in Software Engineering, Artificial Intelligence, Networking, and Parallel/Distributed Computing, 2008. SNPD'08. Ninth ACIS International Conference on, IEEE, pp. 312–317.

53. Gong, T. (2008) Unknown non-self detection & robustness of distributed artificial immune system with normal model, in Intelligent Control and Automation, 2008. WCICA 2008. 7th World Congress on, IEEE, pp. 1444–1448.

54. Zhang, Y., Li, T., and Qin, R. (2008) A dynamic immunity-based model for computer virus detection, in Information Processing (ISIP), 2008 International Symposiums on, IEEE, pp. 515–519.

55. Qin, R., Li, T., and Zhang, Y. (2009) An immune inspired model for obfuscated virus detection, in Industrial Mechatronics and Automation, 2009. ICIMA 2009. International Conference on, IEEE, pp. 228–231.

56. Zeng, J. and Li, T. (2009) A novel computer virus detection method from ideas of immunology, in Multimedia Information Networking and Security, 2009. MINES'09. International Conference on, IEEE, vol. 1, pp. 412–416.

57. Somayaji, A., Hofmeyr, S., and Forrest, S. (1998) Principles of a computer immune system, in Proceedings of the 1997 Workshop on New Security Paradigms, ACM, pp. 75–82.

58. Cilpku08 malware dataset, http://www.cil.pku.edu.cn/malware/.

59. Resource, http://www.cil.pku.edu.cn/resources/.

Chapter 3

Immune Principle and Neural Networks-Based Malware Detection

Detection of unknown malware is one of most important tasks in Computer Immune System (CIS) studies. By using nonself detection, diversity of anti-body (Ab) and artificial neural networks (ANN), this chapter proposes an NN-based malware detection algorithm. A number of experiments illustrate that this algorithm has high detection rate with a very low false positive rate.

3.1 INTRODUCTION

Detection methods of viruses are generally divided into two categories. One is based on signature, which can be used to quickly detect a known virus but doesn't detect unknown and mutated viruses. As the number and classes of the viruses increase, the detection speed of this method will be slowed gradually down because the analysis of virus signature becomes very difficult and time consuming. To cope with this problem, IBM Anti-virus Group proposed an automatic extraction method of virus signatures even though it cannot extract the signature of an encrypted virus [1]. The other method is based on expert knowledge, with which one can construct a classifier to detect unknown viruses [2]. This method can discover some unknown viruses, but its false detection rate is high. To detect unknown viruses, IBM Anti-virus Group also proposes one ANN-based method to detect Boot Sector virus [3] only. Schultz and associates proposed a Bayes method to detect malicious executables, obtaining a good result [4].

Aiming at automation detection malicious executables, this chapter proposes a novel malware detection algorithm (MDA) [5] based on the immune principle and artificial neural networks (ANN) [6]. Extensive experiments show that the algorithm has a better detection performance than Schultz's method.

Artificial Immune System: Applications in Computer Security, First Edition. Ying Tan.
© 2016 the IEEE Computer Society. Published 2016 by John Wiley & Sons, Inc.

3.2 IMMUNE SYSTEM FOR MALICIOUS EXECUTABLE DETECTION

3.2.1 Nonself Detection Principles

To natural immune system, all cells of body are divided into two types of self and nonself. The immune process is to detect nonself from the cell set. To realize the nonself detection, the mature process of the T cell experiences two stages of selection, which are Positive Selection and Negative Selection. Inspired by these two stages, some computer scientists had proposed a few algorithms to detect anomaly information. For example, Forrest and associates proposed a Negative Selection Algorithm (NSA) based on the negative selection process in BIS for computer virus detection [7,8].

3.2.2 Anomaly Detection Based on Thickness

During the anomaly recognition process, cells of the immune system detect antigens and are activated. The activation threshold of immune cells is determined by the thickness of immune cells matching antigens. This property is very useful for improving the anomaly detection power and protecting immune system balance [9,10].

3.2.3 Relationship Between Diversity of Detector Representation and Anomaly Detection Hole

The main function of the anomaly detection utmost decreases the anomaly detection hole, which was efficiently resolved in the natural immune system (BIS). The diversity of the representation of MHC cells determines the diversity of antibody touched in surface of T cells. This property is very useful to increase the power of detecting mutated antigens and decrease the anomaly detection hole [11]. Inspired by this principle in Computer Immune System (CIS) [12] research, we can make use of the diversity of detector representations to decrease the anomaly detection hole.

3.3 EXPERIMENTAL DATASET

The experimental dataset is composed of 4481 executables, which includes 915 benign executables and 3566 virus programs. All files are scanned then classified by a virus cleaner tool. We collected all *.exe files during the windows 2000 operation system and some other application programs were installed in a computer. Through scanning these files by a virus killer, we constructed the benign executable set with 915 executables. The 3566 virus files are collected from the Internet and are also scanned as virus files by a virus killer, that is, the malicious executables set mainly consists of DOS virus, win32 virus, Trojan, Worm, and so on.

3.4 MALWARE DETECTION ALGORITHM

3.4.1 Definition of Data Structures

Definitions include:

B: binary code alphabet, $B = \{0, 1\}$.

$Seq(s, k, l)$: short sequence cutting operation. Suppose s be binary sequence, and $s = b(0)b(1)\ldots b(n-1)$, $b(i) \in B$, then $Seq(s, k, l) = b(k)b(k+1)\ldots b(k+l-1)$, k is the starting position of the short sequence in s.

$E(k)$: executables set, $k \in m, b$, m denotes malicious executable, b denotes benign executable.

E: all executables set, $E = E(m) \cup E(b)$.

$e(f_j, n)$: executable, $e(f_j, n)$ can be expressed as binary sequence that its length is n, and f_j is executable identifier.

l_d: detector code length.

l_{step}: detector generation step length.

d_l: detector, $d_l = Seq(s, k, l)$.

D_l: detector set, detector code length is l, $D_l = d_l(0), d_l(1), \ldots, d_l(n_d - 1)$, $|D_l| = n_d$.

3.4.2 Detection Principle and Algorithm

One executable can be regarded as a binary code sequence. Different binary code sequences of an executable decides that program has a different function. So, we might guess that using the binary sequence allows it to distinguish different programs, and then detect the function of that program. Based on the above principle, we constructed the detectors with short binary sequence and hoped this kind of detector can distinguish malicious executables from benign executables. We tried to build a set of short sequences that included benign executables' properties. These short sequences were used to construct the detector set D_l. Now, the question is how to generate these binary short sequences, that is, detectors, and how to detect nonself by using these binary short sequences.

This algorithm is based on the principle of nonself detection. First of all, the algorithm constructs a gene (G) that is used to generate detectors. The gene is composed of a gene unit, $e(f_j, n)$. These units are composed of benign executables. Here, G is constructed with $E_g(b)$, a subset of $E(b)$. Second, the algorithm extracts anomaly information according to the anomaly detection principle based on thickness. Third, according to the diversity of detector representation, the algorithm detects malicious executables with superior classifier. In summary, this algorithm includes three parts: detector generation, anomaly information extraction, and classification, whose block diagram is shown in Fig. 3.1.

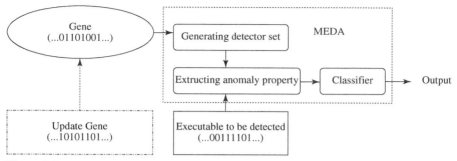

Figure 3.1   Block diagram of the malware detection algorithm.

3.4.3   Generation of Detector Set

3.4.3.1 Detector Code

Detector is encoded as a binary sequence, $d_l = Seq(s, k, l)$. The diversity of detector is realized by changing the code length l [13]. If code length $l = l_0, l_1, l_2, \ldots, l_m$, detector has m kinds, then detector set(D_l) also has m kinds.

3.4.3.2 Generation of Detector Set

Through partitioning the binary sequence of a program into equal lengths, detectors are generated. There are two parameters to be set before the detector set is generated. One is the generating step length l_{step}; the other is detector code length l_d.

3.4.4   Extraction of Anomaly Characteristics

3.4.4.1 Nonself Detection

Nonself detection is the first step of anomaly characteristics extraction. The nonself detection step finds short sequences that are not included in the self-set. Because we construct the detector set with a self short sequence, we use the Positive Selection Algorithm (PSA) [14] to detect nonself. Contrasting with NSA, PSA uses self-units as detectors. On the process of nonself detection, the short sequence not matched by any detector is nonself, otherwise, it is self. Its work process is shown in Fig. 3.2.

Algorithm 6   Detector Generating Algorithm

```
initialize l_step, l_d, k = 0.
repeat
    cutting e(f_k, n) from E_g(b).
    i = 0
    while i ≤ n - l_d - 1 do
        d = Seq(e(f_k, n), i, l_d).
```

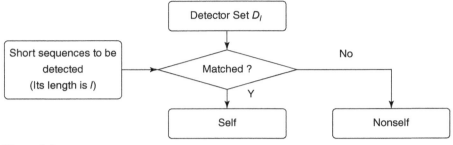

Figure 3.2   Diagram of the anomaly detection with PSA.

```
    if d ∉ D₁_d then
         D₁_d ← d
    end if
    i = i + l_step.
  end while
  k = k + 1.
until cutting e(f_k, n) is over. return D₁_d
```

3.4.4.2 Extraction of Anomaly Property Vector

According to the anomaly detection principle of the immune system based on thickness, we define the percentage of nonself unit number to file binary sequence as Anomaly Property. Anomaly Property is named as Nonself Thickness (NTh) in this chapter, and expressed as p_l. If detectors have m kinds, the file has an Anomaly Property Vector $P = (p_{l_1}, p_{l_2}, \ldots, p_{l_m})$.

Algorithm 7   NTh Extraction Algorithm

```
Open e(f_k, n).
Select l_step, l_d.
Set n_s = 0, n_n = 0.
i = 0.
while i ≤ n − l_d − 1 do
    s = Seq(e(f_k, n), i, l_d).
    if s ∉ D₁_d
        n_n = n_n + 1.
    else
        n_s = n_s + 1.
    end if
    i = i + l_step.
end while
p₁_d = n_n/(n_s + n_n).  return p₁_d
```

To different detector set, this algorithm computes a separate NTh of the file. Finally, all NThs are combined to construct the Anomaly Property Vector $P = \left(p_{l_1}, p_{l_2}, \ldots, p_{l_m}\right)$.

3.4.5 Classifier

We use the Anomaly Property Vector as input of a BP neural network classifier, which consists of two layers. Anomaly Property Vector of the file is the input vector of this network. The number of neurons in the first layer is equal to the dimension of Anomaly Property Vector. The transfer function of input layer uses a Sigmoid-type function, while a liner function is chosen as the transfer function of the output layer of the BP neural network classifier [15].

3.5 EXPERIMENT

The first goal is to verify the detection ability of the malware detection algorithm for malicious executables. The experimental results are all scaled with false positive rate (FPR) and detection rate (DR). The second goal is to calculate the probability of the reducing detection hole with the diversity of detectors. Last, we compare our experimental results with Schultz's results [4].

3.5.1 Experimental Procedure

3.5.1.1 Partitioning Dataset

The whole dataset is divided into benign and malicious executables subsets, $E(b)$ and $E(m)$, respectively. $E(b)$ is composed of 915 program files and is divided into the generating detector dataset $E_g(b)$, which is the gene used to generate the detector data set, and the testing dataset $E_{test}(b)$. Here, $E_g(b)$ includes 613 program files and is constructed by randomly selecting from $E(b)$. The other 302 program files in $E(b)$ are elements of $E_{test}(b)$. In addition, $E(m)$ is composed of 3566 virus files.

3.5.1.2 Generating Detector Set

We select $E_g(b)$ as the gene of generating detectors, $ld \in 16, 24, 32, 64, 96$, and $l_{step} = 8$ bits. By using the detector generating algorithm, we can obtain five detector sets with $D_{16}, D_{24}, D_{32}, D_{64}$, and D_{96}, separately. In order to reduce the space complexity of detector savings, this algorithm uses Bitmap Index technology combined with Tree technology to store detectors.

3.5.2 Experimental Results

3.5.2.1 When to Use a Single Detector Set

Initially, we separately detect malicious executables with a single detector set of five kinds. The experimental result is shown in Figs. 3.3 and 3.4.

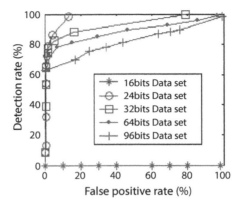

Figure 3.3 ROC curves for five kinds of detector sets.

When $FPS = 0$ and $l_d = 96$, it can be seen from Figs. 3.3 and 3.4 that the best detection effect can be obtained, and the DR becomes worse as the length of l_d becomes longer. The DR becomes better as the FPS becomes worse. When $FPS \geq 1\%$, the detection rate is the highest when $l_d = 24$. Meanwhile, with the length of l_d, the DR will be worse. On the other hand, when $l_d = 16$, the DR is 0 because the number of detectors reaches 2^{16}. When $l_d = 96$, the DR is almost the same regardless of FPS values.

3.5.2.2 When to Use Multi-Datasets and BP Network Classifier

As described in Section 3.4, this experiment uses multi-datasets to detect benign and malicious executables. Here we don't use the D_{16} dataset because the DR is 0 for this

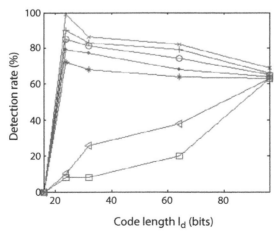

Figure 3.4 When FPR is constant, the curves of DR with l_d. From bottom up, the FPR is 0%, 0.5%, 1%, 2%, 4%, 8%, and 16%, respectively.

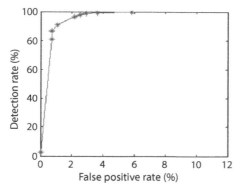

Figure 3.5 Experimental ROC curves with BP network classifier.

dataset. At the same time, we set the upper limit of l_d to be 96 because the DR is almost the same when $l_d = 96$. So, in this experiment, we selected the four datasets of D_{24}, D_{32}, D_{64}, and D_{96}, as anomaly detection sets, and use them for extracting the Anomaly Property Vector. Finally, a BP network with two layers is used as a classifier. In the classification process, we randomly select 30 percent files of $E_{test}(b)$ to train the BP network classifier, and use the other to test the performance of the anomaly detection algorithm. The experimental results are shown with ROCs in Figs. 3.3–3.5 [16].

3.5.3 Comparison With Matthew G. Schultz's Method

3.5.3.1 Comparison of Datasets

Table 3.1 compares experimental sets.

3.5.3.2 Comparison of Algorithmic Performance

Comparison of algorithmic performance includes two aspects—detection rate and the complexity of algorithms.

1. **Detection rates of algorithms:** Known from Schultz's experimental result [4], using the Naive Bayes approach, the DR can reach 97.43 percent when FPR is 3.80 percent. As for MEDA, when FPR is 2 percent, the DR can reach the same value. When to use Multi-Naive Bayes, the detection rate of the algorithm obtains the highest value of 97.76 percent. But for MEDA, the highest DR can reach 99.50 percent. The detailed comparisons are shown in Fig. 3.6.

2. **Complexity of algorithms:** The complexity of algorithms includes both computational complexity and space complexity. The space complexity is mainly about the space size to store detectors and probability information ($P(F_i/C)$) of two kinds of algorithms. The malware detection algorithm used $4000MB$ to store detector set (shown in Table 3.2), while Schultz used about $1\ GB$ to store his probability information [4].

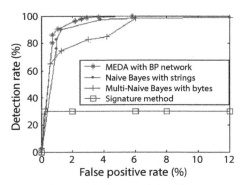

Figure 3.6   Comparison of experiment results for several algorithms.

Table 3.1   Comparisons of Experimental Data Sets

Data set	Operation system	Collection method	Size of data set	$E(b)$	Number	$E(m)$ kinds
M.G. Schultz's data set	Windows	Collecting all *.exe file to construct E(b), and collecting E(m) in Internet	4266	1001	3265	Trojan, virus
Our data set	Windows	As above	4481	915	3566	Trojan, worm and virus

As for the computational complexity, the main operational units in MDA include generating detector, matching short sequence, computing nonself thickness, and classification by BP network. The main operational units of Schultz with Bayes include generating probability information, searching conditional probability $P(F_i/C)$ [4], computing $P(C)\prod_{i=1}^{n}P(F_i/C)$, and classification by probability. In this chapter for simplicity, we won't think about the classification operations. Suppose file size of training dataset is l_{train} bytes, and the size of the file to be detected is l_{test} bytes, the computational complexities of the two algorithms are shown in Table 3.3.

Table 3.2   Generation of Detectors

Detector code length l_d	16	24	32	64	96
$\lvert D_{l_d} \rvert$	65536	10,931,627	8,938,352	12,768,361	21,294,857
Methods to store detectors	Bitmap index	Bitmap index	Tree	Tree	Tree

Table 3.3 Comparison of Computational Complexities of Two Algorithms

Algorithms	Operation type 1		Operation type 2		Operation type 3	
	Name	Operation number	Name	Operation number	Name	Operation number
MDA	Generating detectors	l_{train}	String matching	$\leq 80*l_{test}$[1)]	Computing non-self thickness	$4*l_f$ times addition
Bayes	Generating probability information	$\gg l_{train}$	Searching $P(F_i/C)$	Rest with the number of $P(F_i/C)$	Computing $P(C)\prod_{i=1}^{n}P(F_i/C)$	l_f times float multiplication

3.6 SUMMARY

It turns out from a number of experiments that the detector generated with executable binary short sequences can be used to detect malicious and benign executables. When using a single detector set to detect malicious executables, the best performance with the DR reaches 80.6 percent when FPS is 3 percent. Meanwhile, if a longer code length of detector is used, the DR of single detector set becomes lower. The best detection performance of our algorithm is obtained when a multi-detector set is used to detect malicious executables with 97.46 percent DR when FPS is 2 percent. This verified our claimed principle that diversity of detector representations can decrease the anomaly detection hole, and further it also validated nonself detection and detection based on thickness.

REFERENCES

1. Lo, R.W., Levitt, K.N., and Olsson, R.A. (1995) Mcf: A malicious code filter. *Computers & Security*, **14** (6), 541–566.
2. Arnold, W. and Tesauro, G. (2000) Automatically generated win32 heuristic virus detection, in Proceedings of the 2000 International Virus Bulletin Conference, September 2000, pp.51–58.
3. Wikipedia, Boot sector viruses.
4. Schultz, M.G., Eskin, E., Zadok, E., and Stolfo, S.J. (2001) Data mining methods for detection of new malicious executables, in Security and Privacy, 2001. S&P 2001. Proceedings. 2001 IEEE Symposium on, IEEE, pp. 38–49.
5. Guo, Z., Liu, Z., and Tan, Y. (2004) An NN-based malicious executables detection algorithm based on immune principles, in *Advances in Neural Networks-ISNN 2004*, Springer, pp. 675–680.
6. Dayhoff, J.E. and DeLeo, J.M. (2001) Artificial neural networks. *Cancer*, **91** (S8), 1615–1635.
7. Forrest, S., Perelson, A., Allen, L., and Cherukuri, R. (1994) Self-nonself discrimination in a computer, in Research in Security and Privacy, 1994. Proceedings, 1994 IEEE Computer Society Symposium on, IEEE, pp. 202–212.
8. Guo, Z., Tan, Y., and Liu, Z. (2005) Non-self detector generating algorithm based on negative selection principle. *Journal of Chinese Computer Systems*, **26** (6), 959–964.

9. Guo, Z., Tan, Y., and Liu, Z. (2005) Malicious executables detection algorithm research based on immune system principles. *Journal of Chinese Computer Systems*, **26** (7), 1191–1195.

10. Guo, Z., Liu, Z., and Tan, Y. (2005) Detector generating algorithm based on hyper-sphere. *Journal of Chinese Computer Systems*, **26** (12), 1641–1645.

11. Tan, Y. and Guo, Z. (2005) Algorithms of non-self detector by negative selection principle in artificial immune system, in *Advances in Natural Computation*, Springer, pp. 867–875.

12. Somayaji, A., Hofmeyr, S., and Forrest, S. (1998) Principles of a computer immune system, in Proceedings of the 1997 Workshop on New Security Paradigms, ACM, pp. 75–82.

13. Tan, Y. (2006) Multiple-point bit mutation method of detector generation for SNSD model, in *Advances in Neural Networks-ISNN 2006*, Springer, pp. 340–345.

14. Dasgupta, D. and Nino, F. (2000) A comparison of negative and positive selection algorithms in novel pattern detection, in Systems, Man, and Cybernetics, 2000 IEEE International Conference on, IEEE, vol. 1, pp. 125–130.

15. Ruan, G. and Tan, Y. (2007) Intelligent detection approaches for spam, in Natural Computation, 2007. ICNC 2007. Third International Conference on, IEEE, vol. 3, pp. 672–676.

16. Crawford, R., Kerchen, P., Levitt, K., Olsson, R., Archer, M., and Casillas, M. (1993) Automated assistance for detecting malicious code, *Tech. Rep.*, Lawrence Livermore National Lab., CA (United States).

Chapter 4

Multiple-Point Bit Mutation Method of Detector Generation

In self and nonself discrimination (SNSD) model, it is very important to generate a desirable detector set since it decides the performance and scale of the SNSD model-based task. By using the natural immune system's negative selection principle, a novel detector generating algorithm (i.e., multiple-point bit mutation method) is proposed in this chapter. It utilizes random multiple-point mutation to look for nonself detectors in a large range of the space of detectors, such that we can obtain a required detector set in a reasonable computing time. This chapter describes the work procedure of the proposed detector generating algorithm. Then we tested the algorithm on many datasets and compared it with the Exhaustive Detector Generating Algorithm in detail. The experimental results show that the proposed algorithm outperforms the Exhaustive Detector Generating Algorithm in both detection performance and computational complexity.

4.1 INTRODUCTION

The biological immune system protects the body against harmful diseases and infections by recognizing and discriminating nonself from self. This ability plays very important adjustment functions in the whole lifetime of biological creatures. Recently, many algorithms and architectures were proposed [1–5] in many engineering fields based on natural immune principles. The prevalent model of the immune system is the self and nonself discrimination (SNSD) model [6], which has been used for many years by researchers in the immune community. This SNSD model uses the idea that the immune system functions by making a distinction between bodies native to the system and foreign bodies. Many computer researchers used it as a metaphor to develop artificial immune algorithms and systems for intrusion monitoring and detection, resource change detection, pattern recognition, as well as computation of complex problems [7]. Among them, the negative selection algorithm (NSA) was proposed [2] as a detector generating algorithm by simulating the negative selection

Artificial Immune System: Applications in Computer Security, First Edition. Ying Tan.
© 2016 the IEEE Computer Society. Published 2016 by John Wiley & Sons, Inc.

process of T cells generating in the thymus. However, the generation of detectors is a vital computation burden in NSA and attracts a lot of researchers to explore an efficient algorithm for it. In this chapter, we study the detector generating algorithm and propose a detector generating algorithm based on the SNSD model and negative selection principle from the perspective of optimizing detector generation [8]. The working procedure of the proposed algorithm is presented in detail and then compared to the Exhaustive Detector Generating Algorithm (EDGA).

4.2 CURRENT DETECTOR GENERATING ALGORITHMS

As we know, for biological immune systems, T-cells with essentially random receptors are generated in the thymus. Their generation and maturation undergo a negative selection process. Before they are released to the rest of body, those T-cells matched with self are deleted. This process is called as negative selection process. According to this principle, a number of detector generating algorithms are created in artificial immune systems (AIS) and practical applications. For example, in 1994, Forrest, et al., proposed so-called negative selection algorithm (NSA) inspired by the negative selection principle [2] and applied it to intrusion detection and change detection. NSA primarily consists of two stages of censoring and monitoring. The censoring phase caters for the generation of change detectors. Subsequently, the system being protected is monitored for changes using the detector set generated in the censoring stage.

In the censoring phase, the generation of change detectors needs a large of computational amount which limits the use of NSA in practical applications [9]. Since then, a number of detector generating algorithms with different matching rules applied for self and nonself matching methods are proposed and tested for promoting the application of NSA. For binary code of detector, there are mainly three kinds of matching rules: perfect matching, r-contiguous bits matching and Hamming distance matching [2]. Exhaustive detector generating algorithm (EDGA) is suitable for all of the three matching rules and is used to repeat the negative selection process till the number of detectors meets a presetting requirement or candidate set is vanished. However, negative selection algorithm with mutation [5,10] has different evaluation rules in the negative selection process from EDGA. With the r-contiguous bits matching rule, the related algorithms mainly include the Liner Time Detector Generating Algorithm [4] and the Greedy Detectors Generating Algorithm [5].

4.3 GROWTH ALGORITHMS

The major difference between growth algorithm and NSA is the generating method of candidate detectors. For NSA, each detector candidate in EDGA is randomly selected from the whole candidate space. Thus, after the number of detector candidate space N_{r0} is determined, EDGA randomly selects N_{r0} detectors to construct the detector candidate set R_0. Then, the algorithm generates the detector set R through negative selection process. On the other hand, growth algorithm does not need to

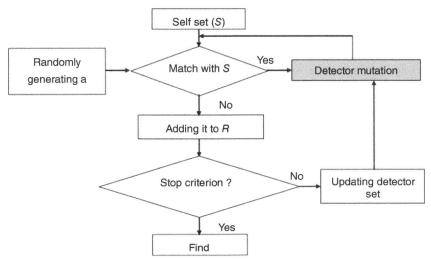

Figure 4.1   Flow chart of detector generation growth algorithm.

maintain a huge detector candidate set R_0. It generates the detector set R directly by utilizing detector mutation or growth in whole shape space, and combining with the negative selection process. The flow chart of the detector generating algorithm is shown in Fig. 4.1.

Algorithm 8   Growth Algorithm

---

1. Generate self set S with its number N_s.
2. Generate one detector generating seed that is randomly selected from the whole shape space.
3. Match the new detector candidate with S.
4. Experience a negative selection process. If the candidate is not matched with S, then a new one is generated and added into R.
5. If the stop criterion is met, then exit.
6. Mutate the candidate and go to step 3.

4.4 MULTIPLE-POINT BIT MUTATION METHOD

As indicated by the name, the proposed method is somewhat similar to the bit muta-tion mechanism of Genetic Algorithm (GA) [11]. But this algorithm mutates multi-ple bits of detector candidate simultaneously, not only one bit. If we let the string length be l and the maximum number of mutation bits be N_m ($N_m = m$), then, at one time, the mutated bits of detector candidate is less than or equal to m.

Algorithm 9   Multiple-Point Bit Mutation Algorithm

---

1. Set the maximum number of mutation bits N_m.
2. Input detector DetectorM to be mutated.
3. Generate mutation seed MutationBits (its length is same as detector): N_m bits of Mutation-Bits are randomly generated at range of 1 and l and set to 1, and others are set to zero.
4. Detector mutation: an exclusive OR operation performed on the corresponding bits of arrays DetectorM and MutationBits.
5. If the stop criterion is met, then exit.
6. Mutate the candidate and going to step 4.

Once the proposed multiple-point bit mutation method is applied to the detector mutation part of the growth algorithm in Fig. 4.1, we can obtain the detector generating algorithm just called multiple-point bit mutation detector generating algorithm (BMDGA) [8–10,12,13].

4.5 EXPERIMENTS

We set two kinds of experiments. One is to choose a random dataset with string lengths 8, 16, and 24 bits, respectively. The other experiment is to detect the changes of static files.

4.5.1 Experiments on Random Dataset

4.5.1.1 8-Bit Dataset

Figures 4.2–4.5 give the experimental results of an 8-bit dataset.

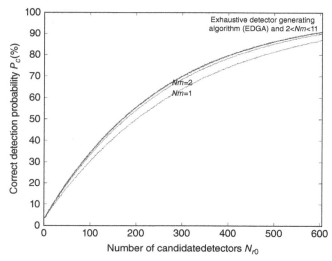

Figure 4.2   Experimental results of Detection rate P_c versus N_{r0} when N_s is constant, where $N_s = 8$, N_{r0} increases from 1 to 604, size of test set is 256, and averaged over 1000 runs.

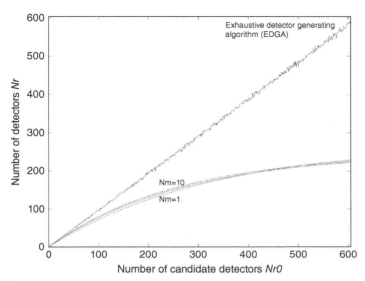

Figure 4.3 Experimental results of N_r versus N_{r0} when N_s is constant, where $N_s = 8$, N_{r0} increases from 1 to 604, size of test set is 256, and averaged over 1000 runs.

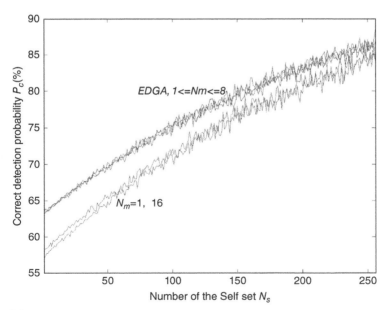

Figure 4.4 Experimental comparisons of EDGA to BMGDGA when $N_{r0} = 256$ and N_s changing from 1 to 256.

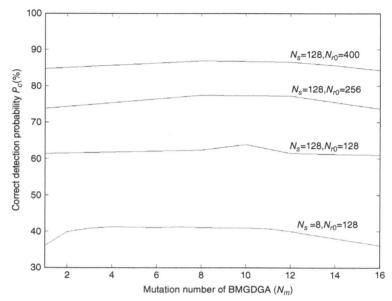

Figure 4.5 Experimental results of detection rate P_c versus mutation number N_m, where N_s, N_{r0} are constants.

4.5.1.2 16-Bit and 24-Bit Datasets

The experimental results of 16-bit and 24-bit datasets are shown in Tables 4.1 and 4.2.

Note that our experimental platform is Intel Pentium 993M CPU, 256M memory and Windows Me. According to the experimental results, it is noted that the detection rate P_c of BMGDGA is not lower than EDGA's under all circumstances, and when $N_m = l/2$, the detection rate reaches the highest value. Its computational complexity is also less than EDGA's, with almost the same memory space. So the overall performance of the proposed BMGDGA is better than EDGA.

4.5.2 Change Detection of Static Files

We conduct two experiments with the algorithm to validate their detection abilities in the change of static files, and then compare to EDGA. First of all, we compare two

Table 4.1 Computational Complexity Comparisons for 16-Bit Dataset

Algorithms	Parameters setting	Computational time (ms)	Note
EDGA	$N_{r0} = 65536, N_{rs} = 2048$	730	
BMGDGA	$N_{r0} = 65536, N_{rs} = 2048, N_m = 8$	594.5	10 runs
BMGDGA	$N_{r0} = 65536, N_{rs} = 2048, N_m = 4$	585	10 runs

Table 4.2   Computational Complexity Comparisons for 24-Bit Dataset

Algorithms		Parameters setting	Detection rate	Computational time (ms)
EDGA		$N_s = 2048, N_{r0} = 16384,$ $N_t = 16384$	0.108154297	183.7
BMGDGA	$N_s = 2048$	$N_m = 1$	0.109436035	128.11
	$N_{r0} = 16384$	$N_m = 16$	0.11151123	151.86
	$N_t = 16384$	$N_m = 24$	0.105224609	188.44

Table 4.3   Results of Anomaly Numbers for File Comparison (First Sub-Column of Last Column), and Anomaly Detection (Second Sub-Column of Last Column)

Algorithms	Parameters setting		Anomaly number	
EDGA	Detector length $l = 16$ *bits*		3775.2	596.9
BMGDGA	Detector length $l = 16$ bits	$N_m = 1$	3389.5	537
		$N_m = 10$	3724.8	561.7
		$N_m = 16$	3709.6	606

different files by using the algorithm. We select two files of FTP.exe and Ping.exe and define Ping.exe as self (S). The experimental results of the anomaly number are listed in the first sub-column of Table 4.3. Second, it is used to detect anomaly detection of the file infected by a virus, where we define a benign file dbeng50.exe as a protected file and detect its changing when infected by the Worm Concept virus. The experimental results of the anomaly number are listed in the second sub-column of Table 4.3. Experimental results are all compared to EDGA and listed in Table 4.3 for convenience.

It can be seen from the experimental results that the same results as random dataset experiments can be obtained. To BMGDGA, when $N_m = 1$, the quality of the detector set generated by this algorithm is the worst. When $N_m = l/2 \sim l$, the performance of BMGDGA is almost same to EDGA. It turns out from our experiments that it is possible to detect the changes of static files with these two algorithms.

4.6 SUMMARY

This chapter proposed a novel detector generating algorithm on the basis of the negative selection principle in natural immune systems. Extensive experimental results show that the proposed algorithm outperformed EDGA in both detection performance and computational complexity.

REFERENCES

1. D'Haeseleer, P., Forrest, S., and Helman, P. (1996) An immunological approach to change detection: Algorithms, analysis and implications, in Security and Privacy, 1996. Proceedings., 1996 IEEE Symposium on, IEEE, pp. 110–119.
2. Forrest, S., Perelson, A., Allen, L., and Cherukuri, R. (1994) Self-nonself discrimination in a computer, in Research in Security and Privacy, 1994. Proceedings., 1994 IEEE Computer Society Symposium on, IEEE, pp. 202–212.
3. Kim, J. and Bentley, P.J. (2002) Immune memory in the dynamic clonal selection algorithm, in Proceedings of the First International Conference on Artificial Immune Systems ICARIS, Citeseer, pp. 59–67.
4. Ayara, M., Timmis, J., de Lemos, R., de Castro, L.N., and Duncan, R. (2002) Negative selection: How to generate detectors, in Proceedings of the 1st International Conference on Artificial Immune Systems (ICARIS), vol. 1, Canterbury, UK:[sn], vol. 1, pp. 89–98.
5. Singh, S. (2002) Anomaly detection using negative selection based on the r-contiguous matching rule, in 1st International Conference on Artificial Immune Systems (ICARIS), University of Kent at Canterbury, UK, DTIC Document.
6. Perelson, A.S. and Oster, G.F. (1979) Theoretical studies of clonal selection: minimal antibody repertoire size and reliability of self-non-self discrimination. *Journal of Theoretical Biology*, **81** (4), 645–670.
7. Dasgupta, D. et al. (1999) *Artificial Immune Systems and Their Applications*, vol. 1, Springer.
8. Tan, Y. (2006) Multiple-point bit mutation method of detector generation for SNSD model, in Advances in Neural Networks-ISNN 2006, Springer, pp. 340–345.
9. Guo, Z., Tan, Y., and Liu, Z. (2005) Non-self detector generating algorithm based on negative selection principle. *Journal of Chinese Computer Systems*, **26** (6), 959–964.
10. Guo, Z., Liu, Z., and Tan, Y. (2005) Detector generating algorithm based on hyper-sphere. *Journal of Chinese Computer Systems*, **26** (12), 1641–1645.
11. Davis, L. et al. (1991) *Handbook of Genetic Algorithms*, vol. 115, Van Nostrand Reinhold, New York.
12. Guo, Z., Liu, Z., and Tan, Y. (2004) An nn-based malicious executables detection algorithm based on immune principles, in Advances in Neural Networks-ISNN 2004, Springer, pp. 675–680.
13. Tan, Y. and Guo, Z. (2005) Algorithms of non-self detector by negative selection principle in artificial immune system, in Advances in Natural Computation, Springer, pp. 867–875.

Chapter 5

Malware Detection System Using Affinity Vectors

This chapter presents a virus detection system (VDS) based on artificial immune system (AIS) [1]. A VDS first generates the detector set from virus files in dataset, negative selection is used to eliminate autoimmunity detectors for the detector set, while clonal selection is exploited to increase the diversity of the detector set in the non-self space. Two novel hybrid distances, called hamming-max and shift r-bit continuous distance, are proposed to calculate the affinity vectors of each file by means of the detector set. The affinity vectors of the training set and the testing set are used to train and test classifiers, respectively. The VDS compares the detection rates of using three classifiers, that is, k-nearest neighbor (KNN), RBF networks [2] and SVM [3] when the length of detectors is 32-bit and 64-bit, respectively. The experimental results show that the proposed VDS is of strong detection ability and good generalization performance.

5.1 INTRODUCTION

Aiming at building light-weight, limited computer resources and an early virus warning system, an immune-based virus detection system using affinity vectors (IVDS) was proposed [1].

At first, the IVDS generates a detector set from viruses in the train set, using negative selection and clonal selection together. Negative selection eliminates autoimmunity detectors and ensures that any detector in the detector set does not match self, while clonal selection increases the diversity of the detector set that helps the model obtain a stronger ability to recognize new variations of viruses and unknown viruses. Then two novel hybrid distances, called hamming-max and shift r-bit continuous distance, are presented to calculate the affinity vectors of each file. Finally, based on the affinity vectors, three classic classifiers, that is, SVM, RBF network and k-nearest neighbor (KNN), are used to verify the performance of the model.

Artificial Immune System: Applications in Computer Security, First Edition. Ying Tan.
© 2016 the IEEE Computer Society. Published 2016 by John Wiley & Sons, Inc.

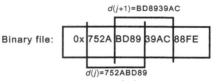

Figure 5.1 The process of extracting data fragments, $\left|x_j^f\right| = L = 32$ bits.

5.2 MALWARE DETECTION USING AFFINITY VECTORS

5.2.1 Sliding Window

Bit slices in a fixed length $L - bit$ (binary data fragments) x_j^f are extracted from each file by using a sliding window. The set of x_j^f of file l is represented by $DF_f = \{x_0^f, x_1^f, \ldots, x_{n-1}^f\}$, $|DF_l| = n^f$, $\left|x_j^f\right| = L$. Two neighboring fragments have an overlap of $[L/2]$ bits. If the size of the file l is N, $|DF_l| = 2N/L$. DF_l is the all information utilized by VDS. The process of extracting data fragments from a binary file is shown in Fig. 5.1.

In the hypothesis of the immune system, antibody T-cells detect antigens using the information of protein portions on the surface of antigen [4,5]. In VDS, x_j^f corresponds to the protein portions of an antigen, and an entire program file is regarded as an antigen.

5.2.2 Negative Selection

In AIS, as the T-cells mature in the thymus, they undergo a censoring process called negative selection [6,7], in which those T-cells that bind self cells are destroyed [8,9]. After censoring, T-lymphocytes that do not bind self are released to the rest of the body and provide a basis for our immune protection against foreign antigens. This mechanism in the immune system is very robust because of its high efficiency and distribution ability.

DTI is the data fragment set extracted from virus files in the training set, it contains immature detectors that will undergo negative selection and clonal selection before they are used to detect virus. Since most viruses insert or append themselves to benign files, DTI contains both benign and virus data fragments that will lead to a false positive during detection process. The purpose of the negative selection to remove x_j^f appears both in DTI and benign files, only virus-specific data fragments are left in DTI. The process of negative selection is shown in Fig. 5.2.

5.2.3 Clonal Selection

The clonal selection algorithm is widely used by AIS to define the basic features of an immune response to an antigenic stimulus [10–12]. It establishes the idea that only those cells that recognize the antigens are selected to proliferate. The selected

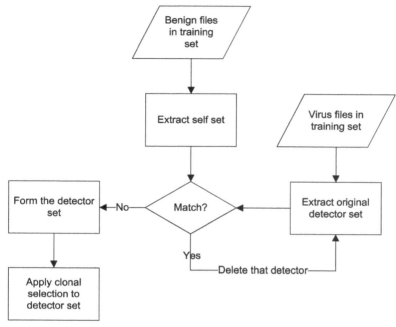

Figure 5.2 Negative selection process for DTI.

cells are subject to an affinity maturation process, which improves their affinity to the selective antigens.

Clonal selection is used to increase the diversity of *DTI* in the nonself space, new detectors are continueously generated from data fragments in *DTI*. The newly generated detectors would not only cover as much nonself space as possible, but would also enhance the ability to detect unknown viruses. The number of clones generated is given by:

$$\left|C\left(x_i^t\right)\right| = \frac{\alpha}{F_{x_i^t}}$$

(5.1)

where α is the coefficient of clone selection, usually $\alpha = 10$. x_i^t represents a single detector in *DTI*, $F_{x_i^t}$ is the occurrence frequency of x_i^t, and $C\left(x_i^t\right)$ is the number of clones generated by x_i^t.

Traditional AIS mutation methods are used in clonal selection, at most 5 bits of x_i^t are randomly changed to produce new detectors. The lower the $F_{x_i^t}$ is, the higher the mutation rate taken.

5.2.4 Distances

After negative selection and clonal selection are applied to *DTI*, the detectors in *DTI* are matured, so it can be used as the detector set *DT* to detect virus. In VDS, the affinity value reflects the similarity between a data fragment from an unknown file and the virus. To calculate the affinity values between x_j^f in DF_l of file l and x_i^t in DT, two novel distances and shift operators are introduced to efficiently detect short noncontinuous but virus-specific assemble code instructions.

5.2.4.1 Hamming-Max Distance

Hamming distance [13] plus cyclic shift operator(called hamming-max distance) is used to find the best matching position between $x_j^f \in DF_l$ and $x_i^t \in DTI$ during the matching process. Hamming-max distance can be evaluated by the following equation:

$$HM\left(x_i^t, x_j^f\right) = \max\left\{HD\left(x_{i'}^t, x_j^f\right)\right\} \tag{5.2}$$

where $HM\left(x_i^t, x_j^f\right)$ and $HD\left(x_{i'}^t, x_j^f\right)$ are the hamming-max and hamming distances between x_i^t and x_j^f, respectively.

$x_{i'}^t \in \{S(x_i^t, 0, left), S(x_i^t, 1, left), S(x_i^t, L-1, left)\}$, $\left|x_{i'}^t\right| = L$, where $S(x_i^t, k, left)$ means left cyclic shift x_i^t k bits.

Hamming-max distance can avoid the influence of bits mismatching to enhance the ability of matching exactly the virus-specific instructions.

5.2.4.2 Shift r-Continuous Bit Distance

The r-continuous bit distance [14,15] is widely used in binary string matching. If two strings contain the same substring with the length of r, they are matched. Shift r-continuous bit distance is aimed at detecting shorter serial assemble instructions that appear rarely in benign programs. It is a supplement to the hamming-max distance. The shift r-continuous bit distance $SR(x_i^t, x_j^f, r)$ between x_i^t and x_j^f can be evaluated by the following equation:

$$SR(x_i^t, x_j^f, r) = max\{R(x_{i'}^t, x_j^f, r)\}, \tag{5.3}$$

where $R(x_{i'}^t, x_j^f, r)$ is the r-continuous bit distance with the length of matching r bits, $x_{i'}^t \in \{S(x_i^t, 0, left), S(x_i^t, 8, left), S(x_i^t, L-8, left)\}$.

The lengths of assemble instructions vary from 8 to 64 bits and shorter instructions appear more frequently than longer ones in most cases, so the VDS selects $r = 12 - bit$ and $r = 24 - bit$, respectively. The length of shift used by shift operator is $8 - bit$ long; it is the minimum length of an assemble instruction.

5.2.5 Affinity Vector

Based on the "immune ball" theory, an antibody has limited detection space, and antigens in that space have closer distance to the antibody than to other antibodies. In VDS, detectors having the identical last $|K|$ bits (K is called the index bit) to data fragment x_j^f are assumed to be neighbors in the detection space of x_j^f. $DTS_{x_j^f}$ represents the sub-detector set of DT, the danger level of x_j^f can be calculated by the following equation:

$$DL\left(x_j^f\right) = \frac{\sum_{i=0}^{n^f} \left\langle HM(x_i^t, x_j^f), SR(x_i^t, x_j^f, 12), SR(x_i^t, x_j^f, 24) \right\rangle}{n^f} \tag{5.4}$$

where $x_i^t \in DTS_{x_j^f}$, detectors in $DTS_{x_j^f}$ have identical $|K|$ bits with x_j^f. $DL(x_j^f)$ is the danger level of x_j^f in DF_l of file l, $|DF_l^t| = n^f$.

The average affinity value of x_j^f in DF_l is the dangerous level of file l. It can be obtained by the following equations:

$$v_l = \frac{\sum_{j=0}^{n^f} DL\left(x_j^f\right)}{n^f} \tag{5.5}$$

$$|DF_l| = n^f \tag{5.6}$$

where v_l is the affinity vector of file l, it reflects the dangerous level of file l from three different distances. The higher v_l is, the more likely file l is a virus.

The calculation process of the dangerous level of $file_l$ is illustrated as follows:

1. Extract the data fragment set DF_l from file l, it is a multi-set because some data fragments may have the same value $x_j^f \in DF_l$, $\left|x_j^f\right| = L$ bits;
2. Calculate v_l using distances described in Section 5.2.4. The pseudo codes are shown in Algorithm 10.

If $DTS_{x_j^f}$ is empty, 0 is assigned to x_j^f. The last part of Algorithm 10 is a normalization process.

5.2.6   Training Classifiers with Affinity Vectors

Three classifiers, including RBF network, SVM [16,17] with a radial basis kernel function(rbf-SVM) and KNN, are used to detect the viruses in the testing set for comparison. They are trained with affinity vectors of files in the training set elaborated in Section 5.2.5. The entire working process of the VDS is shown in Fig. 5.3.

Algorithm 10   Calculation of v_l

```
v₁ = 0
for all  xⱼᶠ ∈ DF₁ do
       v₁' = 0
       if  DTSₓⱼᶠ is empty then
              continue;
       end if
       for all  xᵢᵗ ∈ DTSₓⱼᶠ do
              v₁'+ = ⟨HM(xᵢᵗ, xⱼᶠ), SR(xᵢᵗ, xⱼᶠ, 12), SR(xᵢᵗ, xⱼᶠ, 24)⟩
       end if
       v₁+ = ────
end for      |DTSₓⱼᶠ|
v₁/ = |DF₁|
```

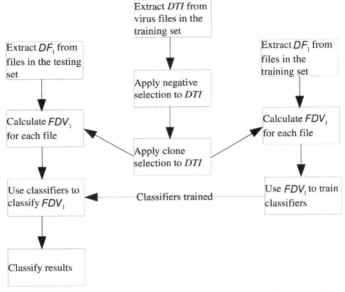

Figure 5.3 The working process of VDS. (a) Extract data fragments DF_l from virus files in the dataset, apply negative selection and clonal selection to DTI to form the detector set DT. (b) Use DT to calculate the dangerous level of all files v_l in the dataset. (c) Train classifiers using v_l in the training set. (d) Classify v_l in the testing set.

5.3 EVALUATION OF AFFINITY VECTORS-BASED MALWARE DETECTION SYSTEM

5.3.1 Dataset

There are 284 benign files with $78MB$ in total, and 3547 virus files with $7.8MB$ in the dataset (DS). Another dataset containing 208 benign files is used for negative selection, totally $189MB$. All the benign files are system files or well-known programs with the extension .exe.

The DS is randomly divided into different percentages of training set and testing set as shown in Table 5.1, there is no overlap in the two datasets.

5.3.2 Length of Data Fragment

The length of data fragments L is critical to VDS. If L is too short, the d_j^f cannot contain enough virus-specific information for detection, because the space 2^L is too small to discriminate self and nonself, On the contrary, if L is too long, the space 2^L is too large so that every x_j^f is rare in the space and x_j^f contains too much information that makes virus-specific data hidden in DF_l. So in either conditions above, the generalization ability of the VDS will be limited.

Table 5.1 The Number of Files in Each Dataset in Our Experiment

	Training set		Testing set	
Datasets	Benign files	Virus files	Benign files	Virus files
Dataset1	71	885	213	2662
Dataset2	142	1773	142	1774
Dataset3	213	2662	71	885

As the length of a single assemble code instruction varies from 1 byte to 7 bytes, L is not necessarily bigger than $64 - bit$ to contain at least one entire instruction. So the experiments choose $L = 64 - bit$ and $L = 32 - bit$, respectively. The overlap of x_j^f is always $\frac{L}{2}$.

5.3.3 Experimental Results

The detection rates by using SVM classifiers with different lengths of L are shown in Table 5.2. Similar performance on all the datasets is observed. $32 - bit$ detectors have better accuracy and generalization ability in detecting virus in the testing sets. So $32 - bit$ data fragments contain enough virus characteristic information for detection, and $64 - bit$ data fragments contain too many benign codes to reduce the thickness of virus information.

The experimental results are compared in Figs. 5.4 and 5.5.

Figures 5.4 and 5.5 show that the RBF network has a better performance than SVM and KNN except on virus files in a testing set. But it has a weaker generalization ability specifically when the training data is small, even though it has a highest detection rate on all other datasets. KNN and SVM have nearly the same detection rates when $L = 32$ bits and SVM has better performance than KNN when $L = 64$. As the training data become larger, the performance of KNN drops down significantly, while the detection rate of SVM is still stable.

Table 5.2 The Average Detection Rate of SVM when $L = 32$ and $L = 64$. The Files are Randomly Selected from the Dataset.

Detection rates		$L = 32$		$L = 64$	
Datasets		Virus	Benign files	Virus	Benign files
Dataset1	Training Set	99.55%	97.18%	100%	97.18%
	Testing Set	91.28%	99.06%	84.44%	99.53%
Dataset2	Training Set	99.38%	98.59%	100%	97.18%
	Testing Set	92.45%	98.59%	89.06%	97.89%
Dataset3	Training Set	99.21%	99.06%	100%	99.53%
	Testing Set	93.46%	95.77%	89.06%	97.18%

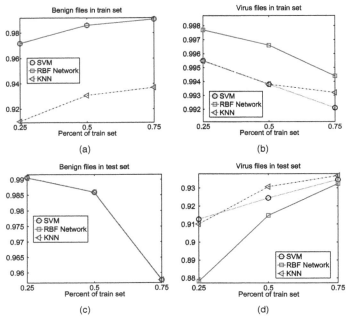

Figure 5.4 The average detection rate of SVM, KNN, and RBF network when $L = 32$, the files are randomly selected from the dataset.

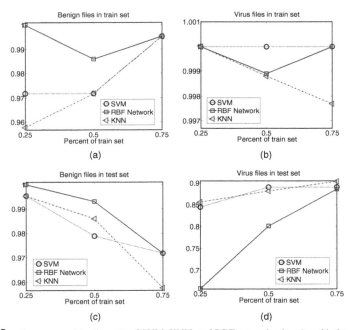

Figure 5.5 The average detection rate of SVM, KNN, and RBF network when $L = 64$, the files are randomly selected from the dataset.

The VDS achieves high accuracy in detecting known and unknown viruses especially in dataset1 where the percentage of training set is 25 percent. But it is shown from Figs. 5.4 and 5.5 that the detection rates of benign files in the testing set decrease as the number of virus files in the training set increases, because some virus files contain an amount of benign codes that reduce the thickness of virus information in the detector set DT. So additional benign files are used in a negative selection process to remove benign information in DT. It is also shown that the detection rate of virus files in the testing set increases as the number of virus files increases in the training set. In the dataset, the size of benign files is much larger than that of virus files which is a common case in the computer software environment. As the size of files in the dataset grows larger, the decreasing part and increasing part neutralize each other, the detection rate stays at a stable point. One aspect of our future work focuses on how to raise this stable point.

5.4 SUMMARY

Inspired by the negative selection and clonal selection algorithms in AIS, an immune-based virus detection system using affinity vectors (IVDS) was proposed for virus detection. Experimental results showed that the IVDS with the rbf-SVM classifier has a strong generalization ability with a low false positive rate in detecting unknown viruses. $64 - bit$ detectors have a better performance than $32 - bit$ detectors to the virus files in the training set, but $32 - bit$ detectors have a better performance on the virus file in the test set. The discrimination error often happens when the size of a file is too small because little information is utilized by IVDS. As the correlation information between data fragments in these files was not completely used here, we will focus on introducing a proper correlation value between data fragments into VDS to reduce the false positive rate further.

REFERENCES

1. Chao, R. and Tan, Y. (2009) A virus detection system based on artificial immune system, in Computational Intelligence and Security, 2009. CIS'09. International Conference on, IEEE, vol. 1, pp. 6–10.
2. Tan, Y., Wang, J., and JM, Z. (2001) Nonlinear blind source separation using radial basis function networks. *IEEE Transaction on Neural Networks*, **12** (1), 124–134.
3. Tan, Y. and Wang, J. (2004) A support vector network with hybrid kernel and minimal vapnik-chervonenkis dimension. *IEEE Trans. On Knowledge and Data Engineering*, **26** (2), 385–395.
4. D'haeseleer, P., Forrest, S., and Helman, P. (1996) An immunological approach to change detection: Algorithms, analysis and implications, in Security and Privacy, 1996. Proceedings., 1996 IEEE Symposium on, IEEE, pp. 110–119.
5. Williams, P.D., Anchor, K.P., Bebo, J.L., Gunsch, G.H., and Lamont, G.D. (2001) CDIS: Towards a computer immune system for detecting network intrusions, in *Recent Advances in Intrusion Detection*, Springer, pp. 117–133.
6. Guo, Z., Tan, Y., and Liu, Z. (2005) Non-self detector generating algorithm based on negative selection principle. *Journal of Chinese Computer Systems*, **26** (6), 959–964.

7. Zhang, P., Wang, W., and Tan, Y. (2010) A malware detection model based on a negative selection algorithm with penalty factor. *Science China Information Sciences*, **53** (12), 2461–2471.

8. Kappler, J.W., Roehm, N., and Marrack, P. (1987) T-cell tolerance by clonal elimination in the thymus. *Cell*, **49** (2), 273–280.

9. Paul, W. (1989) *Fundamental Immunology*, Raven Press. URL http://books.google.com.hk/books?id=HyFrAAAAMAAJ.

10. Kim, J. and Bentley, P. (1999) Negative selection and niching by an artificial immune system for network intrusion detection, in Late Breaking Papers at the 1999 Genetic and Evolutionary Computation Conference, pp. 149–158.

11. Kim, J. and Bentley, P.J. (2001) An evaluation of negative selection in an artificial immune system for network intrusion detection, in Proceedings of GECCO, pp. 1330–1337.

12. Tan, Y. and Xiao, Z. (2007) Clonal particle swarm optimization and its applications, in IEEE Congress on Evolutionary Computation (CEC-2007), IEEE, vol. 4, pp. 2303–2309.

13. Kephart, J.O. et al. (1994) A biologically inspired immune system for computers, in Artificial Life IV: Proceedings of the Fourth International Workshop on the Synthesis and Simulation of Living Systems, pp. 130–139.

14. D'Haeseleer, P., A change-detection algorithm inspired by the immune system: Theory, algorithms and techniques, Tech. Rep. Technical Report CS95-6, The University of New Mexico, Albuquerque, NM.

15. Helman, P. and Forrest, S. (1994) An efficient algorithm for generating random antibody strings, Tech. Rep. Technical Report CS-94-07, The University of New Mexico, Albuquerque, NM.

16. Vapnik, V. and Kotz, S. (2006) *Estimation of Dependences Based on Empirical Data*, Springer.

17. Drucker, H., Burges, C.J., Kaufman, L., Smola, A., and Vapnik, V. (1997) Support vector regression machines. *Advances in neural information processing systems*, **9**, 155–161.

Chapter 6

Hierarchical Artificial Immune Model

As viruses become more complex, current anti-virus methods are inefficient to detect various forms of viruses, especially new variants and unknown viruses. Inspired by the immune system, a hierarchical artificial immune system (HAIS) model, which is based on matching in three layers, is proposed to detect a variety of forms of viruses. Experimental results indicate that the proposed HAIS can recognize obfuscated viruses efficiently with an average recognition rate of 94 percent, including new variants of viruses and unknown viruses.

6.1 INTRODUCTION

A hierarchical artificial immune model (HAIM) for virus detection was presented [1]. The motivation of the HAIM is to make full use of the relativity between viruses' signatures. Generally speaking, a virus usually contains several heuristic signatures, one of which may appear in various viruses. We believe that there is some relativity between these heuristic signatures and the orderly combination of some signatures that make up a virus. The HAIM, taking a virus as an unit, detects viruses based on the simple relativity between signatures in a virus sample.

HAIM is based on matching in three layers to detect a variety of forms of viruses. In the bottom layer, a nonstochastic but guided candidate virus gene library is generated by statistical information of viral key codes. Then a detecting virus gene library is upgraded from the candidate virus gene library using negative selection [2–4]. In the middle layer, a novel storage method is used to keep a potential relevance between different signatures on the individual level, by which the mutual cooperative information of each instruction in a virus program can be collected. In the top layer, an overall matching process can reduce the information loss considerably.

Artificial Immune System: Applications in Computer Security, First Edition. Ying Tan.
© 2016 the IEEE Computer Society. Published 2016 by John Wiley & Sons, Inc.

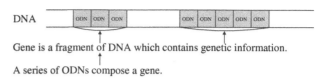

Gene is a fragment of DNA which contains genetic information.

A series of ODNs compose a gene.

Figure 6.1   The relationship among DNA, gene, and ODN.

6.2   ARCHITECTURE OF HAIM

The model is composed of two modules: a virus gene library generating module and self-nonself classification module. The first module is used for the training phase, whose function is to generate a detecting gene library to accomplish the training of given data. The second module is assigned as the detecting phase in terms of the results from the first module for detection of the suspicious programs.

In biology, it is well known that genetic information is mainly stored in DNA, but not all of the fragments of DNA can express useful information. Only a gene is the fragment of DNA containing genetic information. A gene is made up of several deoxyribonucleotides (ODN) [5,6].

In this chapter, the definitions of some notations are:

- *DNA*: The whole bit-string of a procedure.
- *Gene*: Virus detector, a fragment of virus DNA, the compared unit for virus detection.
- *ODN*: Every two bytes of a bit-string.

The relation of DNA, gene and ODN is shown in Fig. 6.1.

The codes of a virus correspond to the DNA in the organism. The small quantity of key codes that perform viral functions are regarded as the genes of a virus. These virus genes are composed of several virus ODNs, which are the smallest units to analyze the virus. An ordered series of ODNs can express one or more program instructions. At this stage, the most important task of the model is to extract the genes of a virus.

6.3   VIRUS GENE LIBRARY GENERATING MODULE

The virus gene library generating module works on the training set consisting of legal and virus programs. The operating principle is shown in Fig. 6.2.

First, this module is to count the ODNs in the DNA of legal and virus programs by a sliding window, in order to extract ODNs which are regarded as representative of the virus. A virus ODN library is built by the obtained statistical information. Second, the DNAs in virus and legal programs are traversed by the ODNs in the virus ODN library to generate a virus candidate gene library and legal virus-like gene library. Finally, according to the negative selection mechanism, we match all the genes in the candidate virus gene library with the genes in the legal virus-like

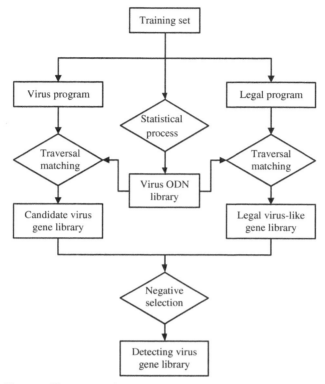

Figure 6.2   Virus gene library generating process.

gene library, and delete those genes that appear in both libraries. In this way, the candidate library is upgraded to the detecting virus gene library.

6.3.1 Virus ODN Library

A sliding window is used to count ODNs in the DNAs to generate this ODN library. For the following DNA fragment:

CD21 C307 1FCD 218C C0B8

Which includes nine ODNs in total such that:

CD21 21C3 C307 071F 1FCD CD21 218C 8CC0 C0B8

The model can obtain the frequency information of ODNs appearing in the legal and virus programs. In the next step, the model can calculate the degree S^i of which each ODN tends to be more representative of the virus based on the frequency information. When S^i exceeds a chosen threshold, ODN i would be added to the virus ODN library. Here we set this threshold to be S_1, called the ODN selection threshold. Apparently S_1 is a constant related to the training set. When the training set is fixed, the value S_1 should be constant, but its choice would vary on different training sets. To choose an appropriate S_1, making the ODNs less but more representative is very important.

6.3.2 Candidate Virus Gene Library

The basic storage block in the virus candidate gene library is the virus sample. All the genes in each sample are stored to make different genes in one virus storage and genes in different virus storage separately. This kind of storage mode is called signature storage on individual level. The gene library mentioned next would apply this storage mode to keep the relevance between different extracted genes in a same virus. Comparison between programs can be made on an individual level with integrated information of virus signatures [7,8].

The model uses continuous matching to match the virus DNA with ODNs in the virus ODN library. It means, from the first matching position, that a sliding window is employed to move forward until a mismatching happens. Then the number, of which ODNs in the virus ODN library take part in the matching from the beginning to the end, is recorded. If this number is larger than a presenting threshold T, the fragment of virus DNA is assigned as a virus gene. Otherwise, the fragment is considered to not contain enough information to be a key code of virus or the genes of a virus. It is clear that this method has one ODN unit fault tolerance.

If T is too small, the generated gene does not contain enough information. Too many invalid redundant genes would cause the loss of system performance and effectiveness. If T is too big, some important information would be lost as the matching length is too long. Let T = 3, the minimum gene is four bytes long and normally one computer instruction is one or two bytes, at the moment the gene may contain one to four instructions that might be regarded as abundant information.

6.3.3 Detecting the Virus Gene Library

Using the same method for generating the candidate virus gene library, this model can also be used to generate a legal virus-like gene library by matching the legal programs with ODNs in the virus ODN library.

Taking the legal virus-like genes as self, and the candidate virus genes as nonself, the NSA is applied to generate the detecting virus gene library. In the candidate virus library, all the genes that match with the gene in the legal virus-like gene library are deleted. In this way, the gene in the detecting virus gene library does not match with any legal virus-like gene library. Therefore these detectors would be able to distinguish all the legal programs in the training set.

R-continuous matching rules [9,10] (as shown in Table 6.1) is a popular matching rule in AIS, where binary string coding is used. It is a fuzzy matching method, allowing some faults in matching. We introduce a new T-successive consistency matching method for the byte strings of the same mechanism. (As shown in Fig. 6.3, gene 1 is a virus gene; gene 2 is a legal virus-like gene.) The rule of T-successive

Table 6.1   R-Continuous Matching

Byte string	Binary string			
68C5	0110	1000	1100	0101
B633	1011	0110	0011	0011

consistency matching is that if there are no less than T successive same ODNs in the two genes and these ODNs belong to the virus ODN library, the two genes are regarded as a successful matching.

When the candidate virus gene library is generated, the threshold T is set to 3, which means that only 3 or more ODNs connections are required to have enough information to form a gene. So only when two genes contain 3 or more ODNs successive consistency matching, can they be considered as having strong similarity, and regarded as a successful matching.

6.4 SELF-NONSELF CLASSIFICATION MODULE

Repeating the method that generates the candidate virus gene library, the ODNs in the detecting virus gene library are used to generate the suspicious virus-like gene library. Then we match virus-like genes in the suspicious program with detectors in the detecting virus gene library to get a matching value. If it is larger than a chosen threshold, the program is regarded as a virus; otherwise it is a legal program (as shown in Fig. 6.4).

6.4.1 Matching Degree Between Two Genes

This module still uses T-successive consistency matching for two genes' matching. A similarity value R is defined to measure the matching degree between two genes. If two genes are mismatched, the value is set to 0; If two genes are matched successfully, $R_1 = R_2 + R_3$, where $R_i \geq T(i = 1, 2, \cdots)$. We consider that the similarity value R_1 of units matching should be larger than the sum of value of R_2 units

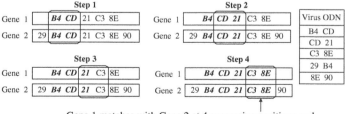

Gene 1 matches with Gene 2 at 4 successive positions and there are 3 virus ODNs belonging to the virus ODN library, not less than T, they are regarded as a successful matching.

Figure 6.3   T-successive consistency matching.

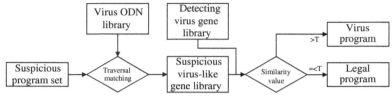

T: classification threshold

Figure 6.4   Self-nonself classification process.

matching and R_3 units matching. Suppose that x_i $(i = 1, 2, \cdots)$ is the similarity value of a matching of i units, the following inequalities hold:

$$x_n > x_{n-i} + x_i; \tag{6.1}$$

The relation between the similarity value and matching length is shown in Table 6.2.

6.4.2 Suspicious Program Detection

If the suspicious program matches with each virus sample in the detecting virus gene library, the similarity value is calculated. All the values for this program are added together as the similarity value between the program and detecting virus gene library. The pseudocode is:

```
initial similarity[M]=0;
initial similarity_indi=0;
for(i=0;I<M;i++)
    for(j=0;j<N;j++)
        temp=get_match_value();
        if(similarity[i]<temp)
        similarity[i]=temp;
    end
    similarity_indi+=similarity[i];
end
```

The proposed hierarchical model works through three layers cooperatively when the model detects an incoming suspicious program. In the gene layer, T-successive consistency matching is used to make a fuzzy matching for a good fault toleration. In the individual layer, virus and legal program are compared on the individual level. The interrelated information of instructions is lost as little as possible, hence the model takes full advantage of the potential relevance between different extracted signatures and recognizes obfuscated viruses effectively and efficiently. Due to the similarity between viruses, it also can detect new variants of known viruses and

Table 6.2   Similarity Value with Matching Length

Matching Length i	1	2	3	$\cdots$	n
Similarity Value	1	3	5	$\cdots$	$2n-1$

recognize unknown viruses accurately. Finally, classification decision is not a single but an overall behavior in the decision layer, which can give a more precise result.

6.5 SIMULATION RESULTS OF HIERARCHICAL ARTIFICIAL IMMUNE MODEL

6.5.1 Dataset

We performed experiments on a virus dataset "cilpku08" [11]. We collected 3547 viruses and the viruses were classified into 685 families, based on their properties.

To determine the performance and possible advantages of the proposed approach, four classes of experiments were carried out on three practical datasets using the Windows operating system. The first dataset contained 538 programs with the self set of 284 legal files and the nonself set of 254 virus files; the second set contained 1815 programs with the self set of 915 legal files and 900 virus files; The third set consisted of the second set and 2647 extra virus files, having 4462 files in total.

6.5.2 Description of Experiments

In this section, four classes of simulation results are described in detail.

In the tables, A denotes the total number of corresponding programs in the certain set; P denotes the number of corresponding programs that are correctly recognized; PR denotes the correct recognition rate of the corresponding programs, $PR = P/A$; APR denotes the average correct recognition rate of the corresponding programs.

$$APR = \frac{P_{legal} + P_{virus}}{A_{legal} + A_{virus}} \tag{6.2}$$

6.5.2.1 Experiments of Class 1

The experiments of class 1 including several tests were carried out on the set of 538 files. The set was divided equally and randomly into the training set and the detecting set. The numbers were both 269, but the particular programs in these sets were different. We pitch upon test 1 and test 2 to perform the simulation results in Table 6.3.

It can be seen from Table 6.3 that two tests have a good correct recognition rate in both the testing (98.9%) and detecting set (around 97%). In the training set, the model can perfectly recognize the legal files, with a recognition rate of around 97 percent for virus files. The trained model can recognize more than 98 percent of the unknown legal files and has a recognition rate of around 95 percent for unknown virus files in the suspicious program set. It is noted that for repeated experiments, the model had a stable performance independent of any particular program in these sets.

Table 6.3   Experimental Results of Class 1

Exp. No.	The training set						
	Legal files			Virus files			APR
	A	P	PR	A	P	PR	
Test 1	142	142	100%	127	124	97.6%	98.9%
Test 2	142	142	100%	127	124	97.6%	98.9%

Exp. No.	The detecting set						
	Legal files			Virus files			APR
	A	P	PR	A	P	PR	
Test 1	142	140	98.6%	127	119	93.7%	96.3%
Test 2	142	140	98.6%	127	122	96.1%	97.4%

6.5.2.2 Experiments of Class 2

The experiments of class 2 are still based on the first dataset. Four divisions of the training and detecting set were made with ratios of 4:1, 2:1, 1:2, and 1:4, respectively. The results are shown in Table 6.4.

The recognition rate of the model does not decrease with the reduction of the training set. In test 6, the number of files in the training set is much less than that of files in the detecting set. However, the correct recognition rate was 98.7 percent of the legal files and 95.1 percent of suspicious virus files in the detecting set. This indicates that the proposed model can learn enough information in a small datset to get a good results in detecting a much bigger corresponding dataset. So, the model has a very strong generalization.

6.5.2.3 Experiments of Class 3

The experiments of class 3 are carried out on the second set, a bigger data set. The ratios of the training set and the detecting set are 2:1, 1:1, and 1:2, respectively. The results are shown in Table 6.5.

The correct recognition rates in this class of experiments were a little lower than that in class 1 and 2, but were still at high levels, with 95 percent in the training set and 94 percent in the detecting set.

All these results show that the proposed model have an excellent stability and generalization.

Table 6.4 Experimental Results of Class 2

Exp. No.	The training set						
	Legal files			Virus files			*APR*
	A	*P*	*PR*	*A*	*P*	*PR*	
Test 3	227	227	100%	203	194	95.60%	97.90%
Test 4	190	190	100%	170	162	95.30%	97.80%
Test 5	94	94	100%	84	82	97.60%	98.90%
Test 6	57	57	100%	51	49	96.10%	98.10%

Exp. No.	The detecting set						
	Legal files			Virus files			*APR*
	A	*P*	*PR*	*A*	*P*	*PR*	
Test 3	57	56	98.20%	51	47	92.20%	95.40%
Test 4	94	93	98.90%	84	82	97.60%	98.30%
Test 5	190	187	98.40%	170	162	95.30%	96.90%
Test 6	227	224	98.70%	203	193	95.10%	97.00%

Table 6.5 Experimental Results of Class 3

Exp. No.	The training set						
	Legal files			Virus files			*APR*
	A	*P*	*PR*	*A*	*P*	*PR*	
Test 7	610	610	100%	600	538	89.70%	94.90%
Test 8	457	457	100%	450	399	88.70%	94.40%
Test 9	305	305	100%	300	279	93.00%	96.50%

Exp. No.	The detecting set						
	Legal files			Virus files			*APR*
	A	*P*	*PR*	*A*	*P*	*PR*	
Test 7	1305	303	99.30%	300	270	90.00%	94.70%
Test 8	458	450	98.30%	450	400	88.90%	93.60%
Test 9	610	601	98.50%	600	543	90.50%	94.50%

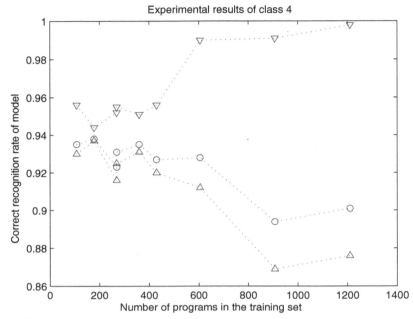

Figure 6.5 The correct recognition rates in the class 4.

6.5.2.4 Experiments of Class 4

The experiments of class 4 used the third set—the biggest dataset with 4462 programs to confirm the model's expansibility. The training set is covered by it and much smaller than the detecting set, so that the expansibility and comprehensive ability of the model could be tested. An outline of the relation between the detecting results and the training set is shown in Fig. 6.5. "○" denotes the correct recognition rate of all the programs on the detecting set; "△" denotes the correct recognition rate of the virus programs; "▽" denotes the correct recognition rate of the legal programs.

6.6 SUMMARY

In this chapter, a hierarchical artificial immune model (HAIM) for virus detection was proposed to overcome three specific shortcomings in traditional AIS models:

1. Randomly generating the detectors leading to the bad efficiency;

2. Poor generalization and poor performance with a big dataset;

3. Ignoring the relevance between different extracted signatures in one virus.

In HAIM, a guided candidate library is made by a priori knowledge. Then a fuzzy matching method is used to dig the similarity between genes out. We store different genes in one virus together to keep all the information on the individual level by taking advantage of the relevance between different extracted signatures in the individual. Finally, classification decision is an overall behavior that greatly reduces the information loss. The model can effectively and efficiently recognize obfuscated virus, detect new variants of known virus and some unknown viruses.

REFERENCES

1. Wang, W., Zhang, P., Tan, Y., and He, X. (2009) A hierarchical artificial immune model for virus detection, in Computational Intelligence and Security, 2009. CIS'09. International Conference on, IEEE, vol. 1, pp. 1–5.
2. Ji, Z. and Dasgupta, D. (2004) Real-valued negative selection algorithm with variable-sized detectors, in Genetic and Evolutionary Computation–GECCO 2004, Springer, pp. 287–298.
3. Dasgupta, D., Krishna, K., Wong, D., and Berry, M. (2004) Negative selection algorithm for aircraft fault detection, in *Artificial Immune Systems*, Springer, pp. 1–13.
4. Taylor, D.W. and Corne, D.W. (2003) An investigation of the negative selection algorithm for fault detection in refrigeration systems, in *Artificial Immune Systems*, Springer, pp. 34–45.
5. Hartl, D., et al. (1997) *Principles of Population Genetics*, vol. 116, Sinauer Associates, Sunderland.
6. Brenner, S. (1974) The genetics of caenorhabditis elegans. *Genetics*, **77** (1), 71–94.
7. Tan, Y. and Guo, Z. (2005) Algorithms of non-self detector by negative selection principle in artificial immune system, in *Advances in Natural Computation*, Springer, pp. 867–875.
8. Guo, Z., Liu, Z., and Tan, Y. (2005) Detector generating algorithm based on hyper-sphere. *Journal of Chinese Computer Systems*, **26** (12), 1641–1645.
9. Tao, C., Shi, J., Wei, Z., and DeJiao, N. (2009) Random r-continuous matching rule for immune-based secure storage system, in Proceedings of the International Workshop on Computational Intelligence in Security for Information Systems CISIS2009, Springer, pp. 294–300.
10. Chao, R. and Tan, Y. (2009) A virus detection system based on artificial immune system, in Computational Intelligence and Security, 2009. CIS'09. International Conference on, IEEE, vol. 1, pp. 6–10.
11. Cilpku08 malware dataset, http://www.cil.pku.edu.cn/malware/.

Chapter 7

Negative Selection Algorithm with Penalty Factor

A malware detection model based on a negative selection algorithm with a penalty factor is proposed to overcome the drawback of traditional negative selection algorithms in defining the harmfulness of self and nonself. Unlike danger theory, the proposed algorithm is able to detect malware through dangerous signatures extracted from programs. Instead of deletingnonself that matches self, the negative selection algorithm with penalty factor (NSAPF) penalizes the nonsel using penalty factor C and keeps these items in a library. In this way, the effectiveness of the proposed model is improved greatly by using the dangerous signatures that would have been discarded in the traditional negative selection algorithm.

7.1 INTRODUCTION

A malware detection model based on a negative selection algorithm with penalty factor (NSAPF) [1] is presented in this chapter. This model extracts a malware instruction library (MIL), containing instructions that tend to appear in malware, through deep instruction analysis with respect to instruction frequency and file frequency. From the MIL, the proposed model creates a malware candidate signature library (MCSL) and a benign program malware-like signature library (BPMSL) by splitting programs into various orderly short bit strings. Depending on whether a signature matches self, the NSAPF further divides the MCSL into two malware detection signature libraries (MDSL1 and MDSL2), and uses these as a two-dimensional reference for detecting suspicious programs. The model classifies suspicious programs as malware and benign programs by matching values of the suspicious programs with MDSL1 and MDSL2. Introduction of a penalty factor C in the negative selection algorithm enables this model to overcome the drawback of traditional negative selection algorithms in defining the harmfulness of self and nonself, and

Artificial Immune System: Applications in Computer Security, First Edition. Ying Tan.

focus on the harmfulness of the code, thus greatly improving the effectiveness of the model and also enabling the model to satisfy the different requirements of users in terms of true positive and false positive rates. Experimental results confirm that the proposed model achieves a better true positive rate on completely unknown malware and a better generalization ability while keeping a low false positive rate. The model can balance and adjust the true positive and false positive rates by adjusting the penalty factor C for better performance.

7.2 FRAMEWORK OF NSAPF

The proposed NSAPF model consists of a malware signature extraction module (MSEM) and a suspicious program detection module (SPDM). A flowchart for the MSEM is shown in Fig. 7.1.

In the MSEM, a malware candidate signature library (MCSL) and a benign program malware-like signature library (BPMSL) are extracted, respectively, from the malware and benign programs of the training set after generating the malware instruction library (MIL). Taking the MCSL as nonself and the BPMSL as self, a NSAPF is introduced to extract the malware detection signature library (MDSL) consisting of MDSL1 and MDSL2. More detailed information is given next.

In the SPDM, signatures of suspicious programs are extracted using the MIL. Then r-contiguous bit matching is computed between the signatures of the suspicious program and the MDSL. If the matching value exceeds the given program classification threshold, we classify the programs as malware; otherwise it is considered a benign program.

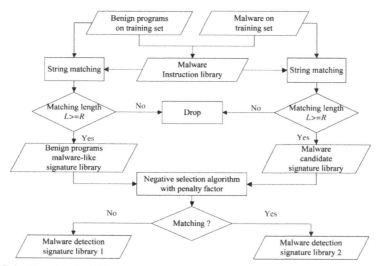

Figure 7.1   Flowchart for MSEM.

7.3 MALWARE SIGNATURE EXTRACTION MODULE

7.3.1 Malware Instruction Library (MIL)

In this chapter, instructions are represented as bit strings with two bytes. Note that in the process of signature extraction, several instructions form one signature, so the length of the instruction does not affect the results greatly. We traverse all the programs in the training set to obtain the frequency statistical information of instruction i in both the malware and benign programs, denoted by I_n^i and I_s^i, respectively. Meanwhile, the numbers of malware and benign programs that contain instructions i are computed and denoted by F_n^i and F_s^i, respectively. Graphs of some real experimental data are shown in Figs. 7.2 and 7.3, where every point denotes an instruction.

As illustrated in Figs. 7.2 and 7.3, the instruction distributions in malware and benign programs differ significantly. If we wish to extract instructions with higher tendencies to malware, we have to select instructions in region B of Fig. 7.2 and region C of Fig. 7.3, and combine the two regions into one through Eq. 7.1. I^i and F^i denote the tendencies of instruction i to malware on instruction frequency and file frequency, respectively. Taking I^i as the x-axis and F^i as the y-axis, the resulting graph is shown in Fig. 7.4.

$$I^i = \frac{I_n^i/I_n}{I_n^i/I_n + I_s^i/I_s}, F^i = \frac{F_n^i/F_n}{F_n^i/F_n + F_s^i/F_s} \tag{7.1}$$

where I_n and I_s denote, respectively, the number of instructions in malware and benign programs in the training set, and F_n and F_s denote the number of the malware and benign programs in the training set.

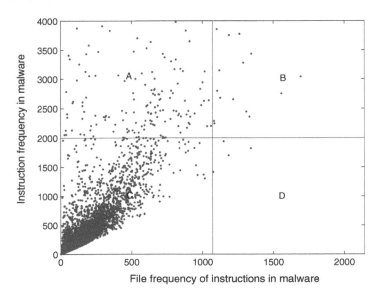

Figure 7.2 Instruction distribution in malware.

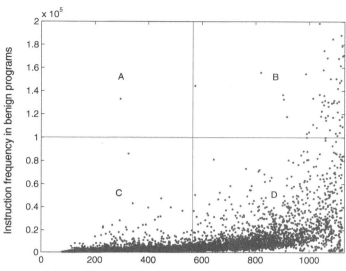

Figure 7.3   Instruction distribution in benign programs.

Equation 7.2 takes both I^i and F^i into consideration:

$$T^i = \sqrt{(I^i)^2 + (F^i)^2}$$ (7.2)

When the tendency of instruction i to malware T^i exceeds the malware instruction threshold T_1, we consider instruction i as tending to appear in malware. All

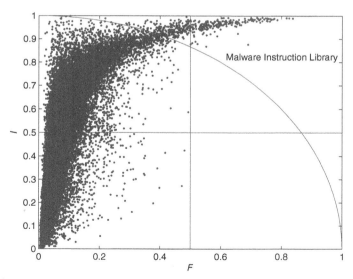

Figure 7.4   Instruction tendencies.

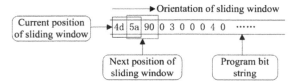

Figure 7.5   Schematic diagram of the sliding window traversing a program bit string.

these instructions make up the MIL. In other words, all instructions excluded by the curve in Fig. 7.4 are included in the MIL.

7.3.2   Malware Candidate Signature Library

In this section, a sliding window is used to split the malware bit string to obtain the Malware Candidate Signature Library (MCSL). We set the window size of the sliding window to two bytes, and the sliding window moves forward one byte at a time. Each program is considered to be a bit string and is traversed by the sliding window as shown in Fig. 7.5.

When the sliding window, in the process of traversing the bit string, encounters the first instruction that belongs to the MIL, it begins to generate a signature. If instructions in two adjacent sliding windows do not belong to the MIL, the next signature cannot be part of the current signature and thus, the current signature is terminated. The sliding window keeps moving forward, and on encountering another instruction belonging to the MIL, it begins to generate the next signature. This process is repeated until the entire bit string has been traversed.

If the number of instructions contained in a signature belonging to the MIL exceeds threshold R, the signature is deemed to contain enough dangerous information to represent malware and it is considered a malware candidate signature. Here $R = 3$. Because the length of a candidate signature auto adjusts according to the program bit string and the MIL, R does not greatly affect the model's accuracy.

By traversing malware and benign programs in the training set, the proposed model can extract the MCSL and BPMSL.

7.3.3   NSAPF and Malware Detection Signature Library

This chapter considers the MCSL as nonself and the BPMSL as self and generates a Malware Detection Signature Library (MDSL) using NSAPF.

The traditional NSA deletes detectors matching self directly and obtains a detector set in which no signatures match self. The traditional NSA is not completely suited to malware detection. Consider formatting a disk as an example. This operation is dangerous and programs implementing this operation are also dangerous. If a program implementing this operation neither reads any command line parameters nor asks the user to confirm, it could be malware. This type of dangerous signature provides some useful information. In fact, the operation of formatting a disk can be included in both malware and benign programs. Deleting such dangerous code snippets from the MCSL, as is done by the traditional NSA, destroys useful information, which is obviously a disadvantage for the malware detection model.

Theoretically, every program, regardless of whether it is a benign program or malware, can use almost any of the instructions and functions in a computer system. Moreover, almost all the functions used in malware are also used by specific benign programs, for example, formatting a disk or modifying the registry. If a "perfect" self set is given, the traditional NSA would be ineffective due to delete too many detectors.

The NSAPF saves nonself signatures that do not match self in the MDSL1 and nonself signatures matching self in the MDSL2. Together the MDSL1 and MDSL2 make up the MDSL.

Signatures in the MDSL1 are characteristic signatures of nonself, whereas signatures in the MDSL2 are dangerous ones belonging to both self and nonself, which should be penalized by penalty factor C after ascertaining, through probabilistic methods, to what extent they represent malware.

7.4 SUSPICIOUS PROGRAM DETECTION MODULE

7.4.1 Signature Matching

It is easy to extract signatures of suspicious programs by adopting the approach used in the process of generating the MCSL. The matching value between a signature of a suspicious program and the malware detection signature is proportional to the matching length and weights of the two signatures.

Equation 7.3 gives the matching value between signatures of suspicious programs and signatures in the MDSL1:

$$M_1 = \begin{cases} 0, & l < R \\ (l - R + 1) \times w_1 \times w_2, & l \geq R \end{cases} \tag{7.3}$$

where l is the number of matching instructions in the two signatures, R is the minimal number of matching instructions for two signatures to match each other and it has the same value as the matching length threshold R, which is set to 3 in this paper, and w_1 and w_2 are the weights of the two signatures expressed as the number of signatures appearing in the files.

Equation 7.4 gives the matching value between signatures of suspicious programs and signatures in the MDSL2:

$$M_2 = \begin{cases} 0, & l < R \\ [(l - R + 1) \times w_1 \times w_2 \times p] \times (1 - C), & l \geq R \end{cases} \tag{7.4}$$

where $p = w_2/(w_2 + w_3)$ (w_2 is the weight of the signature in the MDSL2 and w_3 is the weight of the signature in the BPMSL previously matching the signature before) denotes the probability of representing malware of the signature in the MDSL2, and C is the penalty factor with its interval $[0, 1]$.

As penalty factor C increases, signatures in the MDSL2 are penalized more severely and the extent to which they represent malware decreases. When $C = 1$, the NSAPF degenerates to the traditional NSA.

7.4.2 Matching Between Suspicious Programs and the MDSL

The matching value between a suspicious program and the MDSL is calculated using Eq. 7.5:

$$M = \frac{M_{MDSL1} + (1 - C) \times M_{MDSL2}}{[L_{MDSL1} + (1 - C) \times L_{MDSL2}] \times \sum w} \tag{7.5}$$

where M_{MDSL1} and $(1 - C) \times M_{MDSL2}$ denote the total sum of the matching values of all the signatures in a suspicious program with signatures in the MDSL1 and MDSL2, respectively. L_{MDSL1} and $(1 - C) \times L_{MDSL2}$ are the maximal matching values provided by the MDSL1 and MDSL2, respectively. C is the penalty factor, and $\sum w$ is the sum of the weights of all signatures in a suspicious program.

If the M value of a suspicious program is greater than the program classification threshold T_2, the associated program is classified as malware, otherwise it is deemed to be a benign program.

7.4.3 Analysis of Penalty Factor

L_{MDSL1} and L_{MDSL2} are constants for a specific training set. For a specific suspicious program, M_{MDSL1} and M_{MDSL2} are also constants. At this time, Eq. 7.5 is a function with independent variable penalty factor C and dependent variable matching value M. If the derivation of Eq. 7.5 is greater than 0, we obtain Eq. 7.6:

$$L_{MDSL1}/L_{MDSL2} < M_{MDSL1}/M_{MDSL2} \tag{7.6}$$

In cases where Eq. 7.6 is correct, M is monotonically increasing together with increasing C. When $C = 1$, $(1 - C) \times M_{MDSL2}$ and $(1 - C) \times L_{MDSL2}$ both are 0. The NSAPF is now equivalent to the traditional NSA. Let $C = 1$ be the comparable benchmark.

When $C = 1$, recognizable malware usually has a greater M_{MDSL1} and benign programs have a smaller M_{MDSL1}. By decreasing C, the M values of malware and benign programs would tend to decrease and increase, respectively, making it difficult to recognize such programs. When $C = 1$, unrecognizable malware and benign programs have a smaller M_{MDSL1} and greater M_{MDSL1}, respectively. By decreasing C, the M values of malware and benign programs tend to increase and decrease, respectively. Thus, decreasing C is beneficial for classifying such programs.

An optimal penalty factor C is obtained on the training set and this is helpful to improve the model's performance. Furthermore, two constraints are necessary for penalty factor C to play a positive role: (1) MDSL2 contains enough signatures and (2) the percent of signatures in the MDSL2 relative to the MDSL must be large enough. If and only if these two constraints are satisfied, can the MDSL2 change the matching values of suspicious programs with the MDSL and recognize unknown malware.

7.5 EXPERIMENTS AND ANALYSIS

7.5.1 Experimental Datasets

Experiments were conducted using the three datasets, which were downloaded [2].

7.5.1.1 Henchiri Dataset

The Henchiri dataset consisted of 2994 malware and 1414 benign programs. The malware were provided by Henchiri [3], while the benign programs consisted of executable (EXE) system files from Windows XP and EXE files from a series of applications. These files cover EXE files of mainstream operating systems and applications and are the main targets for attack by malware. Detailed information on the Henchiri dataset is given in Table 7.1.

Here M^* and B^* indicate malware and benign programs, respectively. The units of both the average size and the maximum size is KB, while the unit of minimum size is byte (these units are also applicable to other tables in this paper).

7.5.1.2 CILPKU08 Dataset

We previously used the CILPKU08 dataset [4]. The process of collecting benign programs is the same as in Section 2.4.3.2. The details of this dataset are presented in Table 7.2.

Table 7.1 Henchiri Dataset

	File type	Quantity	Average size	Minimum size	Maximum size
B^*	EXE	1414	107	16	501
M^*	Virus	2880	6.2	22	93.4
	Trojan	88	9.4	49	72.5
	Constructor	6	10	528	33.6
	Other	20	11.6	456	88.5

Table 7.2 CILPKU08 Dataset

	File type	Quantity	Average size	Minimum size	Maximum size
B^*	EXE	915	138.5	817	997
M^*	Virus	3465	4.8	23	59.5
	Trojan	39	4.4	49	5.93
	Other	43	6.8	48	31.2

Table 7.3 Benign Programs in VX Heavens Dataset

File type	Quantity	Average size	Minimum size	Maximum size
DOC	300	103	11000	1587
EXE	300	82.7	6000	498
JPG	300	43.7	447	416
MP3	300	61.5	735	6586
PDF	300	113.3	46	16657
ZIP	300	100	546	2941

Table 7.4 Malware in VX Heavens Dataset

File type	Quantity	Average size	Minimum size	Maximum size
Backdoor	2200	48	3500	9227
Constructor	172	392.9	5060	2391
Trojan	2350	147.7	215	3800
Virus	1048	71.1	1500	1278
Worm	351	199.3	394	11899
Others	1007	151.4	1090	3087

7.5.1.3 VX Heavens Dataset

The benign programs in the VX Heavens dataset are general programs collected from Windows XP and are listed in Table 7.3.

Malware for this dataset comes from the VX Heavens Virus Collection [5]. We only consider malware based on the PE format of Win32. The VX Heavens dataset used contains 7128 malware, details of which are given in Table 7.4.

Here "Others" includes malware such as DoS, Nuker, Exploit, Hacktool, and Flooder.

7.5.2 Experiments on the Henchiri Dataset

Here we adopt five-fold cross validation [6] to estimate the performance of the proposed model as accurately as possible.

7.5.2.1 Cross Validation

According to the malware's name, 2994 malware is divided into 880 families. Based on family, the malware is divided into five folds referred to as $M^i(i = 1, 2, \ldots, 5)$. 1414 benign programs are divided into five folds in a similar manner and are referred to as $B^i(i = 1, 2, \ldots, 5)$. The detailed process of cross validation is shown in Algorithm 11.

Algorithm 11   Cross Validation Algorithm

$M = \bigcup_{i=1}^{5} M^i, B = \bigcup_{i=1}^{5} B^i$
for $i = 1$ to 5 do
  $DS = M^i \cup B^i, TS = (M - M^i) \cup (B - B^i)$;
  Train model on TS;
  Trained model detects suspicious programs in TS and DS;
end for
$FP\_TS = BW\_TS/(4 \times \| B \|), TP\_TS = MC\_TS/(4 \times \| M \|)$
$FP\_DS = BW\_DS/\| B \|, TP\_DS = MC\_DS/\| M \|$

In Algorithm 11, TS and DS denote the training set and test set; BW_TS and MC_TS denote the number of misclassified benign programs and the number of correctly recognized malware in the TS; BW_DS and MC_DS are the number of misclassified benign programs and the number of correctly recognized malware in the DS; FP_TS and TP_TS denote the false positive and true positive rates in the TS, while FP_DS and TP_DS denote the false positive and true positive rates in the DS.

Results for the training and test sets are given in Tables 7.5 and 7.6. Experimental results of Henchiri are shown in Table 7.7 for comparison.

Experimental results on the training set show that when penalty factor C lies within [0.90, 0.99], the proposed model achieves good detection accuracies with lower false positive rates (FPRs) [7], less than 3 percent, and higher true positive rates (TPRs), above 95.9 percent. The proposed model also obtains very good results

Table 7.5   Experimental Results on the Training Set

C	OA	FPR	TPR
0.00	95.5%	7.3%	96.8%
0.50	95.9%	5.9%	96.8%
0.90	96.7%	2.9%	96.6%
0.95	96.7%	1.7%	95.9%
0.99	96.6%	0.8%	95.3%
1.00	95.6%	0.0%	93.6%

Table 7.6   Experimental Results on the Test Set

C	OA	FPR	TPR
0.00	95.0%	7.4%	96.2%
0.50	95.5%	5.9%	96.2%
0.90	96.1%	3.3%	95.8%
0.95	95.8%	2.5%	95.0%
0.99	95.4%	2.5%	94.4%
1.00	94.2%	1.3%	92.0%

Table 7.7 Experimental Results of Henchiri

Classifier	OA	FPR	TPR
ID3	93.29%	4.16%	90.56%
J48	93.65%	5.24%	92.56%
Nave Bayes	69.51%	0.13%	37.17%
SMO	93.39%	5.71%	92.26%

on the test set with an FPR below 4 percent, which is lower than the FPR obtained by Henchiri, and the average TPR at 95 percent. The optimal overall accuracy (OA) on the test set is 96.1 percent, higher than that achieved by Henchiri (93.65%) [2].

It is easy to ascertain from Tables 7.5 and 7.6 that with a decrease in penalty factor C, the penalty to signatures in MDSL2 decreases. The MDSL2 provides more and more false information while still providing correct information. As a result, the FPR of the proposed model increases, while the TPR decreases. The OA increases at first and finally drops. With $C = 0.90$, the OA of the proposed model is at its maximum, 96.1 percent. The results demonstrate that the MDSL2 plays a positive role and improves the effectiveness of the proposed model.

The performance of the proposed model on the test set is similar to its performance on the training set, proving that the model has a good training function.

7.5.2.2 Negative Direction Cross Validation

In this section, we take the training set used in the cross validation as the test set and vice versa. Negative direction cross validation is done to verify the model's generalization ability. Experimental results are shown in Table 7.8.

From Table 7.8, we can see that the OA still remains above 94 percent on the test set. The proposed model trained with a small training set also achieves good performance on a larger test set, showing that this model has strong generalization ability. With $C = 0.90$, the OA on the test set achieves its maximum value: 95.3 percent.

Table 7.8 Experimental Results on the Test Set

C	OA	FPR	TPR
0.00	94.3%	6.8%	94.8%
0.50	94.5%	6.5%	94.9%
0.90	95.3%	4.5%	95.2%
0.95	95.2%	3.8%	94.7%
0.99	94.7%	3.2%	93.6%
1.00	94.2%	3.0%	92.8%

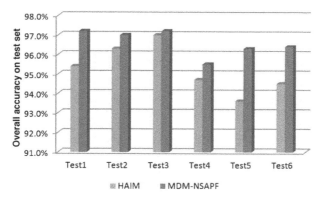

Figure 7.6 Overall accuracy comparison.

7.5.3 Experiments on CILPKU08 Dataset

Comparable experiments were done on the CILPKU08 dataset we used in [4]. In this study, we selected six experiments from our previous study for comparison. The proposed model is referred to as the MDM-NSAPF, while the approach in [4] is referred to as HAIM. The penalty factor is set to 1 and graphs of the experimental results are shown in Figs. 7.6 and 7.7.

In Fig. 7.7, $R = Time_1/Time_2$, $Time_1$ is the training time used by MDM-NSAPF and $Time_2$ is HAIM's training time.

As illustrated in Figs. 7.6 and 7.7, the OA of the proposed model is about 1 percent to 3 percent higher than that of HAIM; yet the training time of the proposed model is only 1/10 of that of HAIM.

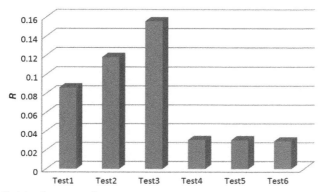

Figure 7.7 Training time comparison.

7.5.4 Experiments on VX Heavens Dataset

The specific training set for virus consists of 50 benign programs and 50 viruses which were randomly selected from the VX Heavens dataset. The remaining benign programs and viruses make up the specific test set for virus. We divided the worm, trojan, backdoor, constructor, and other malware in a similar way. Six datasets were obtained and used to train and verify the proposed model.

To compare the resuluts obtained by Tabish [8], the area under the receiver operating characteristic curve (AUC) [9] was set as the measure of the effectiveness of the proposed model. Table 7.9 gives the experimental results in detail with the bold font in each column indicating the optimal AUC in the corresponding models.

Compared with the results of Tabish [8] shown in Table 7.10, the optimal AUC of the proposed model is on average 0.04 higher. This is because the proposed model generates the MDSL using the NSAPF, which decreases the FPR and achieves a better tradeoff between FPR and TPR by adjusting penalty factor C.

7.5.5 Parameter Analysis

Experimental results demonstrate that when the number of signatures in the MDSL2 is greater than 2000 and the percentage of these signatures contributing to the MDSL is greater than 30 percent, penalty factor C plays a positive role improving the model's performance significantly. This suggests that penalty factor C should be set to a value in the interval $[0.9, 0.99]$.

The malware instruction threshold T_1 usually obtains its value in the interval $[0.9, 1]$, while the malware classification threshold T_2 should be set to a value in the interval $[0.00001, 0.0001]$.

Figure 7.8 shows the detection accuracy of the proposed model for different values of T_1. With $T_1 = 0.95$, the model achieves optimal detection accuracy. When

Table 7.9 Experimental Results on the VX Heavens Dataset

C	Virus	Worm	Trojan	Backdoor	Constructor	Other
0.00	0.918	0.965	0.91	0.739	0.96	0.867
0.50	0.986	0.962	0.908	0.739	0.96	0.912
0.90	**0.987**	0.961	**0.913**	0.923	**0.963**	**0.917**
0.95	0.986	**0.962**	0.911	0.923	0.963	0.917
0.99	0.98	0.961	0.911	**0.924**	0.963	0.907
1.00	0.931	0.939	0.852	0.918	0.922	0.867

Table 7.10 Experimental Results Obtained by Tabish

Virus	Worm	Trojan	Backdoor	Constructor	Other
0.945	0.919	0.881	0.849	0.925	0.903

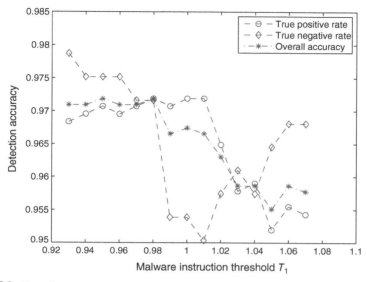

Figure 7.8 Detection accuracy with different T_1.

T_1 is small, malware instructions with lower tendencies increase the FPR. When T_1 is large, there are too few malware instructions to provide enough malware detection signatures to cover the space of malware detection signatures. In summary, an appropriate T_1 ensures that the proposed model contains enough malware instructions

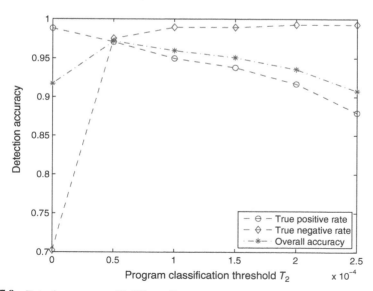

Figure 7.9 Detection accuracy with different T_2.

with marked tendencies, thus generating an optimized MDSL to help the model achieve better performance.

Figure 7.9 shows the effect of the malware classification threshold T_2 on the detection accuracy of the proposed model. By increasing T_2, the TPR of the proposed model decreases monotonically, while the FPR increases monotonically. With $C = 0.00005$, the proposed model achieves optimal overall accuracy.

7.6 SUMMARY

The malware detection model based on the NSAPF overcomes the drawback of the traditional NSA in defining harmfulness of self and nonself. It focuses on the harmfulness of the code and extracts dangerous signatures, which are included in the MDSL. By adjusting the penalty factor C, the proposed model achieved a tradeoff between the TPR and FPR to satisfy the requirements of various users in terms of TPR and FPR. Comprehensive experimental results demonstrated that the proposed model is effective in detecting unknown malware with a lower FPR.

REFERENCES

1. Zhang, P., Wang, W., and Tan, Y. (2010) A malware detection model based on a negative selection algorithm with penalty factor. *Science China Information Sciences*, **53** (12), 2461–2471.
2. Resource, http://www.cil.pku.edu.cn/resources/.
3. Henchiri, O. and Japkowicz, N. (2006) A feature selection and evaluation scheme for computer virus detection, in Data Mining, 2006. ICDM'06. Sixth International Conference on, IEEE, pp. 891–895.
4. Wang, W., Zhang, P., Tan, Y., and He, X. (2009) A hierarchical artificial immune model for virus detection, in Computational Intelligence and Security, 2009. CIS'09. International Conference on, IEEE, vol. 1, pp. 1–5.
5. Vx Heavens virus collection, http://vx.netlux.org.
6. Kohavi, R. et al. (1995) A study of cross-validation and bootstrap for accuracy estimation and model selection, in International Joint Conference on Artificial Intelligence IJCAI, vol. 14, pp. 1137–1145.
7. Fawcett, T. (2006) An introduction to ROC analysis. *Pattern Recognition Letters*, **27** (8), 861–874.
8. Tabish, S.M., Shafiq, M.Z., and Farooq, M. (2009) Malware detection using statistical analysis of byte-level file content, in Proceedings of the ACM SIGKDD Workshop on CyberSecurity and Intelligence Informatics, ACM, pp. 23–31.
9. Hanley, J.A. and McNeil, B.J. (1982) The meaning and use of the area under a receiver operating characteristic (ROC) curve. *Radiology*, **143** (1), 29–36.

Chapter 8

Danger Feature-Based Negative Selection Algorithm

A danger feature-based negative selection algorithm (DFNSA) is presented in this chapter. In the DFNSA, the danger feature space is divided into four parts, and the information of danger features is reserved as much as possible, laying a good foundation for measuring the danger of a sample.

8.1 INTRODUCTION

8.1.1 Danger Feature

A danger feature is a feature with dangerous properties, that is able to identify its corresponding dangerous operations. It is the basic element for an immune system to decide whether an immune response should be produced.

In the malware detection field, a danger feature is a code segment that executes a dangerous operation, such as formatting a diskette or self-replicating.

There are many expressions for a danger feature. For example, we could use binary string, sequences of assembly codes to express a danger feature in the malware detection field. Generally speaking, a danger feature could appear in both nonself and self. It is the foundation of measuring the danger of a sample.

Danger features can be classified into four categories: (1) those only appearing in nonself; (2) those appearing in both nonself and self, but tending to appear in nonself; (3) those appearing in both nonself and self, but tending to appear in self; and (4) those only appearing in self.

Artificial Immune System: Applications in Computer Security, First Edition. Ying Tan.
© 2016 the IEEE Computer Society. Published 2016 by John Wiley & Sons, Inc.

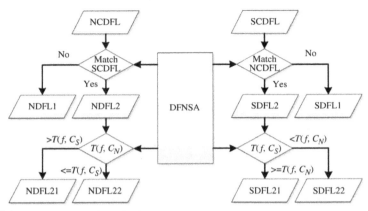

Figure 8.1   The flow chart of the DFNSA.

8.1.2 Framework of Danger Feature-Based Negative Selection Algorithm

The flow chart of the danger feature based negative selection algorithm [1] (DFNSA) is shown in Fig. 8.1, where the NCDFL denotes the nonself candidate danger feature library, which is taken as nonself, and the SCDFL means the self candidate danger feature library, which is self [1–5].

Based on the matching of nonself and self, the DFNSA splits the nonself features, which do not match any self, into the nonself danger feature library 1 (NDFL1), and the other nonself features, which match self, into the NDFL2. According to the class tendency of danger features, the NDFL2 is further divided into the NDFL21 and NDFL22, in which the features tend to appear in nonself and self, respectively. The features in the NDFL22 are extracted from nonself, but tend to appear in self, so they are considered to be invalid and deleted.

The measure of the class tendency of a feature is defined as $T(f, C) = P(f, C)$, where $P(f, C)$ denotes the proportion of feature f appearing in class C. if $T(f, C_N) > T(f, C_S)$, then f is considered to tend to appear in nonself, otherwise self. The C_N and C_S denote the classes of nonself and self, respectively.

In a similar way, the SCDFL is firstly split into the SDFL1 and SDFL2 by the DFNSA. Then the SDFL2 is further divided into the SDFL21 and SDFL22. The SDFL22 is deleted with the same reason as the NDFL22.

Definition: If a danger feature f_1 matches a danger feature f_2, the two features are equivalent to each other, written as $f_1 = f_2$.

According to this definition, since NDFL21 = SDFL22 and NDFL22 = SDFL21, deleting the NDFL22 and SDFL22 merely deletes redundant information, without losing any information of the danger features. The proof about NDFL21 = SDFL22 and NDFL22 = SDFL21 is given next.

Proof

$\because \forall f_S \in SDFL2, \exists f_N \in NDFL2, f_S = f_N$

$\therefore T(f_S, C_S) = T(f_N, C_S) = P(f_S, C_S)$ and $T(f_S, C_N) = T(f_N, C_N) = P(f_N, C_N)$

$\therefore$ if $T(f_S, C_S) >= T(f_S, C_N)$, then $f_S \in SDFL21$ and $f_N \in NDFL22$,

if $T(f_S, C_S) < T(f_S, C_N)$, then $f_S \in SDFL22$ and $f_N \in NDFL21$

$\therefore \forall f'_S \in SDFL21, \exists f'_N \in NDFL22, f'_S = f'_N$

and $\forall f'_S \in SDFL22, \exists f'_N \in NDFL21, f'_S = f'_N,$

Similarly, $\forall f'_N \in NDFL21, \exists f'_S \in SDFL22, f'_N = f'_S$

and $\forall f'_N \in NDFL22, \exists f'_S \in SDFL21, f'_N = f'_S$

$\therefore NDFL21 = SDFL22, NDFL22 = SDFL21$ ∎

The DFNSA divides the danger feature space into four parts, and reserves the information of danger features to the maximum extent, laying a good foundation for measuring the danger of a sample. The four categories of danger features are stored in NDFL1, NDFL21, SDFL21, and SDFL1, respectively.

Compared to the NSAPF [6], the DFNSA does not need to optimize a penalty factor, dramatically dropping down the training time of the DFNSA, and takes full advantage of all the danger features extracted in a training set.

8.2 DFNSA FOR MALWARE DETECTION

In order to incorporate the Danger Feature Based Negative Selection Algorithm (DFNSA) into the procedure of malware detection, a DFNSA-based malware detection (DFNSA-MD) model is proposed. It maps a sample into the whole danger feature space by using the DFNSA. The danger of a sample is measured precisely in this way and used to classify the sample.

8.2.1 Danger Feature Extraction

8.2.1.1 Malware Instruction Library

This section defines an instruction as a binary string of length 2 bytes. The class tendency of an instruction i to malware is measured using Eqs. 8.1, 8.2, and 8.3. The top $P\%$ instructions with the highest tendency value make up the malware instruction library (MIL).

$$I^i = \frac{I_n^i/I_n}{I_n^i/I_n + I_s^i/I_s} \tag{8.1}$$

$$F^i = \frac{F_n^i/F_n}{F_n^i/F_n + F_s^i/F_s} \tag{8.2}$$

$$T^i = \sqrt{(I^i)^2 + (F^i)^2} \tag{8.3}$$

where I_n^i and I_s^i denote the instruction frequencies of an instruction i in nonself and self, respectively, and F_n^i and F_s^i are the document frequencies of i in nonself and self. I_n and I_s indicate the number of instructions in the nonself and self, respectively. F_n and F_s are the number of samples in nonself and self. I^i and F^i measure the tendency of i to the nonself in the perspectives of instruction frequency and document frequency. T^i is the tendency of i to the nonself.

Since the instructions in the MIL tend to appear in malware, they are dangerous. If the length of a binary string constructed by these instructions exceeds a threshold R bytes, the binary string contains enough danger information and is a danger feature. All the danger features make up the danger feature space.

8.2.1.2 NCDFL and SCDFL

On the basis of the MIL, the NCDFL and SCDFL are generated by traversing all the malware and benign programs in a training set, respectively. The way to traverse a sample is described next.

A sliding window of length two bytes is used to traverse a sample to extract candidate danger features. It moves forward one byte at a time. When the window encounters an instruction contained in the MIL, it begins to generate a feature. If the instructions in two adjacent windows do not belong to the MIL, the current feature is terminated as the next feature would not connect with it. If the length of the current feature exceeds R bytes, it is taken as a candidate danger feature. The sliding window keeps on moving to the end of the sample.

This chapter sets $R = 4$. The length of a candidate danger feature would be adjusted based on the specific sample and MIL as described above, so R would not affect the result significantly. The frequency of a feature is taken as its weight.

8.2.1.3 Detecting Feature Library

Taking the NCDFL and SCDFL as the inputs of the DFNSA, four danger feature libraries are generated: NDFL1, NDFL21, SDFL1, and SDFL21, which make up the detecting feature library (DFL) of the proposed DFNSA-MD model. The features in the DFL are the basic elements to construct the danger feature vector of a sample.

8.2.2 Danger Feature Vector

In this chapter, a sample is expressed as a danger feature vector to measure the danger of the sample. The danger feature vector is defined as:

$$\left\langle \frac{M_{NDFL1}}{L_{NDFL1}}, \frac{M_{NDFL21}}{L_{NDFL21}}, \frac{M_{SDFL1} + M_{SDFL21}}{L_{SDFL1} + L_{SDFL21}} \right\rangle$$

where M_i denotes the matching value of a sample and a library i, and L_i is the sum of weights of features in a library i, $i = $ NDFL1, NDFL21, SDFL1, SDFL21.

The r-bit continuous matching [7] is taken as the feature matching criteria. Here $r = R*8$, that is, the matching part of two features is also a danger feature. The matching value of a sample and a danger feature library is the sum of weights of the features in the library that match any feature of the sample.

The danger feature vector maps a sample into the whole danger feature space and characterizes a sample efficiently and completely, making the DFNSA-MD model perform well. Every sample in a training set is expressed as a danger feature vector, which is taken as the input of a classifier.

8.3 EXPERIMENTS

Eight groups of experiments on three public malware datasets were exploited to evaluate the effectiveness of the proposed DFNSA-MD model using cross validation. Comprehensive experimental results suggest that the DFNSA is able to reserve as much information about the danger features as possible, and the DFNSA-MD model is effective to detect unseen malware. It outperforms the traditional negative selection algorithm based and the negative selection algorithm with penalty factor-based malware detection models in all the experiments for about 5.34 percent and 0.67 percent on average, respectively.

8.3.1 Datasets

The experiments in this chapter were conducted on three public malware datasets: CILPKU08, Henchiri, and VX Heavens [8] datasets. The three datasets and their composition documents can be downloaded [9].

The benign program dataset used here consists of files of Windows XP and a series of applications, which are the main punching bag of malware.

8.3.2 Experimental Setup

The support vector machine (SVM) [10,11], implemented in LibSVM [12], is taken as the classifier of the proposed DFNSA-MD model, and the area under the receiver operating characteristic curve (AUC) [13,14] is utilized as the performance evaluation criteria. The information of the experimental platform is shown in Table 8.1.

In the experiments described in Section 8.3.4, eight groups of experiments were made with the three public malware datasets using five-fold cross validation [15], and the 95 percent confidence intervals are computed to look into the stability of the proposed DFNSA-MD model. Both the CILPKU08 and Henchiri datasets mainly consist of computer viruses, so two experiments were carried out on in the two datasets directly, ignoring the categories of malware. The VX Heavens dataset

Table 8.1 Experimental Platform

CPU	Core 2 Duo 3.00 GHz
RAM	8 GB
Operating system	Win 7 64-bit

contains 7128 malware that fall into six categories, so we split this dataset into six smaller datasets: backdoor, constructor, miscellaneous, trojan, virus, and worm. The miscellaneous includes DoS, Nuker, Hacktool, and Flooder, while the malware in the other five smaller datasets, respectively, fall into a category. Six experiments were carried out with the six smaller datasets.

In all the experiments, there was no overlap between a training set and a test set. That is to say, to a training set, the malware in a test set were unseen malware. This setting increased the reliability of the experiments.

The TNSA-based malware detection (TNSA-MD) model and the NSAPF-based malware detection (NSAPF-MD) model were imported for comparison.

8.3.3 Selection of Parameters

This section selects the instruction proportion: P percent used in the MIL, using liner search, where $P = 0.5, 1.0, \ldots, 10.0$. We did not try larger P, since when $P = 10$, the MIL contains 6553 instructions and already covers a huge danger feature space. The experimental results are shown in Fig. 8.2.

Figure 8.2 illustrates that, with the growth of P, the performance of the DFNSA-MD model shows a steady downward trend because the MIL contains more and more instructions with unremarkable tendencies to malware. When $P = 1$, the DFNSA-MD model obtained the optimal AUC $= 0.9039$.

Generally speaking, the instruction proportion P percent varied with different datasets. Hence we set the optimization interval of P as $[0.5, 3]$ in the rest of experiments, instead of setting $P = 1$. In the rest of experiments, the P, which makes the DFNSA-MD model perform best in a training set, was set as the optimal P.

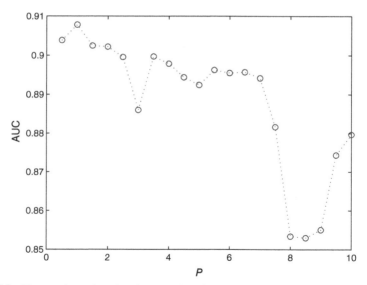

Figure 8.2 The experimental results of the selection of parameters.

Table 8.2 Experimental Results

	TNSA-MD model	NSAPF-MD model	DFNSA-MD model
CILPKU08	0.9684 ± 0.00568	0.9688 ± 0.00907	0.9761 ± 0.00781
Hechiri	0.9634 ± 0.00755	0.9679 ± 0.01404	0.9808 ± 0.00428
Backdoor	0.8100 ± 0.02060	0.8190 ± 0.01764	0.8247 ± 0.01024
Constructor	0.9095 ± 0.03120	0.9202 ± 0.01545	0.9244 ± 0.01213
Miscellaneous	0.8243 ± 0.01603	0.8255 ± 0.01912	0.8394 ± 0.01028
Trojan	0.7901 ± 0.01332	0.8729 ± 0.01897	0.8735 ± 0.01714
Virus	0.6275 ± 0.01738	0.8746 ± 0.01187	0.8774 ± 0.01784
Worm	0.8252 ± 0.03697	0.8430 ± 0.04788	0.8489 ± 0.04101

8.3.4 Experimental Results

The experimental results of the proposed DFNSA-MD model are listed in Table 8.2. The experimental results of the TNSA-MD and NSAPF-MD models are also given in Table 8.2 for comparison.

From Table 8.2, the NSAPF-MD model is 4.67 percent better than the TNSA-MD model in all the experiments on average by taking advantage of danger features extracted from malware. The detailed analysis will be given in Section 8.4.

The DFNSA-MD model outperforms the TNSA-MD and NSAPF-MD models by about 5.34% and 0.67% in all the experiments on average, respectively. The DFNSA-MD model makes use of all the danger features extracted from a training set, regardless of their categories. Hence the DFNSA-MD model is considered to be able to measure the danger of a sample more precisely and achieves the best performance.

The 95% confidence intervals of the three models are relatively small from Table 8.2, indicating that the results of these models are very stable and believable.

8.4 DISCUSSIONS

8.4.1 Comparison of Detecting Feature Libraries

Table 8.3 lists the composition of the DFLs of the TNSA-MD, NSAPF-MD and DFNSA-MD models. It is easy to see that the DFL of the TNSA-MD model is the smallest DFL, consisting of NDFL1, that is, the features merely appearing in nonself.

Table 8.3 The Composition of the DFLS of the Three Models

	Detecting feature library
TNSA-MD Model	NDFL1
NSAPF-MD Model	NDFL1, NDFL21, NDFL22
DFNSA-MD Model	NDFL1, NDFL21, SDFL1, SDFL21

Since the TNSA discards lots of danger features that are believed helpful, the performance of the TNSA-MD model is relatively bad.

The DFL of the NSAPF-MD model consists of NDFL1, NDFL21. and NDFL22, that is, all the danger features appearing in nonself. The NSAPF reserves the nonself danger features that match self danger features by punishing these features, and obtains a larger DFL. Based on this DFL, the NSAPF-MD model detects malware by measuring the danger of a sample and achieves good results.

The DFNSA-MD model owns the largest DFL, which consists of all the danger features extracted from a training set. The DFNSA divides the danger feature space into four parts and reserves the information of danger features to the maximum extent. It makes the danger feature vector of a sample contain as much information as possible and measure the danger of a sample better. In this way, the DFNSA-MD model outperforms the TNSA-MD and NSAPF-MD models in all the experiments.

8.4.2 Comparison of Detection Time

The detection time of a sample is proportional to the number of the features in a DFL. We analyzed the average detecting time of the three models for a sample in the virus dataset, in which the average size of a sample is 104 KB:

- The DFL of the TNSA-MD model is the smallest DFL, so it is faster than the other two models to detect a sample, assuming 0.05 seconds on average.

- The size of the DFL of the NSAPF-MD model lays between that of the TNSA-MD and DFNSA-MD models, taking 0.12 seconds on average for detecting a sample.

- The DFNSA-MD model has the largest DFL, which consists of all the danger features extracted in a training set, so its detecting time is the longest, 0.15 seconds on average, basically meeting the demand of a real-time system.

8.5 SUMMARY

In this chapter, the danger feature negative selection algorithm (DFNSA) was used for malware detection. The DFNSA divided the danger feature space into four parts, and reserved the information of danger features to the maximum extent. Comprehensive experimental results suggested that the DFNSA is able to reserve as much information of danger features as possible, and the DFNSA-MD model is effective in detecting unseen malware by precisely measuring the danger of a sample. It turns out that NFNSA-MD outperformed the TNSA-MD and NSAPF-MD models by about 5.36 percent and 0.67 percent, respectively.

REFERENCES

1. Zhang, P. and Tan, Y. (2012) A danger feature based negative selection algorithm. Advances in Swarm Intelligence, pp. 291–299.

2. Matzinger, P. (2002) The danger model: A renewed sense of self. *Science's STKE*, **296** (5566), 301.
3. Aickelin, U. and Cayzer, S. (2002) The danger theory and its application to artificial immune systems. Artificial Immune Systems, pp. 141–148.
4. Zhu, Y. and Tan, Y. (2011) A danger theory inspired learning model and its application to spam detection. Advances in Swarm Intelligence, pp. 382–389.
5. Zhang, C. and Yi, Z. (2010) A danger theory inspired artificial immune algorithm for on-line supervised two-class classification problem. *Neurocomputing*, **73** (7–9), 1244–1255.
6. Zhang, P., Wang, W., and Tan, Y. (2010) A malware detection model based on a negative selection algorithm with penalty factor. *Science Chins Information Sciences*, **53** (12), 2461–2471.
7. Cai, T., Ju, S., Zhong, W., Niu, D. (2009) Random r-continuous matching rule for immune-based secure storage system, in Proceedings of the International Workshop on Computational Intelligence in Security for Information Systems (CISIS2009), Springer, pp. 294–300.
8. Vx Heavens virus collection, http://vx.netlux.org.
9. Resource, http://www.cil.pku.edu.cn/resources/.
10. Suykens, J.A. and Vandewalle, J. (1999) Least squares support vector machine classifiers. *Neural Processing Letters*, **9** (3), 293–300.
11. Furey, T.S., Cristianini, N., Duffy, N., Bednarski, D.W., et al. (2000). Support vector machine classification and validation of cancer tissue samples using microarray expression data. *Bioinformatics*, **16** (10), 906–914.
12. LibSVM. URL http://www.csie.ntu.edu.tw/~cjlin/libsvm/.
13. Fawcett, T. (2006) An introduction to ROC analysis. *Pattern Recognition Letters*, **27** (8), 861–874.
14. Hanley, J.A. and McNeil, B.J. (1982) The meaning and use of the area under a receiver operating characteristic (ROC) curve. *Radiology*, **143** (1), 29–36.
15. Kohavi, R. et al. (1995) A study of cross-validation and bootstrap for accuracy estimation and model selection, in International Joint Conference on Artificial Intelligence (IJCAI), vol. 14, pp. 1137–1145.

Chapter 9

Immune Concentration-Based Malware Detection Approaches

In this chapter, the immune concentration is applied to malware detection. The local concentration-based malware detection method connects a certain number of two-element local concentration vectors as the feature vector. To achieve better detection performance, particle swarm optimization (PSO) is used to optimize the parameters of local concentration. Then the hybrid concentration-based feature extraction (HCFE) approach is presented by extracting the hybrid concentration (HC) of malware in both the global resolution and the local resolution.

9.1 INTRODUCTION

Immune concentration-based malware detection approaches are mainly divided into three parts [1–6]:

1. Generate self and nonself detector libraries from the randomly selected training set;

2. Extract the immune concentration for each training sample to construct a feature vector;

3. Use three trained classifiers, including KNN, RBF neural networks, and SVM, to detect the testing sample characterized by the ordered concentration vector.

The overview of the proposed algorithm is outlined in Algorithm 12. The approach computes a statistical and information-theoretic feature in a manner of immune concentration on the byte-level file content. The generated feature vector of a program is then given as an input to standard data mining classification algorithms that classify the file as malware or not.

Artificial Immune System: Applications in Computer Security, First Edition. Ying Tan.
© 2016 the IEEE Computer Society. Published 2016 by John Wiley & Sons, Inc.

9.2 GENERATION OF DETECTOR LIBRARIES

The operation principle of generating self detector library and nonself detector library is shown in Fig. 9.1. The concrete step is to divide all detectors into two sets by their tendency value and calculate these detectors' importance, with important detectors retained.

Algorithm 12   Algorithm for Malware Detection

Generate self and nonself *detector libraries* from training set.
The sizes of the libraries are decided by parameter m that corresponds to proportional selection of the *potential detectors.*

for each the sample in training set **do**.
   Extract the *immune concentration-based feature vector* from each training sample through the two detector libraries.

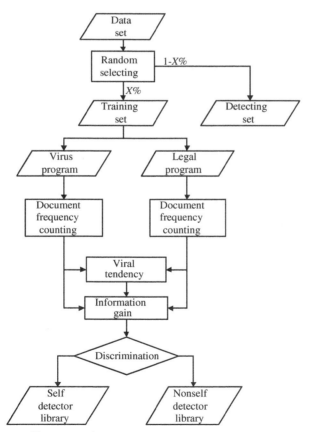

Figure 9.1   Detector library generating process.

end for

Use these *feature vectors* to train a certain classifier.

while Algorithm is running **do**.
   if a program is detected **then**.
      Characterize the sample by *immune concentration-based feature vector* through trained self and nonself *detector libraries*
      Use trained classifier to predict the *label* of the program.
   end if.
end while.

Self detector library are composed of detectors with maximum representative of benign files and nonself detector library are composed of those detectors with maximum representative of malware. Intuitively, the fragment that appears most in malware programs while seldom in benign programs is a good representative of malware.

The detectors in the library are a set of fixed-length fragments. Here a fixed length L-bit fragment of binary data that is considered containing appropriate information of functional behaviors is taken as the detector to discriminate malware from benign program. The length L is set not too short to discriminate self and nonself and not too long to make malware-special data hidden in the binary data of files. Considering that one meaningful computer instruction is 8 or 16 bits normally, it is reasonable to set L as 16, 32, or 64. A sliding window (shown in Fig. 9.2, the overlap of sliding window is $[L/2]$ bits) is used to count the document frequency of a detector in the malware programs and benign programs. The difference of its document frequency in the malware programs and benign programs can reflect its tendency to be a malware or a benign file.

After counting the document frequency of each fragment, the tendency $T(X)$ of fragment X is defined by Eq. 9.1.

$$T(X) = P(X = 1|C_v) - P(X = 1|C_s) \tag{9.1}$$

$P(X = 1|C_v)$ means document frequency of fragment X appears in malware samples of training set;

$P(X = 1|C_s)$ means document frequency of fragment X appears in benign samples of training set.

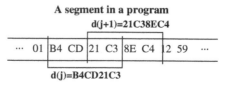

Figure 9.2   Document frequency counting process, L = 32bits.

If we define the number of malware files as N_v, the number of benign files as N_s, the number of malware files that contain fragment X as n_v, and the number of benign files that contain fragment X as n_s, then

$$P(X = 1|C_v) = \frac{n_v}{N_v} \tag{9.2}$$

$$P(X = 1|C_s) = \frac{n_s}{N_s} \tag{9.3}$$

If each fragment is extracted to form a dictionary, the size of this dictionary would be very large. The detectors that appear in most of files are not relevant to separate these files because all the classes have instances that contain these detectors. So with the increasing number of detectors, the cost of computing would increase but the effect may not improve and could even be worse. We reduce the number of fragments to generate self and nonself detector libraries by evaluating the importance of each detector. Here the detector's importance is calculated based on Information Gain (IG). The detectors are sorted based on IG values in descending order, P percent of them are retained. Moreover, besides IG, other detector importance measures such as document frequency, term-frequency variance, χ^2 statistic can be applied to the model, enbuing it with promising development. The preprocess of statistical and information-theoretic feature generation is done.

The generation process of detector libraries is described in Algorithm 3, in which m is a adjusting parameter used for the proportional selection of all the fragments. The information gain is defined in Eq. (9.4).

$$IG(X, C) = \sum_{x \in \{0,1\}, c \in \{C_v, C_s\}} P(X = x \land C = c)$$
$$\cdot \log_2 \frac{P(X = x \land C = c)}{P(X = x) \cdot P(C = c)} \tag{9.4}$$

It should be added that,

$P(X = 1)$ means document frequency of fragment X that appears in the training set;

$P(X = 0)$ means document frequency of fragment X that doesn't appear in the training set;

$P(C = C_v)$ means document frequency of malware files;

$P(C = C_s)$ means document frequency of benign files;

$P(X = 0|C_v)$ means document frequency of fragment X that doesn't appear in malware samples of training set;

$P(X = 0|C_s)$ means document frequency of fragment X that doesn't appear in benign samples of training set.

$$P(X = 1) = \frac{n_v + n_c}{N_v + N_c} \tag{9.5}$$

$$P(X = 0) = \frac{N_v + N_c - n_v - n_c}{N_v + N_c} \tag{9.6}$$

$$P(C = C_v) = \frac{N_v}{N_v + N_c} \tag{9.7}$$

$$P(C = C_s) = \frac{N_s}{N_v + N_c} \tag{9.8}$$

$$P(X = 0|C_v) = \frac{N_v - n_v}{N_v} \tag{9.9}$$

$$P(X = 0|C_s) = \frac{N_s - n_s}{N_s} \tag{9.10}$$

Algorithm 13   Algorithm for Generation of Detector Libraries

---

Initialize self and nonself *detector libraries* as ∅

while Algorithm is running **do**
    for each fragment X in the sample of training set **do**
        Calculate the *tendency* of fragment X by Eq. (9.1)
        Calculate the *information gain* of fragment X by Eq. (9.2)
    end for

    for each fragment X in the sample of training set **do**
      if $IG(X) > m$ **then**
        if $T(X) < 0$ **then**
            add fragment X into self *detector library*
        else
            add fragment X into nonself *detector library*
        end if
      end if
    end for
end while

Extract P percent front of fragments to form self *detector library* and nonself *detector library*, P is decided by parameter m.

9.3 CONSTRUCTION OF FEATURE VECTOR FOR LOCAL CONCENTRATION

For constructing a feature vector, a jumping window is moved to plot out several fixed length W-bit segments. Inside a fixed length W-bit segment in the program, a sliding window with $[L/2]$ bits overlap is used to get the self local concentration and

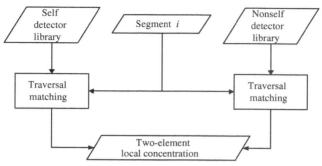

Figure 9.3   Local concentration construction.

nonself local concentration (shown in Fig. 9.3). In every window, the local concentration of segment i is defined in Eqs. (9.3) and (9.4).

$$VC_i = \frac{VN_i * L}{W} \tag{9.11}$$

$$BC_i = \frac{BN_i * L}{W} \tag{9.12}$$

Where VC_i and BC_i denotes the nonself and self local concentration, respectively; VN_i is the number of detectors appearing in both the detecting segment of the file and the nonself detector library; BN_i is the number of detectors appearing in both the detecting segment of the file and the self detector library.

After self and nonself local concentration are constructed in every window, these two-element local concentrations of the program are connected to form a feature vector:

$$\langle(VC_1, BC_1), (VC_2, BC_2), \ldots (VC_n, BC_n)\rangle \text{(shown in Fig. 9.4)}.$$

In order to use these feature vectors as the input of successive classifiers for detecting, the dimensionality of the vector should be consistent. In this chapter, a truncated operation is applied and some rear dimensionality is discarded. We use $N * W$ bits information of each program, N is the number of segments that is covered by the jumping window. Algorithm 14 is for feature construction and Fig. 9.4 shows the process of the feature vector construction.

Algorithm 14   Algorithm for Feature Construction

For a program to be detected, truncate front $N*W$ bits of the file and discard rear dimensionality of the file

for each segment inside W-bit jumping windows **do**
  Traverse the segment i using a L-bit sliding window with $[L/2]$ bits overlap

  Initialize $BN_i = 0$, $VN_i = 0$
  for each different L-bit fragment in the segment i **do**

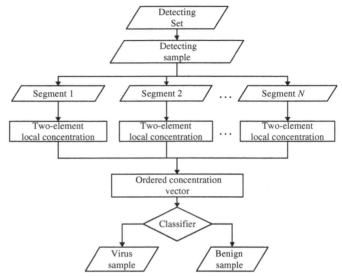

Figure 9.4   Feature vector construction.

> **if** it appears in self *detector library* **then**
> BN_i++;
> **else if** it appears in nonself *detector library* **then**
> VN_i++;
>   **end if**
> **end for**
>
> *self-local concentration* = BN_i**L/W*
> *nonself-local concentration* = VN_i**L/W*
> **end for**

Connect these ordered two-element local concentrations to construct a feature vector.

9.4   PARAMETERS OPTIMIZATION BASED ON PARTICLE SWARM OPTIMIZATION

The feature vector constructed by an ordered two-element local concentration is the input of a classifier, and one binary value is the output. The generation of self and nonself detector libraries, the jumping window size W setting, the window number N setting, which in turn determine the feature vector, is an optimization problem.

The vector that we need to optimize $P^* = \{m, W, N, P_1^*, P_2^*, \cdots, P_n^*\}$ is composed of detector library determinant m, jumping window size W, window number N, and parameters $P_1^*, P_2^*, \cdots, P_m^*$ associated with a certain classifier.

When m is set to different values, P would take different values, different detector libraries are obtained. With different W and N, for a file to be characterized, self local concentrations that represent their similarity to benign program and nonself local concentrations that represent their similarity to malware are different, a unique feature vector can be constructed. $P_1^*, P_2^*, \cdots, P_m^*$ are classifier-related parameters that influence the performance of a certain classifier. Different classifiers hold different parameters and lead to different performance. For examples, parameters associated with KNN include number of nearest neighbors and the ways of distance measures. SVM-related parameters that determine the position of optimal hyperplane in feature space, include cost parameter C and kernel parameters.

The optimal vector is the one whose cost function associated with classification is minimum, namely the one that makes the accuracy of classification maximum. The cost function $CF(P)$ can be defined as:

$$CF(P) = Err(P) \tag{9.13}$$

where $Err(P)$ is the classification error on the training set.

The input vector includes two parts: LC feature vector determinant m, W, N, and $P_1^*, P_2^*, \cdots, P_m^*$ the classifier-related parameters. Output is to find a P^*, so that

$$CF(P^*) = Err(P^*) = \min_{\{m,W,N,P_1^*,P_2^*,\cdots,P_m^*\}} Err(P) \tag{9.14}$$

Several robust optimization approaches can be employed to optimize the input vector, like particle swarm optimization (PSO) and genetic algorithm (GA). Here we use a CPSO (as shown in Fig. 9.5) to design the LC feature vector and corresponding classifier. The detailed optimization process is referred in the References [7].

9.5 CONSTRUCTION OF FEATURE VECTOR FOR HYBRID CONCENTRATION

9.5.1 Hybrid Concentration

Based on the immune concentration, importing the concept of multi-resolution, the hybrid concentration (HC) is proposed in this section.

Definition: A hybrid concentration is constructed by the immune concentration vectors which are extracted in more than one resolution, for example, both the global resolution and the local resolution.

In this chapter, the HC is written as $\langle IC_1, \ldots, IC_m \rangle$, where $IC_i(i = 1, 2, \ldots, m)$ denotes the concentration vector extracted in the i-th resolution, and m is the number of the resolutions in the HC. We make use of the GC extracted in the global resolution and the LC extracted in the local resolution to construct the HC. The HC is a two-resolution concentration, expressed as:

$$HC = \langle GC, LC \rangle,$$
$$GC = \langle GC_1, GC_2, \ldots, GC_M \rangle,$$
$$LC = \langle LC_1, LC_2, \ldots, LC_N \rangle,$$
$$LC_i = \langle LC_{i1}, LC_{i2}, \ldots, LC_{iM} \rangle$$

where M is the number of the classes in a classification problem, and N is the number of the local areas defined in the LC. $GC_j(j = 1, 2, \ldots, M)$ is the global concentration

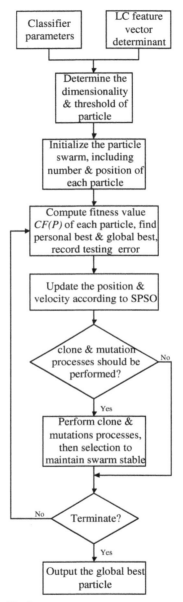

Figure 9.5 CPSO-based classification process.

value of class j in the whole sample. $LC_i (i = 1, 2, \ldots, N)$ is the local concentration vector in local area i, and the LC_{ij} is the local concentration value of class j in local area i.

It is easy to see that the HC consists of the GC and LC, which are extracted in the global and local resolutions, respectively. So the HC contains both the global and local information of a sample. Through the co-operation of the global and local information, the HC overcomes the disadvantages of the GC and LC which only characterizes a sample in a single resolution. In this way, the HC characterizes a sample more precisely and completely than the GC and LC alone.

The dimension of the HC is $(1 + N)^* M$. To a specific classification problem, M is a constant. Hence the dimension of the HC is determined by the number of the local areas N defined in the LC. Furthermore, we could extract the LC in different local resolutions by different N, to obtain more coarse or detailed local information.

9.5.2 Strategies for Definition of Local Areas

In this chapter, a local area is defined as a gene string with variable length. The length of a local area is determined by the length of a sample and the number of local areas defined in the LC.

There are two strategies of defining local areas [3]: local area with fixed length and local area with variable length. In the field of spam filtering, both the two strategies result in good performance without marked difference [3]. In one malware detection method [8], a local area is defined as a local area with fixed length that is set to 500 bytes. The number of local areas is 40. This method performs very well using these parameters. However, this method only extracts the concentration information from the top $500 ^* 40 = 20{,}000$ bytes ≈ 20 KB of a sample and ignores the remaining content. In the anti-malware field, we cannot make sure that the malicious codes in a malware appear in its top 20 KB binary string, and we have to traverse a sample. As a result of the local area with fixed length, it is easy for a malware to evade from the method [8]. Actually, other fields, such as spam filtering, have a similar problem. Hence the local area in this chapter is defined as the local area with variable length, and the set of all the local areas covers the whole sample.

9.5.3 HC-Based Malware Detection Method

The HCMD method is proposed in this section. Its two main stages are shown in Fig. 9.6.

In the HCMD method, a gene is defined as a binary string of length four bytes. The gene in this length contains enough information to identify a meaningful operation and is the same as the 4-Gram [9,10]. Set $\theta = 0$.

In the training stage, a sliding window is used to traverse the whole training set to obtain the document frequency of every gene. The length of the sliding window is set to four bytes, so the content in a sliding window is a gene. The sliding window moves forward one byte at a time. There is an overlap of three bytes between two adjacent sliding windows. The overlap allows the gene to capture not only genes of four-byte length, but also longer genes implicitly. Then the HCFE approach outputs the HC set of all the training samples. The HC set are taken as the input of a classifier to train the classifier.

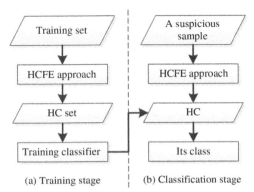

Figure 9.6   The training and classification stages of the HCMD method.

In the classification stage, the trained classifier makes classification to the HC of a suspicious sample.

9.5.4 Discussion

To date, the experimental results suggest that the HC extracted by the HCFE approach is a discriminating feature that characterizes a sample more precisely and completely than the GC and LC, and the proposed HCMD method is able to detect unseen malware effectively and stably.

9.5.4.1 Advantages of the HC

Inspired by the human immune system, the GC, as an effective feature, was proposed and applied to the field of spam filtering and malware detection successfully. The GC, which is a two-element vector, is very simple but effectively characterizes a sample. The value of the GC is independent of the distribution of the genes in a sample. This independent attribute of the GC is comparably important for detecting malware. There are three main ways for malware to infect benign programs: insertion in the head of a benign program, insertion in the tail of a benign program, and insertion in the cavity of a benign program—the space that is useless and filled by 0 among different segments in a program. All the three ways of infection are widely used, so it is not possible to predict the distribution of the malware genes in an infected executable. Furthermore, the distribution of the malware genes in a malware loader is also not predictable. Hence the independent attribute of the GC becomes its vital attribute. However, the GC only characterizes a sample in the global resolution, so the value of the GC is closely related to the size of the sample. Hence, there is a high dilute risk for the GC. Considering two samples containing the same malware genes that are 1 KB and 1 MB, respectively, the values of the GCs in the malware dimension of the two samples are different from each other for about 1000 times. Obviously, it is not reasonable.

Taking inspiration from the GC, the LCFE approach extracts the concentration information in a local area with fixed length or variable length, and stores the local information in the LC. With the help of the local areas, the LC overcomes the dilute risk of the GC to a certain extent. The local area helps to zoom out the gene concentration and effectively extract the position-correlated information that is believed helpful for the classification. However, the LC is closely related to the distribution of the genes in a sample by using the local area. Just like the example of an infected executable, the position-correlated information is unstable in many cases. What is more, the LC is extracted in the local resolution, resulting in its bias to the local information, ignoring the global information.

On the basis of the GC and LC, the HC tries to characterize a sample in two different resolutions, taking global information and local information into account at the same time. In this way, the HC is able to characterize a sample more precisely and completely. Through the co-operation between the global and local information, the HC has the potential ability to discard the bias of the GC and LC to the global information and local information, respectively. Furthermore, the HC is considered to be able to overcome the unstable position-correlated information contained in the LC by making use of the independent attribute of the GC, and reduce the dilute risk of the GC using the local information in the LC. However, there is still a dilute risk in the HC.

9.5.4.2 Advantages of the HCMD Method

Table 9.1 shows the classification relationship of the GCMD, LCMD, and HCMD methods. When both the GCMD and LCMD methods classify a sample S into the class 0 or 1, the HCMD method would make the same classification. When the GCMD method believes that the S belongs to class 0 and the LCMD method regards the S as a sample of class 1, for example, the GC value of the S is relatively smaller and the LC value of the S is larger, the HCMD method would classify the S into class 0 or 1 in terms of the global and local information of the S reasonably, vice versa. That is, when different results are obtained by the GCMD and LCMD methods, respectively, the HCMD method is probably able to make a better classification by means of the co-operation of the global and local information in the HC implicitly.

The HCMD method would outperform the GCMD and LCMD methods in most cases for the following reasons:

Table 9.1 The Classification Table of the GCMD, LCMD, and HCMD Methods

GCMD method	LCMD method	HCMD method
0	0	0
0	1	0,1
1	0	0,1
1	1	1

- As we know, $HC = \langle GC, LC \rangle$. If the correct information brought in by the GC and LC is more than the false information brought in by them, then the correct information contained in the HC is more than that in the GC and LC alone.

- A number of studies [1–3,5,8] had proved that the GC and LC were effective features, so the correct information in the GC and LC is more than the false information in them.

- The HCMD method is constructed on the basis of the HC. And the GCMD and LCMD methods are constructed on the basis of the GC and LC, respectively. All three methods use the same classifier.

To summarize, with more correct information, the HCMD method would outperform the GCMD and LCMD methods in most cases.

9.5.4.3 Time Complexity

The time complexity of the HCFE approach is the same as the CFC and LCFE approaches: $O(L)$, where L is the length of a sample. In the three approaches, we have to traverse a sample to extract its feature. To a single gene in the sample, we only need to execute several operations, such as query and addition, in several hash tables. The number of the hash tables is a constant in a specific approach. The time complexity of query and addition in a hash table is $O(1)$. Hence all the time complexities of the three approaches are $O(L)$.

9.6 EXPERIMENTS

9.6.1 Experiments of Local Concentration

Experiments were conducted on a public malware dataset in the pervious works. The CILPKU08 dataset, which can be obtained from the web site http://www.cil.pku.edu. cn/malware, including 3547 malwares classified to 685 families based on their properties, comprises six different types: virus, trojan, worm, backdoor, constructor, and miscellaneous. This dataset is divided into three subsets. The first dataset contains 538 programs with the self set of 284 legal files and the nonself set of 254 malware files; the second set contains 1815 programs with the self set of 915 legal files and 900 malware files; The third set consists of the second set and 2647 extra malware files, having 4462 files in total, the training set is covered by the detecting set and even much smaller than it, so that the expansibility and comprehensive ability can be tested.

The test platform for experiments is shown in Table 9.2.

9.6.1.1 Experiments for Different Window Size and Number of Windows

Different window size W and number of windows N, which correspond to dimension of the feature vector, were tested using three different classifiers, aiming to find the

Table 9.2 The Test Platform

Operating system	Windows XP
Computer hardware	CPU: Pentium IV 1.5GHz RAM: 512M
Programming language	C & Matlab language
Compiling environment	Microsoft Visual C++ 6.0 & Matlab R2007a

parameters with the best performance. The tested W ranges from 100 to 500 with a step size 100 and N ranges 20 to 60 with a step size 10. The average results of ten experiments with different partitions of the second dataset are used to measure the performance. Figures 9.7 to 9.9 show that when $W = 400$ and $N = 50$ three methods perform considerably stable and good on the dataset, so these two parameters are fixed in the following discussion.

9.6.1.2 Experiments for Different Proportional Selection of All the Fragments

The size of detector dictionary is decided by the proportional selection of the fragments. A suitable chosen proportional selection parameter m may reduce a lot of the computing cost without the loss of its discriminatory power. The experiments for

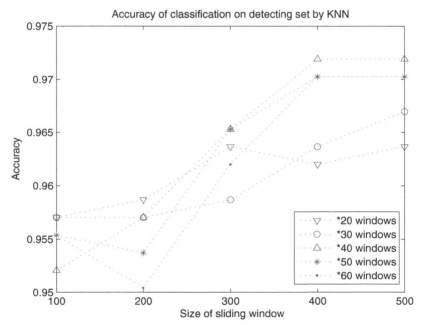

Figure 9.7 Accuracy with different window size and number of windows on the second data set by KNN.

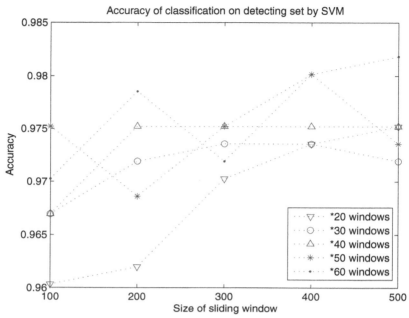

Figure 9.8 Accuracy with different window size and number of windows on the second data set by SVM.

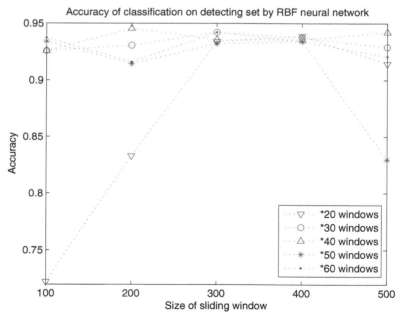

Figure 9.9 Accuracy with different window size and number of windows on the second data set by RBF NN.

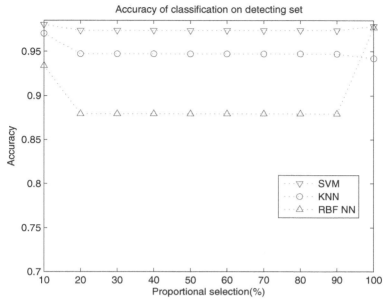

Figure 9.10 Accuracy with different proportional selection of the fragments on the second data set.

different *m* are also conducted on the second dataset, *m* is chosen from 10 percent to 100 percent with a step 10 percent. The results are shown in Fig. 9.10. When m = 10%, the detecting rate perform best. At the same time, the size of detector dictionary is smallest.

9.6.1.3 Length of the Detector

The length of the chosen detector *L*-bit is critical to discriminate malwares from benign programs. Because the length of a meaningful program instruction is usually 16 bits, 32 bits, or 64 bits, *L* is not necessarily bigger than 64 to contain at least one entire instruction. The length of the detector is taken as 32 or 64 in this chapter in order to make it not too long to contain some hidden viral information and not too short to get enough representative viral information. The overlap of sliding window is [*L*/2] bits. The detection rate using a SVM classifier with a different length of the detector are shown in Tables 9.3 and 9.4.

9.6.1.4 Contrast Experiments

To determine the performance and possible advantages of the proposed approach, nine contrast experiments against the method in [11] are carried out on these three practical datasets using the windows operating system; the same partitions are made using the same data. Test 1,2,3 are carried on the first data set with a partition ratio of 4:1,1:1,1:4 for training set and detecting set, test 4,5,6 are carried on it with a

Table 9.3 Average Detection Rate by SVM when $L = 64$

Exp.	Detection rate with 64-bit detector (%)					
	Training set			Detecting set		
	All	*Malware*	*Benign*	*All*	*Malware*	*Benign*
Test1	100.00	100.00	100.00	97.22	96.08	98.25
Test2	100.00	100.00	100.00	97.40	95.28	99.30
Test3	100.00	100.00	100.00	94.19	87.68	100.00
Test4	100.00	100.00	100.00	97.75	96.43	98.94
Test5	100.00	100.00	100.00	97.03	94.49	99.30
Test6	100.00	100.00	100.00	95.56	90.59	100.00
Test7	99.92	100.00	99.84	98.02	97.67	98.36
Test8	100.00	100.00	100.00	96.04	94.00	98.03
Test9	100.00	100.00	100.00	95.12	91.83	98.36

partition ratio of 2:1,1:1,1:2 for training set and detecting set. Test 7,8,9 are carried on the second data set with a partition ratio of 2:1,1:1,1:2 for training set and detecting set.

As shown in Figs. 9.11 and 9.12, our proposed method outclasses the hierarchical AIS method in all the tests, and achieves a detection rate of more than 97 percent on the detecting set. With the growth of the set size, the proposed method does not deteriorate. The runtime performance of our method is also better than the hierarchical AIS method. In Fig. 9.13, the training time of the new method varies linearly with the number of files, unlike the H-AIS method that makes the training time have an explosive growth with the file number. What is more, the runtime of new method (several minutes) and H-AIS method (several hours) are not of the same order of magnitude.

Table 9.4 Average Detection Rate by SVM when L = 32

Exp.	Detection rate with 32-bit detector (%)					
	Training set			Detecting set		
	All	*Malware*	*Benign*	*All*	*Malware*	*Benign*
Test1	99.53	99.51	99.56	95.37	98.04	92.98
Test2	99.63	99.21	100.00	98.51	96.85	100.00
Test3	99.07	98.04	100.00	96.74	95.57	97.80
Test4	99.44	98.82	100.00	96.07	92.86	98.94
Test5	100.00	100.00	100.00	97.03	98.43	95.77
Test6	100.00	100.00	100.00	95.00	90.59	98.95
Test7	99.09	99.50	98.69	98.02	97.67	98.36
Test8	99.78	99.56	100.00	97.91	97.33	98.47
Test9	99.67	99.33	100.00	97.27	95.83	98.69

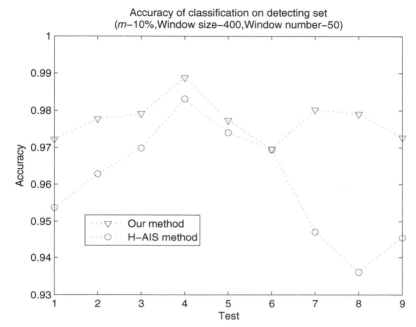

Figure 9.11 Detection Rate on the detecting sets of Contrast Experiments.

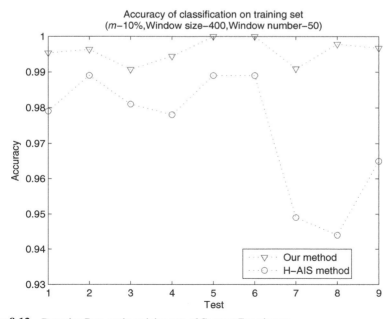

Figure 9.12 Detection Rate on the training sets of Contrast Experiments.

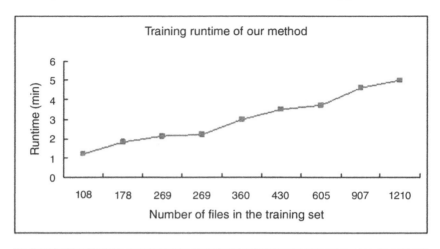

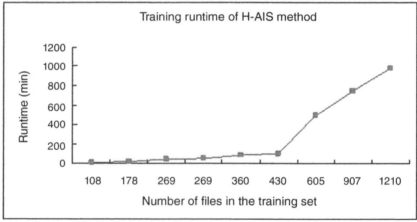

Figure 9.13 Training runtime of two methods.

An experiment on the third dataset was used to confirm the model's expansibility, the training set is much smaller than the detecting set. The results are shown in Fig. 9.14.

9.6.1.5 Parameters Optimization Based on PSO

The selection of LC feature vector determinant m, W, N and the classifier-related parameters, P_1^*, P_2^*, $\cdots$, P_m^*, is a dynamic optimization process. Parameters associated with KNN include number of nearest neighbors K and the ways of distance measures, K is optimized in the integer number interval [1, 20], the ways of distance measures are chosen among *euclidean*, *cityblock*, *cosine*, *correlation*. For SVM, the cost parameter C is optimized in real number interval [1, 200]. For RBF neural network, the number of nodes of hidden layers ranged from 3 to 15, kernel center and

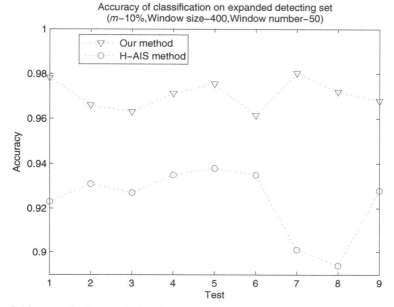

Figure 9.14 Detection Rate on the detecting sets of expanded Contrast Experiments by SVM.

spread σ in real number interval [1, 20] are optimized. m is optimized in the integer number interval [5, 100], W, N range in [100, 600] and [10, 100], respectively. The maximum number of generations is set to be 200 as the stop criterion; the number of particles in a swarm is 20.

The randomness of CPSO leads to the performance and obtained parameters varying slightly, therefore the results of nine independent classes of experiments on the expended third dataset are used to evaluate tests, which is more reasonable. The average performances of empirical and optimized classification designs are reported in Tables 9.5 and 9.6. FP means false positive rate.

The results show that the optimized classification design resulted in about a 1 percent increase in detection rate compared with the empirical classification design on average. The CPSO method improved the accuracy performance and reduced the false positive rate but a trade-off decision has to be made between the result and a much longer training time.

9.6.2 Experiments of Hybrid Concentration

9.6.2.1 Experimental Datasets

Comprehensive experiments were conducted on three public malware datasets: CIL-PKU08, Henchiri, and VXHeavens. The three datasets and their composition documents can be download from www.cil.pku.edu.cn/resources/. The benign program dataset used here consists of the files in portable executable format from Windows XP and a series of applications, which are the main punching bag of malware.

Table 9.5   Average Detection Rates on the Detecting Set with Empirical and Optimized Classification Designs Under Optimum Conditions by SVM

Exp.	Optimized designs		Empirical designs	
	All (%)	*FP (%)*	*All (%)*	*FP (%)*
Test1	97.83	4.37	97.83	4.37
Test2	98.51	0.00	96.59	2.95
Test3	96.74	2.20	96.30	3.61
Test4	97.75	1.06	97.13	3.17
Test5	97.56	3.93	97.56	3.93
Test6	96.15	3.17	96.15	3.17
Test7	98.03	1.64	98.03	1.64
Test8	97.91	1.53	97.20	1.09
Test9	97.27	1.31	96.80	1.20
Average	97.53	2.14	97.06	2.79

9.6.2.2 Experimental Setup

The support vector machine (SVM), realized by libSVM [12], is taken as the classifier of the proposed HCMD method. Other classifiers, such as k-nearest neighbor, naive Bayes, and decision tree, can also be used. The parameters of the SVM are set as follows: $g = 0.25$, $c = 4$. We do not take many works to optimize the parameters of the SVM as it is not the focus of the HCMD method. The detailed information of the experimental platform is listed in Table 9.7.

The area under the receiver operating characteristic curve (AUC), which is widely used to evaluate the classification performance in the field of data mining, is utilized as the performance evaluation criteria in this chapter.

Table 9.6   Average Detection Rates on the Detecting Set with Empirical and Optimized Classification Designs Under Optimum Conditions by KNN

Exp.	Optimized designs		Empirical designs	
	All (%)	*FP (%)*	*All (%)*	*FP (%)*
Test1	97.78	4.04	97.78	4.04
Test2	97.77	0.70	96.08	2.84
Test3	97.91	0.00	96.23	3.06
Test4	98.88	1.06	97.69	4.04
Test5	96.65	0.00	96.12	2.73
Test6	95.94	3.61	95.94	3.61
Test7	97.02	0.00	96.68	0.44
Test8	97.47	1.31	96.30	1.20
Test9	96.94	1.15	95.47	0.87
Average	97.37	1.32	96.48	2.54

Table 9.7 Experimental Platform

CPU	Core 2 duo 3.00 GHz
RAM	8 GB
Operating system	Win 7 64-bit
Programming language	C# (.NET Framework 3.5), Matlab 2010a
Thread	Single thread
Compiler	Visual studio 2008

In the experiments of Section 8.3.4, all the experiments are taken using five-fold cross validation to get a more precise and believable evaluation of the proposed HCMD method. In both the CILPKU08 dataset and the Henchiri dataset, most of the malware are computer viruses. Hence we ignore the categories of the malware and carry on five-fold cross validation directly in the two datasets, respectively. The VXHeavens dataset contains 7128 malware which fall into six categories, so we split the dataset into six smaller datasets: backdoor, constructor, miscellaneous, trojan, virus, and worm. The miscellaneous includes malware such as DoS, Nuker, Hacktool, and Flooder, while the malware in the other five smaller datasets, respectively, fall into a category. We take five-fold cross validation on each of the six smaller datasets.

In all the experiments, there is no overlap between a training set and a test set. That is to say, to a training set, the malware in a test set are unseen malware. This setting increases the reliability of the experiments.

In summary, eight groups of experiments were done using three public malware datasets using five-fold cross validations. The 95 percent confidence intervals were computed to look into the stability of the proposed HCMD method.

The GC-based malware detection (GCMD) method [5] and the LC-based malware detection (LCMD) method [8] are imported for comparisons.

9.6.2.3 *Selection of Parameters*

This section selects the two parameters in the HCFE approach, that is, the proportion of the genes ($P\%$) and the number of the local areas (N).

The dataset used in this section consists of 1048 benign programs, randomly selected from the benign program dataset, and 1048 computer viruses from the VXHeavens dataset. We randomly split the benign programs into two sets with 524 programs for each set, one for training and the other for testing. The same partition was done to the computer viruses. The 524 benign programs and 524 viruses made up the training set, and the test set consisted of the remaining benign programs and viruses.

We optimized the two parameters using the grid search method, where $P = 5, 10, \ldots, 50$ and $N = 10, 20, \ldots, 100$. We do not try larger P. As we know, the larger P means that more genes with less information content are selected into the gene library. The class tendencies of these poor genes are unclear. They bring less information content for the classification and lead to false positives or false negatives. The above analysis is supported by the experimental results that follow.

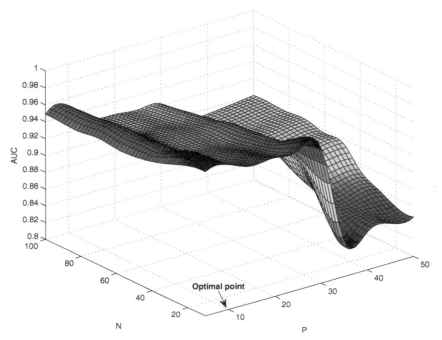

Figure 9.15   The experimental results in the selection of parameters.

The experimental results on the dataset just described are plotted in Fig. 9.15 with the cubic spline interpolation method.

Figure 9.15 illustrates that when $P = 10$, regardless of the value of the N, the AUCs of the HCMD method are fairly good and stable. The AUCs of the HCMD method drop down dramatically when $P > 30$. It is because there are too many genes with less information content in all the gene libraries. These poor genes are helpless for the classification, and bring in harmful information that confuses the classifier. This result proves the above analysis about the larger P. When we set $P = 10$, we found the influence of the N to the AUC of the HCMD method was not remarkable. When $N = 10$, the dimension of the HC is relatively lower, only 22 dimensions, which is much lower than that of the features reported [9,10] which are usually hundreds of dimensions, and the HCMD method gets the optimal AUC: 0.9724. Hence we set $P = 10, N = 10$.

In order to compare to the GCMD and LCMD methods fairly, we optimize the parameters of the two methods in the same way. When $P = 10$, the GCMD method gets the best AUC. And the optimal parameters for the LCMD method are: $P = 10, N = 10$.

9.6.2.4 Experimental Results

Eight groups of experiments were conducted on three public malware datasets. The experimental results of the proposed HCMD method are shown in Table 9.8. The

Table 9.8 Experimental Results of the HCMD Method

Dataset	Training set	Test set
CILPKU08	**0.9991 ± 0.000234**	**0.9984 ± 0.000758**
Henchiri	**0.9992 ± 0.000053**	**0.9981 ± 0.001113**
Backdoor	**0.9921 ± 0.000654**	**0.9749 ± 0.006304**
Constructor	**0.9810 ± 0.001016**	**0.9687 ± 0.007591**
Miscellaneous	**0.9804 ± 0.005168**	**0.9494 ± 0.009814**
Trojan	**0.9847 ± 0.001185**	**0.9596 ± 0.004817**
Virus	**0.9904 ± 0.000976**	**0.9731 ± 0.008639**
Worm	**0.9546 ± 0.011265**	**0.9331 ± 0.016261**

experimental results of the GCMD method and the LCMD method are shown in Tables 9.9 and 9.10, respectively, for comparison. The results in the bold font indicate the best results among the three methods.

In all the training sets, the HCMD method performed better than the GCMD and LCMD methods. The results suggest that the HCMD method is able to learn much better than the other two methods since the HC extracted by the HCFE approach contains much more information than the GC and LC, which characterizes a sample in two resolutions and has a strong discriminating ability.

Tables 9.9 and 9.10 show that the GCMD method is 0.03 percent better than the LCMD method in the test sets of the CILPKU08 dataset and Henchiri dataset, whereas the LCMD method is better than the GCMD method in the test sets of the other six experiments by about 1.04 percent on average. These results demonstrate that the GCMD method and LCMD method do not have any advantage over the HCMD method.

The proposed HCMD method is very stable and always better than the other two methods from Table 9.8, regardless of the training sets and test sets. In all the test sets of the whole experiments, the HCMD method is 1.05 percent better than the GCMD method which is a big increase, and the average AUC of the HCMD method is 0.28 percent larger than that of the LCMD method.

Table 9.9 Experimental Results of the GCMD Method

Dataset	Training set	Test set
CILPKU08	0.9984 ± 0.000209	0.9976 ± 0.000526
Henchiri	0.9984 ± 0.000109	0.9970 ± 0.001283
Backdoor	0.9887 ± 0.000777	0.9711 ± 0.007953
Constructor	0.9759 ± 0.001725	0.9651 ± 0.011248
Miscellaneous	0.9624 ± 0.004145	0.9288 ± 0.014902
Trojan	0.9753 ± 0.001397	0.9525 ± 0.004842
Virus	0.9851 ± 0.001288	0.9650 ± 0.009839
Worm	0.9156 ± 0.016786	0.8942 ± 0.032133

Table 9.10 Experimental Results of the LCMD Method

Dataset	Training set	Test set
CILPKU08	0.9983 ± 0.000259	0.9973 ± 0.000559
Henchiri	0.9983 ± 0.00018	0.9966 ± 0.001944
Backdoor	0.9908 ± 0.000685	0.9740 ± 0.006196
Constructor	0.9800 ± 0.000861	0.9672 ± 0.00904
Miscellaneous	0.9739 ± 0.005254	0.9438 ± 0.009501
Trojan	0.9802 ± 0.001742	0.9527 ± 0.003589
Virus	0.9888 ± 0.001037	0.9692 ± 0.008283
Worm	0.9537 ± 0.011121	0.9322 ± 0.016678

Without increasing the time complexity, the HCMD method performs very well and stably with a little more computing, so the HC is considered to be able to characterize a sample more precisely and completely than the GC and LC alone, and could be regarded as a replacement of the GC and LC. The time complexity to extract the GC, LC and HC, that is, the time complexity of the CFC, LCFE and HCFE approaches, will be discussed in detail in the next chapter.

The 95 percent confidence intervals of the three methods were relatively small from Tables 9.8–9.10. They suggested that the results of these methods were very stable and believable.

Table 9.11 gives the average detecting time of the GCMD, LCMD, and HCMD methods for a single program in the virus dataset of the VXHeavens dataset. The average size of the programs in this dataset is 104 KB.

From Table 9.11, the detecting time of the LCMD method is the shortest: 0.15 s. The hash tables in the LCMD method only need to keep all the distinct genes in a local area, so the elements in the hash tables are relatively small. Hence the query time and addition time would be shorter. These factors result in the shortest detecting time of the LCMD method.

To detect a sample, the HCMD method consumes the longest time: 0.18 s on average. In the HCMD method, the elements in the hash tables of a local area need to be loaded to the hash tables of the global resolution after traversing a local area. Hence the detecting time of the HCMD method is the longest. The detecting time of the GCMD method is between the LCMD method and the HCMD method.

Although the detecting time of the HCMD method is longer than the other two methods, it is still only 0.18 s, basically meeting the demand of a real-time system.

Table 9.11 Comparisons of the Detecting Time (in Second)

GCMD method	LCMD method	HCMD method
0.16	0.15	0.18

9.7 SUMMARY

This chapter applies two types of immune concentration to malware detection—local concentration and hybrid concentration.

The local concentration-based malware detection method connects a certain number of two-element local concentration vectors as feature vector. Experimental results demonstrate that the proposed approach not only has a very much faster speed but also gives around 98 percent accuracy over the CILPKU08 dataset.

The hybrid concentration-based feature extraction approach extracts the hybrid concentration of a sample in both the global resolution and the local resolution. Extensive experimental results have demonstrated that the hybrid concentration outperforms the global concentration and local concentration method in the eight groups of experiments on the three public malware datasets by about 1.08 percent and 0.28 percent on average, respectively.

REFERENCES

1. Tan, Y., Deng, C., and Ruan, G. (2009) Concentration-based feature construction approach for spam detection, in Neural Networks, 2009. IJCNN 2009. International Joint Conference on, IEEE, pp. 3088–3093.
2. Ruan, G. and Tan, Y. (2010) A three-layer back-propagation neural network for spam detection using artificial immune concentration. *Soft Computing*, **14** (2), 139–150.
3. Zhu, Y. and Tan, Y. (2011) A local concentration based feature extraction approach for spam filtering. *Information Forensics and Security, IEEE Transactions on*, **6** (2), 486–497.
4. Wang, W., Zhang, P., Tan, Y., and He, X. (2011) An immune local concentration based virus detection approach. *Journal of Zhejiang University-Science Part C*, **12** (6), 443–454.
5. Wang, W., Zhang, P., and Tan, Y. (2010) An immune concentration based virus detection approach using particle swarm optimization, in *Advances in Swarm Intelligence*, Springer, pp. 347–354.
6. Mi, G., Zhang, P., and Tan, Y. (2013) A multi-resolution-concentration based feature construction approach for spam filtering, in The International Joint Conference on Neural Networks (IJCNN 2013), IEEE, vol. 1, pp. 1–8.
7. Tan, Y. and Xiao, Z. (2007) Clonal particle swarm optimization and its applications, in Evolutionary Computation, 2007. CEC 2007. IEEE Congress on, IEEE, pp. 2303–2309.
8. Wang, W., Zhang, P., Tan, Y., and He, X. (2011) An immune local concentration based virus detection approach. *Journal of Zhejiang University Science C*, **12** (6), 443–454.
9. Kolter, J. and Maloof, M. (2004) Learning to detect malicious executables in the wild, in Proceedings of the Tenth ACM SIGKDD International Conference on Knowledge Discovery and Data Mining, KDD '04, pp. 470–478.
10. Kolter, J. and Maloof, M. (2006) Learning to detect and classify malicious executables in the wild. *Journal of Machine Learning Research*, **7**, 2721–2744.
11. Wang, W., Zhang, P., Tan, Y., and He, X. (2009) A hierarchical artificial immune model for virus detection, in Computational Intelligence and Security, 2009. CIS'09. International Conference on, IEEE, vol. 1, pp. 1–5.
12. Chang, C. and Lin, C. (2011) Libsvm: a library for support vector machines. *ACM Transactions on Intelligent Systems and Technology (TIST)*, **2** (3), 27.

Chapter 10

Immune Cooperation Mechanism-Based Learning Framework

Inspired from the immune cooperation (IC) mechanism in biological immune systems (BIS), this chapter presents an IC mechanism-based learning (ICL) framework. In this framework, a sample is expressed as an antigen-specific feature vector and an antigen-nonspecific feature vector, simulating the antigenic determinant and danger features in the BIS. The antigen-specific and antigen-nonspecific classifiers score the two vectors and export real-valued Signal 1 and Signal 2. With the cooperation of the two signals, the sample is classified by the cooperation classifier, which resolves the signal conflict problem at the same time. The ICL framework simulates the BIS in the view of immune signals and takes full advantage of the cooperation effect of the immune signals, which improves the performance of the ICL framework. It does not involve the concept of the danger zone and further suggests that the danger zone is considered to be unnecessary in an artificial immune system (AIS).

10.1 INTRODUCTION

The adaptive immune system is one of the most important parts of BIS. It allows for a stronger immune response as well as immunological memory [1]. There are two kinds of immunities in the adaptive immune system—humoral immunity and cellular immunity. The humoral immunity is mediated by antibodies secreted in the B lymphocytes (B-cell), which can be found in the body fluids, while the cellular immunity is the immunity mediated by cells, involving the macrophages, natural killer cells, T lymphocytes (T-cell), and cytokines [2].

In the adaptive immune system, the cooperation mechanism between the first signal (Signal 1) and the second signal (known as co-stimulation signal, referred to

---

Artificial Immune System: Applications in Computer Security, First Edition. Ying Tan.
© 2016 the IEEE Computer Society. Published 2016 by John Wiley & Sons, Inc.

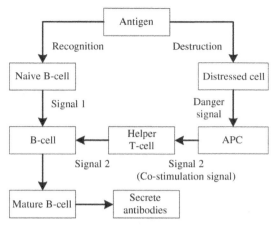

Figure 10.1 The danger model.

as Signal 2), which are antigen specific and nonspecific respectively, is usually crucial for BIS to produce an effective immune response to an antigen. This mechanism is called the immune cooperation (IC) mechanism. From the perspective of the IC mechanism, there are no remarkable differences between the humoral immunity and cellular immunity in the procedure of antigen recognition. Hence this chapter illustrates the IC mechanism by using the humoral immunity.

The danger model is shown in Fig. 10.1, which illustrates an immune response in the humoral immunity [3]. First, the naive B-cell recognizes the antigenic determinant of an antigen, which is able to identify a specific kind of antigen by using the antibody molecule in its surface and sends Signal 1 to activate this kind of B-cells. At the same time, the normal cells intruded by the antigens die abnormally and release the intracellular products, which are believed to be danger features. These danger features are considered to be able to send a danger signal, which is antigen nonspecific, to their neighboring antigen present cells (APCs). After receiving the danger signal, the APCs move into immune tissues and transform it to corresponding helper T-cells (Th, for short), CD4+ Th1 in this case, as the co-stimulation signal, referred to as Signal 2. Then the helper T-cells release various kinds of cytokines, which act as Signal 2, to activate the corresponding B-cells. Finally, under the cooperation of the two signals, the B-cell is fully activated and secretes antibodies to produce an effective immune response.

There are two signals acting on the lymphocytes, B-cell and T-cell, in an effective immune response: antigen-specific Signal 1 provided by the antibody molecules of B-cell or T-cell receptors, and antigen-nonspecific Signal 2, which is able to stimulate the antigen-specific lymphocytes to proliferate and differentiate. Since both signals are considered to own two states, presence or absence, in an immune response, the two signals are regarded as binary-valued signals. A lymphocyte could be fully activated if and only if the two signals cooperate with each other and work on it.

Although there are many differences between the danger signal and Signal 2, taking different senders and receivers as an example, Signal 2 is considered to come from the danger signal and could be regarded as a danger signal in another form. Hence we merge the danger signal into Signal 2. The IC mechanism drops down the probability of the auto-immunity in BIS, and helps to recognize and clear antigens more precisely. It is one of the most important mechanisms to keep BIS working stably and effectively.

Many researchers have shown that Signal 2 plays an important role in an adaptive immune response [4–7]. It is necessary for the proliferation, differentiation, and survival of the lymphocytes. It is also able to increase the immunological effect dramatically in an adaptive immune response.

It is important to note that the APCs send Signal 2 to corresponding helper T-cells by moving in BIS, rather than its neighboring helper T-cells. For example, after receiving a danger signal, an APC delivers itself to the lymphatic tissue through lymphatic channels in cellular immunity. In the lymphatic tissue, it transforms the danger signal to corresponding helper T-cells in the form of Signal 2. The helper T-cells further transform this signal to corresponding effector T-cells to activate these T-cells.

Many DT-based AIS assume that there is a danger zone in an AIS. It indicates the spread range of a danger signal and defines a specific way for a danger signal to interact with other signals. According to the BIS, this assumption is considered to be unreasonable. The APC, which is antigen nonspecific and could engulf a wide range of antigens, has lower diversity. It is different from the B-cells and T-cells, which are antigen specific and own many classes. Because there are plenty of APCs that could be found everywhere in the BIS, it is reasonable to assume that any danger signal is able to be sent to any kind of APC. After receiving a danger signal, an APC would load the information of the antigen into its major histocompatibility complex (MHC) molecule and further send this information to corresponding helper T-cells in the form of Signal 2. As mentioned, these helper T-cells need not be phyically near the APC. The APC could move in the immune system with the information of the antigen and find the appropriate helper T-cells. That is to say, although the immune signals only spread among adjacent immune cells, the immune cells with the antigen information are able to move in the immune system. This mechanism disagrees with the assumption of the danger zone that suggests that the danger signal spreads itself in a local zone. Hence, we regard the danger signal, referred to as Signal 2, as a global signal. There is no need to define a danger zone in AIS, which simplifies the framework of AIS dramatically.

We can illustrate this analysis using an example. When the same antigens intrude on an immune system from any position, the immune system almost always produces an effective immune response. This phenomenon suggests that there is not a danger zone in the immune system and the danger signal, Signal 2, could be regarded to spread in the whole immune system. In an AIS, every APC usually only has one copy, which represents a kind of APC. No matter how far an antigen is from an APC physically, a danger signal activated by the antigen is sent to all the APCs.

10.2 IMMUNE SIGNAL COOPERATION MECHANISM-BASED LEARNING FRAMEWORK

Inspired by the IC mechanism in BIS, this chapter proposes a novel IC mechanism-based learning (ICL) framework. The definitions of the concepts used in the ICL framework are:

- **Antigen-specific feature** is the antigen feature that occurs only in antigens, simulating the basic unit of the antigenic determinant of a biological antigen. Because it is antigen-specific, it is able to identify a specific kind of antigen.

- **Antigen-nonspecific feature**, also called danger feature, is able to measure the danger of a sample and discriminate antigens from non-antigens. Because it appears in both antigens and non-antigens, it is antigen-nonspecific, simulating the basic element of the danger features in BIS.

A flowchart of the ICL framework is shown in Fig. 10.2. First, the ICL framework expresses a sample as an antigen-specific feature vector by using the antigen-specific feature library L_1. This feature vector simulates the antigenic determinant of a biological antigen and is considered to contain the antigen-specific information of the sample. It is taken as the input of the antigen-specific classifier C_1, in which the antigen-specific information contained in the sample is measured. At the same time, the sample is further expressed as an antigen-nonspecific feature vector based on the antigen-nonspecific feature library L_2. This feature vector simulates the

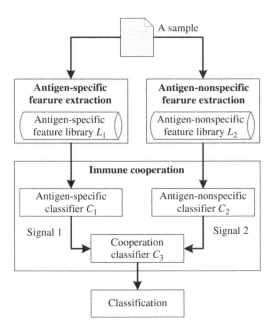

Figure 10.2   The flowchart of the ICL framework.

danger features in BIS, and is used to measure the danger information of the sample by the antigen-nonspecific classifier C_2.

Second, the classifiers C_1 and C_2 score their input features. The scores of the two features are taken as the real-valued Signal 1 and Signal 2, corresponding to the binary-valued Signal 1 and Signal 2 in BIS. The two signals here are real numbers in the interval [0, 1]. They are taken as the input of the cooperation classifier C_3.

Finally, according to the cooperation information of Signal 1 and Signal 2, the cooperation classifier C_3 classifies a sample into a class. In this phase, the classifier C_3 resolves the classification problem and immune signal conflict problem at the same time on the basis of the knowledge learned in its training procedure. It increases the efficiency of the ICL framework greatly. Furthermore, the IC mechanism used here helps to drop down the false positive rate and false negative rate, and improves the performance of the proposed ICL framework.

The mathematical model of the proposed ICL framework could be written as:

$$f(V_S, V_N) = f_{C_3}(f_{C_1}(V_S), f_{C_2}(V_N)) \tag{10.1}$$

where the V_S and V_N denote the antigen specific and nonspecific feature vectors of a sample. And the f_{C_1}, f_{C_2}, and f_{C_3} represent the classifiers C_1, C_2 and C_3, respectively.

Different from the method proposed by Zhu and Tan [8], there is no uncorrelated requirement for the machine-learning classifiers used in the classifiers C_1 and C_2 because their data sources are considered to be independent. That is to say, any machine-learning classifier is able to be used in the classifiers C_1 and C_2. Their training feature vectors determine their properties, antigen-specific and antigen-nonspecific, respectively.

The proposed ICL framework utilizes the real-valued signals instead of the binary-valued signals in BIS. The real-valued signals are believed to bring many advantages, including:

- The real-valued signals are able to transform the characterization information of a sample more precisely to the cooperation classifier C_3 without information loss. Base on this property, the real-valued signals have the potential ability to improve the performance of the ICL framework.

- The ICL framework does not need to set the binary thresholds for the classifiers C_1 and C_2, which brings down the number of parameters in this framework.

- With the help of the real-valued signals, there is no need to resolve the immune signal conflict problem here, which further simplifies the structure of this framework.

Signal 1 and Signal 2 in the proposed ICL framework are emitted based on the antigen-specific and antigen-nonspecific feature vectors of a sample by the classifiers C_1 and C_2. The data sources of the two signals almost exactly correspond to those in BIS. It makes the emission of the signals more natural. Table 10.1 lists the mapping between the BIS and the ICL framework. Inspired from BIS, the ICL framework

Table 10.1 The mapping between the BIS and the ICL framework

BIS	ICL framework
Antigenic determinant	Antigen-specific feature vector
Danger feature	Antigen-nonspecific feature vector
Binary-valued Signal 1	Real-valued Signal 1
Binary-valued Signal 2	Real-valued Signal 2
B-cell, T-cell	Antigen-specific classifier C_1
APC, helper T-cell	Antigen-nonspecific classifier C_2
B-cell, T-cell	Cooperation classifier C_3

simulates the BIS in the view of immune signals reasonably and takes full advantage of the IC mechanism. It is believed to be able to measure the danger of a sample more precisely and make a better classification.

In the ICL framework, Signal 1 and Signal 2 cooperate with each other. The cooperation effect is considered to help the ICL framework express and measure the class information of a sample more accurately and precisely. Actually the two branches in the ICL framework (i.e. the classifiers C_1 and C_2 which emit Signal 1 and Signal 2), could be regarded as two independent learning methods, written as M_1 and M_2, respectively. The mathematical models of the M_1 and M_2 are $f(V_S) = f_{C_1}(V_S)$ and $f(V_N) = f_{C_2}(V_N)$. With the cooperation of the immune signals, the ICL framework is expected to outperform both the M_1 and M_2, and further exceed the sum of the two methods. The sum of the M_1 and M_2 is written as $M_{1 \cup 2}$, the mathematical model of which is $f(V_S, V_N) = f_{C_1}(V_S) \cup f_{C_2}(V_N)$.

In this chapter, $F(M_i)$ is used to denote the performance of the method M_i, where $i = 1, 2, 1 \cup 2, 3$. In particular, $F(M_3)$ indicates the performance of the ICL framework. According to the IC mechanism:

$$F(M_3) > F(M_{1 \cup 2}) \tag{10.2}$$

$$F(M_{1 \cup 2}) >= F(M_1) \tag{10.3}$$

$$F(M_{1 \cup 2}) >= F(M_2) \tag{10.4}$$

The area under the receiver operating characteristic (ROC) curve (AUC), which is widely used to evaluate the classification performance in the field of machine learning, is utilized as the performance evaluation criteria in this chapter. Let $f_i(x)$ denote the ROC curve of the method M_i, where x is the false positive rate and $f_i(x)$ is the true positive rate, then:

$$F(M_i) = \int_0^1 f_i(x)dx \tag{10.5}$$

From the definition:

$$F(M_{1 \cup 2}) = \int_0^1 max\{f_1(x), f_2(x)\}dx \tag{10.6}$$

it is easy to see that Eqs. 10.3 and 10.4 are always true. We will verify Eq. 10.2 in the experiments, thereby proving that the IC mechanism helps to improve the performance of the ICL framework.

10.3 MALWARE DETECTION MODEL

The ICL-MD model involves two modules, feature extraction and classification. In the malware detection problem, malware are taken as antigens, while benign programs are non-antigens.

In the ICL-MD model, the 4-Grams are taken as the candidate features which are binary strings of length four bytes. N-Gram is a concept from text categorization, which indicates N continuous words or phrases. Kolter and Maloof took 4-Grams as candidate features in their previous works [9,10]. They believed that the 4-Gram is able to capture not only binary strings of length four bytes, but also longer strings.

The way to extract the feature libraries L_1 and L_2 is introduced next. First, the ICL-MD model collects the statistical information of the 4-Grams by traversing the training set. It is the data basis to evaluate the goodness of a 4-Gram. Second, the goodness of every 4-Gram is measured by using a feature goodness criteria. The information gain (IG) is taken as the feature goodness criteria in this chapter. Other feature goodness criteria, such as document frequency, mutual information, χ^2 statistic, and term strength [11] could also be used. Then all the 4-Grams are sorted in descending order based on their IG values. Finally, the ICL-MD model traverses the ordered 4-Grams. If a feature f only occurs in malware, it is considered to be antigen-specific and added to the L_1. Otherwise, we regard it as an antigen-nonspecific feature and add it to the L_2. Iterate this process until there are N_1 features in the L_1 and N_2 features in the L_2 until the two feature libraries are generated.

The features in the L_1 occur only in malware that are antigens, hence they are considered to be antigen-specific. However, the features in the L_2 appear in both malware and benign programs with high IG value, so they are believed to be antigen-nonspecific features and have the ability to discriminate malware from benign programs.

In the procedure of feature extraction, a sample is expressed as a binary feature vector of length N_1, which consists of 0s for absence of the features in the L_1 and 1s for presence of the features in the L_1. This feature vector is the antigen-specific feature vector that is taken as the input of the classifier C_1. In a similar way, the antigen-nonspecific feature vector of length N_2 is extracted on the basis of the L_2.

In the classification module, the three classifiers C_1, C_2 and C_3 adopt the same machine learning classifier: the support vector machine (SVM) with the same parameters realized in LibSVM. Other classifiers, such as k-nearest neighbor, naive Bayes and decision tree, can also be used.

' In the malware detection field, the M_2 is actually the method proposed [9,10], which is imported in for comparison.

10.4 EXPERIMENTS USING THE MALWARE DETECTION MODEL

10.4.1 Experimental Setup

Comprehensive experiments were conducted on three public malware datasets: CILPKU08 dataset, Henchiri dataset, and VXHeanvens dataset, which can be download from www.cil.pku.edu.cn/resources/.

The benign program dataset used here consists of the files in portable executable format from Windows XP and a series of applications, which are the main punching bag of malware.

We optimize the following two parameters for the SVM, the gamma g in kernel function and the cost c, by traversing the whole combinations of g and c, where $g = 0.005, 0.010, \ldots, 1$ and $c = 1, 2, \ldots, 64$. According to the experimental results, the parameters of the SVM are finally set as follows: $g = 0.125, c = 4$. We did not emphasize optimizing the SVM parameters because that was not our main focus.

In the experiments in this section, eight groups of experiments were carried out on the three public malware datasets using five-fold cross validation, and the 95% confidence intervals were computed to look into the stability of the proposed ICL-MD model. Because both the CILPKU08 and Henchiri datasets mainly consist of computer viruses, two experiments were exploited in the two datasets, ignoring the categories of malware. There were six categories of malware in the VXHeavens dataset, so it was split into six smaller datasets: backdoor, constructor, trojan, virus, worm, and Others. Others includes DoS, Nuker, Hacktool, and Flooder, while the malware in the other five smaller datasets fall into a separate category. Six groups of experiments were taken in the six smaller datasets.

There is no overlap between a training set and a test set in all the experiments. To a training set, the malware in a test set are unseen malware. This setting increases the reliability of the experiments.

In the experiments, we verified that the IC mechanism plays the cooperation effect and improves the performance of the proposed ICL-MD model. The immune global concentration-based malware detection (GC-MD) approach [12] and the immune local concentration based malware detection (LC-MD) approach [13], which perform very well, were imported in for comparison.

The average detecting time for a sample is very important for a real-time system, hence it will be given and discussed in next Section. The detailed information of the experimental platform is listed in Table 10.2.

Table 10.2 The experimental platform

CPU	Core 2 Duo 3.00 GHz
RAM	8 GB
Operating system	Win 7 64-bit

10.4.2 Selection of Parameters

The two parameters in the ICL framework, N_1 and N_2, are selected by using the grid search in this section, where $N_1, N_2 = 100, 200, \ldots, 1000$. The larger N_1 and N_2 are not considered as the higher dimension of the feature vectors.

The dataset used here consists of 1048 benign programs, randomly selected from the benign program dataset, and 1048 computer viruses from the VXHeavens dataset. The benign programs were randomly split into two sets with 524 programs for each set, one for training and the other for testing. The same partition was done to the computer viruses. The 524 benign programs and 524 viruses made up the training set, and the test set consisted of the remaining benign programs and viruses.

The experimental results on this dataset are further processed using the cubic spline interpolation method and plotted in Fig. 10.3, which illustrates the influence of the two parameters, N_1 and N_2, to the performance of the ICL-MD model. It is easy to see that the N_1 has a greater influence to the performance of the ICL-MD model, so selecting a proper N_1 would help the ICL-MD model perform better. With the increase of the N_1, more and more discriminating antigen-specific features are included in the L_1, which are considered to help to improve the performance of the ICL-MD model, whereas more misleading information are also brought in which lead to the decrease of the performance of the ICL-MD model. According to the experimental results, the N_1 is set to 400 as the ICL-MD model performs well and stably with this parameter. The influence of the N_2 is less than that of the N_1. With the $N_1 = 400$, we set $N_2 = 400$.

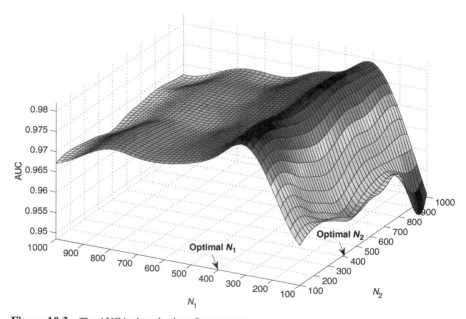

Figure 10.3 The AUC in the selection of parameters.

10.4.3 Experimental Results

Eight groups of experiments were conducted on the three public malware datasets in this section. Table 10.3 lists the experimental results of the M_1, M_2, $M_{1 \cup 2}$, and the proposed ICL-MD model. The bold entries indicates the best results of the four models.

Table 10.3 suggests that the ICL-MD model outperforms both the M_1 and M_2 in all the experiments. It performs better than the M_1 and M_2 for about 13.46 percent and 0.58 percent on average in the experiments taken in the VXHeavens dataset. Since both the M_1 and M_2 achieved good results in the CILPKU08 and Henchiri datasets, the ICL-MD model outperforms the M_1 and M_2 slightly in the two datasets.

The ICL-MD model also outperforms the $M_{1 \cup 2}$, which indicates the sum of the M_1 and M_2, with minor superiority in the experiments on the CILPKU08 and Henchiri datasets, while it is better than the $M_{1 \cup 2}$ for about 0.42 percent on average in the other six groups of experiments. In the experiment to detect worm, the ICL-MD model outperforms the $M_{1 \cup 2}$ for about 0.92 percent, which proves that the IC mechanism in the ICL framework uses the cooperation effect effectively.

The proposed ICL-MD model characterizes and analyzes a sample from the antigen-specific perspective and antigen-nonspecific perspective at the same time, which lays a good foundation for the classification later. The ICL-MD model achieves excellent performance with the help of the cooperation of the two immune signals, which are considered to help to decrease the false positive and false negative rates.

The experimental results of the GC-MD and LC-MD approaches are given in Table 10.4. The proposed ICL-MD model outperforms the GC-MD and LC-MD approaches by about 3.28 percent and 2.24 percent on average, respectively, in the experiments taken in the VXHeavens dataset, while it is a little better than the two approaches in the other two experiments. These experimental results suggest that the ICL framework is an effective immune-based learning framework and introducing the IC mechanism into AIS has the potential ability to improve its performance.

Table 10.3   The AUCs of the $M_1, M_2, M_{1 \cup 2}$, and the ICL-MD model

Datasets	M_1	M_2	$M_{1 \cup 2}$	ICL-MD model
CILPKU08	0.9564 ± 0.003228	0.9992 ± 0.000910	0.9995 ± 0.000410	$\mathbf{0.9997 \pm 0.000249}$
Henchiri	0.9606 ± 0.006053	0.9990 ± 0.000862	0.9994 ± 0.000361	$\mathbf{0.9995 \pm 0.000276}$
Backdoor	0.8509 ± 0.004976	0.9794 ± 0.003280	0.9825 ± 0.003355	$\mathbf{0.9846 \pm 0.002036}$
Constructor	0.8996 ± 0.047044	0.9794 ± 0.014825	0.9808 ± 0.013594	$\mathbf{0.9820 \pm 0.014933}$
Trojan	0.7741 ± 0.036341	0.9644 ± 0.005274	0.9665 ± 0.005665	$\mathbf{0.9702 \pm 0.004172}$
Virus	0.8439 ± 0.023959	0.9770 ± 0.004391	0.9775 ± 0.004147	$\mathbf{0.9833 \pm 0.002757}$
Worm	0.8691 ± 0.035813	0.9708 ± 0.006525	0.9726 ± 0.006626	$\mathbf{0.9818 \pm 0.002969}$
Others	0.8282 ± 0.025178	0.9676 ± 0.007042	0.9688 ± 0.006974	$\mathbf{0.9717 \pm 0.006097}$

Table 10.4   The AUCs of the GC-MD approach and LC-MD approach

Datasets	GC-MD approach	LC-MD approach
CILPKU08	0.9976 ± 0.000526	0.9973 ± 0.000559
Henchiri	0.9970 ± 0.001283	0.9966 ± 0.001944
Backdoor	0.9711 ± 0.007953	0.9740 ± 0.006196
Constructor	0.9651 ± 0.011248	0.9672 ± 0.009040
Trojan	0.9525 ± 0.004842	0.9527 ± 0.003589
Virus	0.9650 ± 0.009839	0.9692 ± 0.008283
Worm	0.8942 ± 0.032133	0.9322 ± 0.016678
Others	0.9288 ± 0.014902	0.9438 ± 0.009501

The 95 percent confidence intervals in all the experiments of the ICL-MD model are relatively small (Table 10.3), and they are less than that of the M_1, M_2, and $M_{1 \cup 2}$ in most cases. These results suggest that the proposed ICL-MD model is very stable.

10.4.4 Statistical Analysis

In order to ensure that the experimental results are reliable and the proposed ICL-MD model outperforms the GC-MD and LC-MD approaches statistically, an analysis of variance (ANOVA) was done followed by two t hypothesis tests (t-test).

As the malware in the CILPKU08 and Henchiri dataset come from the Disk Operating System (DOS) which are easier to be detected, all the GC-MD approach, LC-MD approach, and the proposed ICL-MD model perform well on the two datasets. Here all the statistical analysis has been done with the six groups of experiments on the VXHeavens dataset.

We regard the performances of the three malware detection models as a random variable, which is distributed normally with the same variance. According to the six groups of independent experimental results, the ANOVA/P-value table is given in Table 10.5.

Table 10.5 suggests that the P-value is 0.034, which is less than the default $\alpha = 0.05$ significance level. It indicates that the performances of the three malware detection models are not the same statistically. Hence the null hypothesis that all the three models have a common performance is rejected.

Table 10.5   The ANOVA/P-value table

Source	SS[a]	Df[b]	MS	F	P
Experiments	0.00338	2	0.00169	4.27	0.034
Error	0.00592	15	0.00039		
Total	0.00930	17			

[a] The SS denotes the sums of squares, and the df is the degrees of freedom.

[b] The MS represent the mean squares (SS/df) and the P is the P-value.

In order to make sure that the proposed ICL-MD model outperforms the GC-MD and LC-MD approaches statistically, two t-tests have been further carried out. There are six groups of independent experimental results, written as (X_i, Y_i, Z_i) where X_i, Y_i, Z_i are the AUCs of the GC-MD, LC-MD and ICL-MD models, respectively, $i = 1, 2, \ldots, 6$. Let $D^i_{xz} = X_i - Z_i$, $D^i_{yz} = Y_i - Z_i$. As there is only a Z, in the different malware detection models, which affects the values of the D^i_{xz} and D^i_{yz}, the D^i_{xz} and D^i_{yz} are considered to be distributed normally. Suppose that $D^i_{xz} \sim N(\mu_{D_{xz}}, \sigma^2_{D_{xz}})$, $i = 1, 2, \ldots, 6$. Three hypothesis tests are needed to be exploited based on the samples D^{xz}_i, which are:

$$H_0 : \mu_{D_{xz}} = 0, H_1 : \mu_{D_{xz}} \neq 0 \qquad (10.7)$$

$$H_0 : \mu_{D_{xz}} \leq 0, H_1 : \mu_{D_{xz}} > 0 \qquad (10.8)$$

$$H_0 : \mu_{D_{xz}} \geq 0, H_1 : \mu_{D_{xz}} < 0 \qquad (10.9)$$

According to the t-test, $t_{0.05/2}(5) = 2.5706, t_{0.05}(5) = 2.0150$, the critical region of the three hypothesis tests are:

$$(-\infty, -2.5706] \cup]2.5706, +\infty), [2.0150, +\infty), (-\infty, -2.0150]$$

As $t_{xz} = -2.7839$, the t_{xz} refuses the hypothesis H_0 in Eq. 10.7 and 10.9, but accepts the hypothesis H_0 in Eq. 10.8. These results suggest that the ICL-MD model outperforms the GC-MD approach at the $\alpha = 0.05$ significance level. In a similar way, we know $t_{yz} = -3.7712$, which also demonstrates that the ICL-MD model outperforms the LC-MD approach at the $\alpha = 0.05$ significance level. On the basis of the above t-tests, the improvement of the ICL-MD model is considered to be statistically significant, and the experimental results are reliable.

10.5 DISCUSSION

10.5.1 Advantages

Inspired by BIS, the danger zone is considered to be unnecessary in AIS. As a result, the proposed ICL framework does not define a danger zone. It is different from the previous danger theory-based learning models that almost always define a danger zone to limit the spread range of the danger signal. Hence, the ICL framework does not need to optimize the size of the danger zone. It diminishes the complexity of the ICL framework. Compared to the BIS, the ICL framework without a danger zone is more natural.

The proposed ICL framework takes advantage of the real-valued signals instead of the binary-valued signals in BIS. The ICL framework need not define the binarization thresholds for the classifiers C_1 and C_2, and nor resolve the signal conflict problem here. The complexity of the ICL framework is reduced dramatically in this way. What is more, the real-valued signals are able to be sent to the cooperation classifier C_3 more precisely without information loss which lays a good foundation for the cooperation of the immune signals later.

The ICL framework defines a new way to emit the immune signals. The antigen-specific classifier C_1 sends out Signal 1 based on the antigen-specific feature vector of a sample, while Signal 2 is emitted by the antigen-nonspecific classifier C_2 according to the sample's antigen-nonspecific feature vector. The different properties of the two immune signals, that is, antigen-specific and antigen-nonspecific, do not rely on the uncorrelated machine-learning classifiers used in the classifiers C_1, C_2 and C_3. In fact, they come from the two different and independent training data sources: antigen-specific and antigen-nonspecific feature vector sets.

The IC mechanism is introduced into AIS successfully by the ICL framework. The ICL framework characterizes a sample more precisely from the antigen-specific and antigen-nonspecific perspectives with the help of the IC mechanism, which is believed to help to reduce the false positive and false negative rates. With the cooperation effect of the immune signals, the ICL framework outperforms the M_1, M_2 and $M_{1\cup2}$, and it further outperforms the GC-MD and LC-MD approaches statistically.

10.5.2 Time Complexity

The time complexity of the ICL framework is the same as the GC-MD and LC-MD approaches: $O(N)$, where N is the length of a sample. There are N 4-Grams at most in a sample of length N. In the procedure of feature extraction, every 4-Gram needs to be queried in a hash table, the capacity of which is a constant, $N_1 + N_2$ in this context. The query complexity in the hash table is $O(1)$. Hence the time complexity to extract the antigen-specific and antigen-nonspecific feature vectors of a sample is $O(N)$. Comparing to the time complexity of the feature extraction, the time complexity of the classification module in the ICL framework is very low, which could be ignored. Hence, the time complexity of the proposed ICL framework is $O(N)$.

The average detecting time for a sample of the ICL-MD model is measured in the virus dataset of the VXHeavens dataset, where the average size of the samples is 104 KB. The average detecting time is given in Table 10.6.

Table 10.6 shows that the average detecting time for a sample of the four models is almost the same. In the feature extraction procedure, the ICL-MD model and the $M_{1\cup2}$ store the feature libraries L_1 and L_2 in a hash table, the capacity of which is $N_1 + N_2$, while the capacity of the hash tables used in the M_1 and M_2 are N_1 and N_2, respectively. Actually a query in these hash tables consumes nearly the same time. Compared to the time used in the feature extraction procedure, the time of classification is quite short. Hence the ICL-MD model runs as fast as the M_1, M_2, and $M_{1\cup2}$.

The proposed ICL-MD model is twice as fast as the GC-MD and LC-MD approaches that consume 0.16 and 0.15 seconds for a sample on average, respectively. It basically meets the requirement of a real-time system.

Table 10.6   The average detecting time for a sample (seconds)

M_1	M_2	$M_{1\cup2}$	ICL-MD model
0.07179	0.06968	0.07236	0.07256

10.6 SUMMARY

The ICL framework was applied to malware detection. Comprehensive experimental results demonstrate that the ICL framework is an effective learning framework. The ICL framework-based malware detection model outperforms the global concentration-based malware detection approach and the local concentration-based malware detection approach by about 3.28 percent and 2.24 percent with twice the speed, respectively.

REFERENCES

1. Pancer, Z. and Cooper, M. (2006) The evolution of adaptive immunity. *Annual Review Immunology*, **24**, 497–518.
2. Janeway C., Travers, P., Walport, M., Shlomchik, M. (2001) Immunobiology: The Immune System in Health and Disease, Garland Science.
3. Matzinger, P. (2002) The danger model: a renewed sense of self. *Science's STKE*, **296** (5566), 301.
4. Golovina, T., Mikheeva, T., Suhoski, M., Aqui, N., Tai, V., et al. (2008) Cd28 costimulation is essential for human T regulatory expansion and function. *Journal of Immunology*, **181** (4), 2855–2868.
5. Vincenti, F. (2008) Costimulation blockade in autoimmunity and transplantation. *Journal of Allergy and Clinical Immunology*, **121** (2), 299–306.
6. Nurieva, R., Liu, X., and Dong, C. (2009) Yin–yang of costimulation: crucial controls of immune tolerance and function. *Immunological Reviews*, **229** (1), 88–100.
7. Ford, M. and Larsen, C. (2009) Translating costimulation blockade to the clinic: lessons learned from three pathways. *Immunological Reviews*, **229** (1), 294–306.
8. Zhu, Y. and Tan, Y. (2011) A danger theory inspired learning model and its application to spam detection. Advances in Swarm Intelligence, pp. 382–389.
9. Kolter, J.Z. and Maloof, M.A. (2004) Learning to detect malicious executables in the wild, in Proceedings of the Tenth ACM SIGKDD International Conference on Knowledge Discovery and Data Mining, KDD '04, pp. 470–478.
10. Kolter, J. and Maloof, M. (2006) Learning to detect and classify malicious executables in the wild. *Journal of Machine Learning Research*, **7**, 2721–2744.
11. Yang, Y. and Pedersen, J. (1997) A comparative study on feature selection in text categorization. International Conference on Machine Learning, pp. 412–420.
12. Wang, W., Zhang, P., and Tan, Y. (2010) An immune concentration based virus detection approach using particle swarm optimization, in *Advances in Swarm Intelligence*, Springer, pp. 347–354.
13. Wang, W., Zhang, P.t., Tan, Y., and He, X.g. (2011) An immune local concentration based virus detection approach. *Journal of Zhejiang University Science C*, **12** (6), 443–454.

Chapter 11

Class-Wise Information Gain

This chapter presents a new statistic: the class-wise information gain (CIG). Different from information gain (IG), which only selects global features for a classification problem, the CIG is able to select the features with the highest information content for a specific class in a problem. On the basis of the CIG, a novel malware detection method is proposed to detect malware loaders and infected executables in the wild.

11.1 INTRODUCTION

Malware is a general term for all the malicious code that is a program designed to harm or secretly access a computer system without the owners' informed consent [1], such as computer virus, backdoor, Trojan, and worm. Some malware is used to steal private information or open a backdoor for the intruders. Malware has been one of the most terrible threats to the security of the computers worldwide [2].

Malware is present generally in two forms: malware loader and infected executable. Malware loader is the pure malware only containing malicious code. Infected executable is a combination of a malware loader and a benign program. An infected executable could be a benign program infected by a computer virus or binding with a malware loader. The infected executable is the main form of malware in the wild empirically.

A variety of malware detection methods have been proposed so far, while various commercial anti-virus software is available to purchase. These solutions can be classified into two categories: static techniques and dynamic techniques. The static techniques are mainly based on machine-learning techniques, data-mining techniques, and heuristic theories (such as artificial immune theory [3,4]). The static techniques work on the binary string or application programming interface (API) calls of a program without running the program. They are usually portable and can be deployed on personal computers. The dynamic techniques keep watch over the execution of every program during run-time and stop the program once it tries to harm the system. The dynamic techniques bring extra load that significantly degrades the performance of the system. Hence the dynamic techniques are usually used to analyze malware in the corporate environment instead of in personal computers.

Artificial Immune System: Applications in Computer Security, First Edition. Ying Tan.
© 2016 the IEEE Computer Society. Published 2016 by John Wiley & Sons, Inc.

Machine-learning methods based on statistical and information-theoretic features, such as information gain (IG) [5] which is used to select global features (i.e., N-Grams) with the highest information content in a classification problem, have been widely used in the anti-malware field in the past decade. Most of these methods make use of statistical features to select global features and are able to classify malware loaders and benign programs efficiently. However, most of the statistical and information-theoretic features do not take the class information of the features into account, hence the classes of the global features selected are unknown. Furthermore, the distribution of the features of each class in the detecting feature set is out of control. Actually, most of statistical and information-theoretic features are just able to select global features for a whole classification problem, but cannot select the features for a specific class, such as the IG. The global features only have discriminative information and can perform very well for the ordinary classification problem. However, they do not have the recognition information to a specific class, which is expressed by the features of the class. The accuracy of these methods drops down dramatically for detecting infected executables.

This chapter proposes a new statistics named class-wise information gain (CIG) and a CIG-based malware detection method to detect malware loaders and infected executables in the wild. Based on document frequency and class information, the CIG is able to select the features with the highest information content for each class. These features have the information to express and recognize their corresponding classes. We believe similar work could be done for other statistical and information-theoretic features to make them take class information into account. With the help of the CIG, the features tending to appear in malware are selected and used to recognize malware loaders and infected executables from benign programs. The experimental results demonstrate that the malware features selected by the CIG performed much better than the global features selected by the IG for detecting infected executables.

In the feature selection stage, we take N-Grams as the candidate feature and sort all the N-Grams based on their values of CIG for each class. We select the top M N-Grams as the detecting features. The set of all the detecting features is called detecting feature set (DFS). Based on the DFS, a program is able to be expressed as a binary vector of length M (0 and 1 represent the absence and presence of a feature of DFS in a program, respectively.).

We use Support Vector Machine (SVM) as the classifier in the classification stage. The trained SVM can be used to recognize malware loaders and infected executables from benign programs.

11.2 PROBLEM STATEMENT

11.2.1 Definition of the Generalized Class

Definition 1: If a feature f appears in a class C and does not appear in any other classes, we define f as a special feature (SF) of C, and the special class (SC) of f as C.

The special class is the traditional class. The special features of C are able to recognize C. The malware signatures are the special features of the malware.

Definition 2: If a feature f tends to appear in a class C and does not appear in any other classes, we define f as a generalized feature (GF) of C, and the generalized class (GC) of f as C.

The set of the GF of C contains the set of the SF of C from Definition 2. We make use of the following example to interpret Definition 2. For example, 90 percent programs containing the function of formatting diskette are malware and the other 10 percent are benign programs. That is, the function of formatting diskette tends to appear in malware and does not appear in benign programs. According to Definition 2, this function is a GF of malware. The feature would regard a program containing this feature as malware, so it can recognize the malware containing this feature. Just like the SF of C, the GF of C has the ability to recognize C.

The class of a feature mentioned in this chapter is the GC of the feature.

11.2.2   Malware Recognition Problem

As mentioned, malware is present in two forms: malware loader and infected executable. The infected executable is the main form of malware in the wild empirically. Hence detecting infected executable becomes one of the most important tasks in the anti-malware field.

An infected executable is a combination of a benign program and a malware loader, so it theoretically would take all the features of benign programs. When the features of benign programs are used to detect infected executables, these features tend to recognize an infected executable as a benign program and make a false negative. It is easy to see that the features of benign programs are helpless, even bring misleading information, for detecting infected executables. Hence the features of benign programs are not suitable to detect malware in the wild.

In order to detect malware loaders and infected executables effectively, we take the malware detection problem as the malware recognition problem rather than the classification problem of benign programs and malware. Actually the commercial anti-malware software also regards the malware detection program as the malware recognition problem. How to select the malware features becomes the key of the malware detection problem.

Many works regarded the malware detection problem as a classification problem of benign programs and malware loaders, ignoring the form of infected executable of malware. These works made use of the statistical and information-theoretic features to select the global features that contain discriminative information for the whole classification problem. These works performed very well for classifying benign programs and malware loaders.

However, the global features in these works only contain discriminative information, ignoring the class information. The GCs of the features are unknown. The effectiveness of these methods drops down dramatically for detecting infected executables because the global features contain too many features of benign programs.

According to the IG, this chapter designs a new statistic named CIG that could select the features with the highest information content for a specific class. Furthermore, we proposed a CIG-based malware detection method. With the help of the CIG, the proposed method gets a DFS consisting of malware features. The experimental results suggest that the proposed method is an effective and universal way to detect both malware loaders and infected executables.

11.3 CLASS-WISE INFORMATION GAIN

In this section, we define and analyze a new concept of class-wise information gain (CIG, for short).

11.3.1 Definition

Information gain (IG) is one of the most widely used information-theoretic statistics to select features for various kinds of classification problems in the field of machine learning [5]. Generally, the IG is expressed as

$$IG(f) = \sum_{v_f \in \{0,1\}} \sum_{C \in \{C_i\}} P(v_f, C) \log \frac{P(v_f, C)}{P(v_f)P(C)} \tag{11.1}$$

where f is a candidate feature. v_f is the value of feature f. $v_f = 1$, if feature f occurs in a program and $v_f = 0$, otherwise. C is one of the classes, taking malware and benign program as an example. $P(v_f, C)$ is the probability that feature f in class C has the value v_f. $P(v_f)$ is the probability that feature f in the training set takes the value v_f. $P(C)$ is the probability of the training data belonging to class C.

$IG(f)$ is a metric to measure how much information content a feature f brings in. The more information content the feature f brings in, the larger $IG(f)$ is. For a classification problem, the features with the highest $IG(f)$ are desirable.

However, the IG considers all the values of feature f in all the classes, so the class information of feature f is "flooded". That is, the IG only measures the information content of the features bringing in, but ignores the classes of the features. Although we select the features with the highest $IG(f)$, we do not know which classes the features tend to belong to, that is, the GCs of the features. Hence the IG could not select the features for a specific class. In the malware detection problem, the IG could not select malware features, which is the key for detecting malware as mentioned in the previous Section.

Here, according to the IG, we define a new concept, the class-wise information gain (CIG) as

$$CIG(f, C_i) = P(v_f = 1, C_i) \log \frac{P(v_f = 1, C_i)}{P(v_f = 1)P(C_i)}$$
$$+ \sum_{C_j \in \{C_i\} \wedge i \neq j} P(v_f = 0, C_j) \log \frac{P(v_f = 0, C_j)}{P(v_f = 0)P(C_j)} \tag{11.2}$$

where $P(v_f = 1, C_i)$ denotes the probability of feature f appearing in C_i, whereas $P(v_f = 0, C_j)$ denotes the probability of feature f absenting from C_j. The other symbols are the same as used in Eq. 11.1.

There are two terms in Eq. 11.1. The first term and the second term denote the statistical information of feature f occurring in class C_i, but which is absent from other classes.

The value v_f of feature f in class C_i and C_j is related to the class of feature f by $P(v_f = 1, C_i)$ and $P(v_f = 0, C_j)$ in Eq. 11.2. Based on this relation, we obtain the CIG from the IG by importing the class information of feature f. The $CIG(f, C_i)$ selects the features tending to appear in class C_i but not occur in the other classes. According to Definition 2, these features are the GF of C_i, called the features of C_i in this chapter. Hence the $CIG(f, C_i)$ could measure the information content of feature f to recognize class C_i and select the features for a specific class.

The $CIG(f, C_i)$ measures the discrimination and class information of feature f at the same time. The more information content a feature f brings in for recognizing C_i, the larger the $CIG(f, C_i)$. With the CIG, we are able to select the features with the highest information content for each class. To some extent, the CIG could be understood as the disassembly of the IG in the perspective of the classes of the features. Hence the CIG is able to select the features with the highest information content for a specific class. It could be applied to recognition problems directly, extending the application field of the IG. What is more, the CIG allows people to balance or adjust the proportions of the features in the DFS freely, so it could replace the IG to get more stable or effective models in some classification problems.

In the malware detection problem, the formula of $CIG(f, C_i)$ could be further rewritten as:

$$CIG(f, C_B) = P(v_f = 1, C_B) log \frac{P(v_f = 1, C_B)}{P(v_f = 1)P(C_B)}$$
$$+ P(v_f = 0, C_M) log \frac{P(v_f = 0, C_M)}{P(v_f = 0)P(C_M)}$$
(11.3)

$$CIG(f, C_M) = P(v_f = 0, C_B) log \frac{P(v_f = 0, C_B)}{P(v_f = 0)P(C_B)}$$
$$+ P(v_f = 1, C_M) log \frac{P(v_f = 1, C_M)}{P(v_f = 1)P(C_M)}$$
(11.4)

where C_B and C_M denote benign program and malware, respectively.

11.3.2 Analysis

We regard Eqs. 11.3 and 11.4 as a function $CIG(f, C)$, $C \in \{C_B, C_M\}$, of two variables $P(v_f = 1, C_B)$ and $P(v_f = 1, C_M)$. Set $P(v_f = 1) = 0.5$ and $P(C_B) = 0.5$. The two functions are drawn in Fig. 11.1. Furthermore, we plot the $IG(f)$ in Fig. 11.2.

From Fig. 11.1, we found when a feature f got a larger $CIG(f, C_B)$, its $CIG(f, C_M)$ would be smaller relatively, and vice versa. In the experiments in

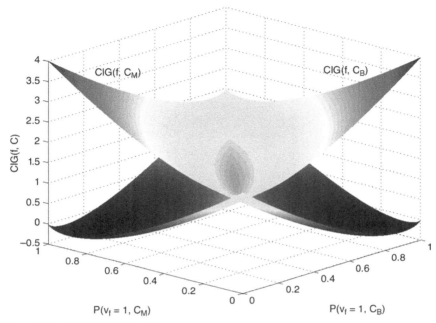

Figure 11.1   The $CIG(f, C)$ function.

Section 8.3.4, we would show there is not even one same feature in the top 1000 features selected by the $CIG(f, C_B)$ with those selected by the $CIG(f, C_M)$. Furthermore, different from the intervals of the $IG(f)$, the $CIG(f, C)$ could be less than 0 which means feature f brings harmful information to recognize class C.

The $IG(f)$ is equivalent to $CIG(f, C_B) + CIG(f, C_M)$ in the malware detection problem. Although the IG is very effective to select the global features with the highest information content for a classification problem, it does not have the ability to express "the information content of a feature f brings in when to recognize a class C" Figures 11.1 and 11.2 illustrate that the features with the highest $IG(f)$ may have good $CIG(f, C_B)$ with bad $CIG(f, C_M)$, or bad $CIG(f, C_B)$ with good $CIG(f, C_M)$. The distribution of the features with good $CIG(f, C_B)$ and good $CIG(f, C_M)$ selected by the IG depends on a specific dataset and is out of the researchers' control. For example, the distribution of the features of benign programs and malware in the DFS selected by the IG is up to a training set.

To recognize a specific class C, what we need are the features of C. Nevertheless, to classify two classes, the features that could discriminate the two classes are desirable. In this situation, the classes of these features are ignored. These features may come from one class or both classes. In order to get a more stable model, the proportions of the features of the two classes should be balanced in most cases. However, the constitution of the features in the DFS selected by the IG is up to a specific training dataset based on the previous analysis. The CIG proposed in this chapter, extending from the IG, allows people to pay more attention to a specific

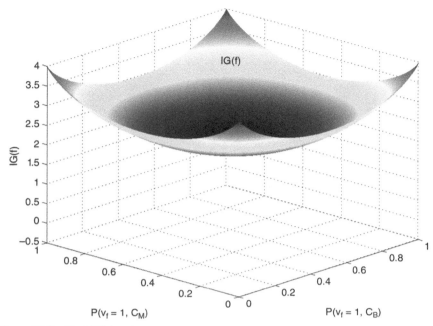

Figure 11.2 The $IG(f)$ function.

class and select the features for each class to balance or adjust the proportions of the features in the DFS freely.

In our study, we found the features tending to appear in benign programs, that is, the GFs of benign programs, usually had larger $IG(f)$ than the features tending to appear in malware, that is, the GFs of malware. Because the benign programs use more general instructions, the distribution of the features in the benign programs is more centralized. Intuitively, the features of benign programs are more remarkable than the malware features and bring much more information content to the classification problem of benign programs and malware. Hence the IG usually selects the GFs of benign programs. This deduction will be proved by the experimental results in Section 11.8. As we know, an infected executable is a combination of a benign program and a malware loader. The features of benign programs would make an infected executable be a benign program rather than a malware because it has all the features of benign programs. A false negative is made in this situation. Hence the features of benign programs would bring no information, even misleading information, to detect infected executables. The IG cannot select the features for a specific class, while the CIG proposed in this chapter solves this problem.

The CIG could be computed based on two kinds of statistics: (1) document frequency and (2) feature frequency.

Document frequency is widely used in many fields, for example, text categorization. Here the document frequency of feature f in class C is the number of files in class C containing feature f. In the document frequency based class-wise

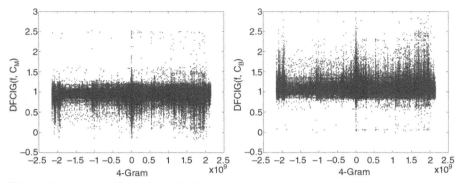

Figure 11.3   The distribution of $DFCIG(f, C)$ of 4-Grams.

information gain (DFCIG), $P(v_f)$ is the probability of the files in which feature f takes the value v_f, and $P(v_f, C)$ is the probability of the files in class C in which feature f takes the value v_f.

The feature frequency of feature f in class C is the occurrence number of feature f in all the files in class C. In this context, $P(v_f)$ is the probability of the number of feature f taking the value v_f to the number of features in the training set. And $P(v_f, C)$ is the probability of the number of feature f taking the value v_f in class C to the number of features in class C. We denote the feature frequency based class-wise information gain as FFCIG.

We plotted the distribution of the DFCIG and FFCIG of 4-Grams in the training set used in Section 11.6 in Figs. 11.3 and 11.4, respectively. Figures 11.3 and 11.4 illustrate that the distribution of DFCIG of 4-Grams is discrete, which is helpful to select better 4-Grams, whereas FFCIG of 4-Grams stays together, which is detrimental to the feature selection process. In order to select features with higher CIG, we prefer DFCIG to FFCIG based on their distributions.

In addition, the distribution of the IG of 4-Grams in the training set used in Section 11.6 is also shown in Fig. 11.5. It is regarded as the combination of every N-Gram in Fig. 11.3(a) and (b). The top M features in Fig. 11.5 are mixed up by a part of top M features in Fig. 11.3(a), a part of top M features in Fig. 11.3(b), and

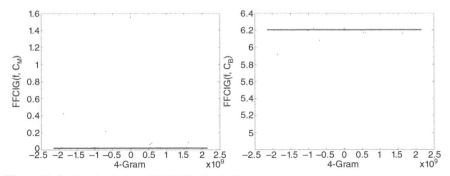

Figure 11.4   The distribution of $FFCIG(f, C)$ of 4-Grams.

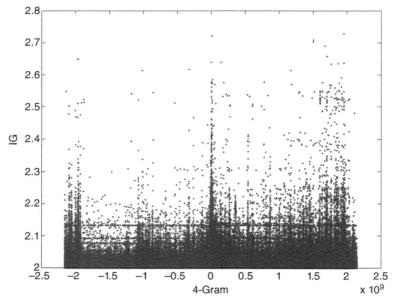

Figure 11.5   The distribution of IG of 4-Grams.

other features. The experimental results demonstrate the top 1000 4-Grams of malware are completely different from the top 1000 4-Grams of benign program.

    In the rest of this chapter, we make use of IG-A, DFCIG-B, and DFCIG-M, respectively, to denote the top M features selected using $IG(f)$, $DFCIG(f, C_B)$ and $DFCIG(f, C_M)$. The features in the DFCIG-B and DFCIG-M tend to be features of benign programs and malware, respectively, referred to as the features of benign programs and malware, individually.

11.4   CIG-BASED MALWARE DETECTION METHOD

The CIG-based malware detection method involves two modules: (1) feature selection module and (2) classification module.

11.4.1   Feature Selection Module

In this chapter, a gram is defined as a binary string of length L. Here we set $L = 8$, that is, one byte, because the smallest unit of an instruction in the Intel Architecture-32 bit set (IA-32) is one byte. N-Gram means N-continuous grams. Here a N-Gram is a binary string of length N bytes. The number of N-Grams in its feature space is $(2^8)^N$. We take N-Grams as the candidate features that are the basis of feature selection.

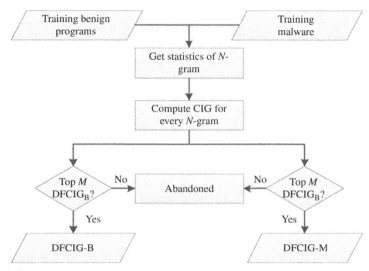

Figure 11.6 The flow chart of the feature selection module.

An N-Gram is saved as a three-dimensional vector $\langle$content, $DFCIG_B$, $DFCIG_M\rangle$. The field "content" keeps the string of the N-Gram. And the field "$DFCIG_B$" and "$DFCIG_M$" keep the values of the $DFCIG(f, C_B)$ and $DFCIG(f, C_M)$, respectively.

The flow chart of the feature selection module is shown in Fig. 11.6. First, the document frequency of every N-Gram is counted by traversing benign programs and malware in the training set using a sliding window. The size of the sliding window is set to N bytes. The content in a sliding window is an N-Gram. The sliding window moves forward one byte at a time. The adjacent two N-Grams have an overlap of $N - 1$ bytes. With the help of the overlap, N-Gram is able to capture not only strings of length N bytes, but also longer strings implicitly. We count how many benign programs an N-Gram appears in, so the same procedure is used for malware.

Second, we compute the $DFCIG_B$ and $DFCIG_M$ for every N-Gram gathered from the training set using Eqs. 11.3 and 11.4, respectively. Until now, all the information of the whole N-Grams has been obtained.

Finally, the top M N-Grams with the highest $DFCIG_B$ are selected to make up the DFCIG-B. The N-Grams in this set are supposed to be the features of benign programs. After sorting the N-Grams by $DFCIG_M$ in descending order, the top M N-Grams with the highest $DFCIG_M$ are selected as DFCIG-M, which is the set of the malware features. The DFCIG-B and DFCIG-M will be used to map a program into a binary vector of length M based on the presence and absence of the features in the two sets.

It is necessary to mention that the DFCIG-B is brought in just for comparisons. What we would use here is only the DFCIG-M. We will show that the features in the DFCIG-B are helpless for detecting infected executables. The

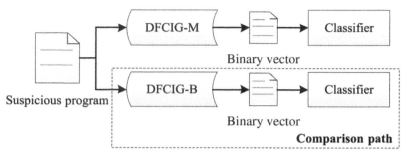

Figure 11.7   The flow chart of the classification module.

accuracy of the DFCIG-B-based classifier is almost equal to random classification for detecting infected executables, while it is fairly good for detecting malware loaders.

11.4.2 Classification Module

The classification module accomplishes the classification on the basis of the DFCIG-M and DFCIG-B. The flow chart is given in Fig. 11.7.

There are two paths for every suspicious program. The first one is mapping the program by the DFCIG-M, which would be used in the real world. The other one makes use of the DFCIG-B for the purpose of making a comparison with the first path.

A suspicious program is expressed as a binary vector of length M that consists of 0s for absence of the features in the DFS, and 1s for presence of the features in the DFS. A classifier is trained to detect the suspicious programs.

The support vector machine (SVM) is chosen as the classifier in this chapter. Other classifiers, such as instance-based learner, naive Bayes, decision tree, and boosted classifiers, could be also used. Here we utilize the libSVM [6] on the platform of Matlab 2010a.

11.5 DATASET

This section describes the datasets used in this chapter that are available online at http://www.cil.pku.edu.cn/resources/.

11.5.1 Benign Program Dataset

The benign program dataset consists of portable executable (PE) system files from Windows XP and PE files from a series of applications. These files cover PE files of mainstream operating systems and applications and are the main punching bag of malware. The detailed information of the dataset is listed in Table 11.1.

Table 11.1 Benign Program Dataset*

Filetype	Quantity	Avg. size	Min. size	Max. size
PE	1458	126.2	16	993

*Note that the unit of Avg. Size and Max. Size is KB and the unit of Min. Size is Byte. The units are also applicable for the tables in the rest of the chapter.

11.5.2 Malware Dataset

We conducted our experiments on three malware datasets are available online at http://www.cil.pku.edu.cn/resources/.

11.5.2.1 VXHeavens Dataset

The VXHeavens dataset is a famous dataset in the anti-malware field that can be downloaded from http://vx.netlux.org. Many researchers estimated their methods based on this dataset.

In this chapter, we focus on the malware in PE format of Win32. The VXHeavens dataset used here contains 7128 malware, detailed information about the dataset is given in Table 11.2.

11.5.2.2 Henchiri Dataset

The Henchiri dataset consists of 2994 malware. Henchiri made use of this dataset in his previous work [7]. The detailed information about this dataset is given in Table 11.3.

11.5.2.3 CILPKU08 Dataset

The CILPKU08 dataset was collected by our CIL laboratory at Peking University (PKU) in 2008 [8,9]. There are 3547 malware in this dataset whose details are listed in Table 11.4.

Table 11.2 VXHeavens Dataset

Filetype	Quantity	Avg. size	Min. size	Max. size
Backdoor	2200	48	3500	9227
Constructor	172	392.9	5060	2391
Trojan	2350	147.7	215	3800
Virus	1048	71.1	1500	1278
Worm	351	199.3	394	11899
Others	1007	151.4	1090	3087

Table 11.3   Henchiri Dataset

Filetype	Quantity	Avg. size	Min. size	Max. size
Virus	2880	6.2	22	93.4
Trojan	88	9.4	49	72.5
Constructor	6	10	528	33.6
Other	20	11.6	456	88.5

Table 11.4   CILPKU08 Dataset

Filetype	Quantity	Avg. size	Min. size	Max. size
Virus	3465	4.8	23	59.5
Trojan	39	4.4	49	5.93
Other	43	6.8	48	31.2

11.6   SELECTION OF PARAMETERS

We selected the two parameters in the proposed CIG-based malware detection method—the length of N-Gram (N) and the number of the features in the DFS (M).

11.6.1   Experimental Setup

The dataset used here consists of 1048 benign programs, randomly selected from the benign program dataset, and 1048 computer viruses from VXHeavens dataset. We randomly split the benign programs into two sets with 524 programs for each set, one for training and the other for testing. The same partition was done to the viruses. The 524 benign programs and 524 viruses made up test set 1 (referred to as T_1). We let the computer viruses in the T_1 infect all the benign programs in the T_1. In this way, we got 524*524 = 274576 infected executables. The infected executables and the benign programs in the T_1 made up test set 2 (written as T_2). Hence the T_1 includes benign programs and malware loaders, whereas the T_2 includes benign programs and infected executables. All the experiments in this section were taken on this dataset. In the rest of the chapter, all the experiments include two test sets: T_1 and T_2. All the T_2 are generated from the T_1 in the same way. "In the wild" in the title means the infected executables are the main form of malware in the wild and all of them used in this chapters are not preprocessed.

In this chapter, we make use of the area under the receiver operating characteristic curve (AUC) to measure the effectiveness of the proposed method. The AUC is widely used to compare classification capability of different algorithms in data mining.

The parameters of SVM was set as: $g = 0.125, c = 4$. We did not attempt to optimize the parameters of SVM because it was not the focus of the proposed method.

The method using IG-A was used for a comparison [10,11].

11.6.2 Experiments of Selection of Parameter

Optimizing two parameters at the same time is time consuming. Here we optimized the parameters by traversing the whole combinations of N and M. We set $N = 2, 3, 4$ and $M = 100, 200, \ldots, 1000$. We did not try a larger N because we knew that the space of N-Grams is exponential with respect to the value of N: $(2^8)^N$. For example, the space of 5-Grams is $2^{40} = 1TB$. A one-MB program contains 2^{10} 5-Grams at most when every 5-Gram in it is different from the others. When we tried to map the program into the 5-Gram space, we found the grams contained in the program were comparatively sparse to the space of 5-Grams. Furthermore, when N is set to a larger value, an N-Gram turns out to be special. However, what we want are general grams that could cover as much space as possible with larger information content. Based on the above reasons, we just set N in the interval [2,4]. In addition, Kolter and Maloof also set $N = 4$ [10,11].

From the experimental results shown in Figs. 11.8–11.10, we set $N = 4$ and $M = 400$ as the optimal parameters. From the perspective of M, the influence of M

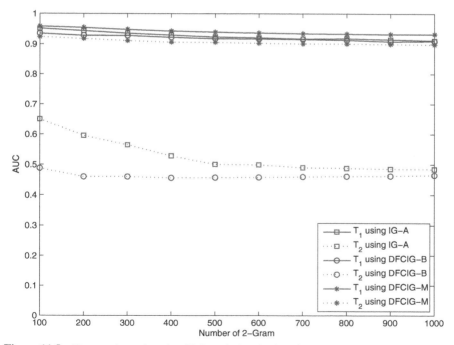

Figure 11.8 The experimental results of 2-Gram in the selection of parameter.

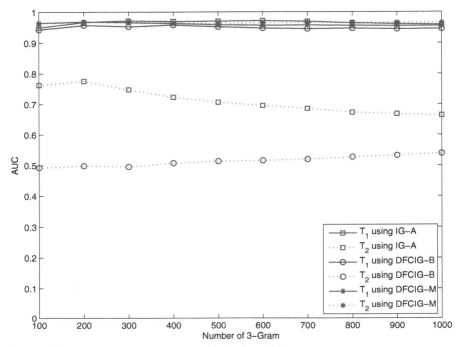

Figure 11.9 The experimental results of 3-Gram in the selection of parameter.

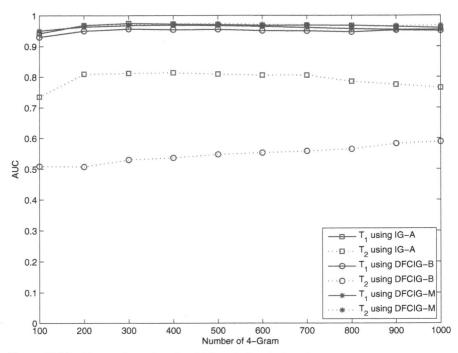

Figure 11.10 The experimental results of 4-Gram in the selection of parameter.

to the results was not significant regardless of the values of N. Considering the different values of N, the effectiveness of the method with $N = 4$ outperformed that when N had other values.

The methods using IG-A and DFCIG-B both give excellent AUCs on the T_1, whereas very bad AUCs on the T_2. However, the method using DFCIG-M obtains excellent AUCs on both the T_1 and T_2. Section 8.3.4 showed the similar results. The detailed analysis and discussion will be given in Section 11.8.

11.7 EXPERIMENTAL RESULTS

We conducted three series of experiments on three malware datasets to evaluate the effectiveness and stability of the proposed method through five-fold cross validation. With the standard error, we computed 95 percent confidence intervals. The parameters of the SVM are the same as used in the previous Section.

11.7.1 Experiments on the VXHeavens Dataset

There are six categories of malware in the VXHeavens dataset. We trained six different models, one model for one category. Taking computer virus as an example, we split the benign program dataset and computer viruses in the VXHeavens dataset randomly into five folds without any overlapping sample for each fold. Then one fold was taken as the test set and the others were taken as the training set. We iterated the process five times until every fold had been taken as a test set. In this way, the effectiveness of the proposed CIG-based malware detection method was evaluated. The 95 percent confidence intervals were computed to look into the stability of the proposed method.

The experimental results of the methods using IG-A, DFCIG-B, and DFCIG-M on the VXHeavens dataset were given in detail, respectively, in Tables 11.5–11.7. The results jn bold indicate the optimal AUCs for a specific category in the three methods.

Table 11.5 shows that the method using IG-A performed fairly well on the T_1 and dropped down dramatically on the T_2, just like its performance in Section 11.6. The AUC of the method using IG-A on the T_2 is about 0.75 on

Table 11.5 Experimental Results of the Method Using IG-A

Filetype	T_1	T_2
Backdoor	0.9792 ± 0.002875	0.5335 ± 0.005042
Constructor	0.9794 ± 0.015314	0.9098 ± 0.019567
Miscellaneous	$\mathbf{0.9675 \pm 0.007014}$	0.7821 ± 0.013041
Trojan	$\mathbf{0.9642 \pm 0.005419}$	0.7007 ± 0.051600
Virus	0.9770 ± 0.004388	0.8292 ± 0.013479
Worm	$\mathbf{0.9708 \pm 0.006474}$	0.7706 ± 0.008077

Table 11.6 Experimental Results of the Method Using DFCIG-B

Filetype	T_1	T_2
Backdoor	**0.9810 ± 0.001373**	0.5052 ± 0.001869
Constructor	0.9614 ± 0.014976	0.5554 ± 0.008020
Miscellaneous	0.9587 ± 0.005232	0.5885 ± 0.004380
Trojan	0.9600 ± 0.004146	0.5479 ± 0.007324
Virus	0.9746 ± 0.005017	0.5773 ± 0.006360
Worm	0.9611 ± 0.012944	0.5834 ± 0.009375

Table 11.7 Experimental Results of the Method Using DFCIG-M

Filetype	T_1	T_2
Backdoor	0.9669 ± 0.008422	**0.9601 ± 0.009563**
Constructor	**0.9818 ± 0.014519**	**0.9505 ± 0.008022**
Miscellaneous	0.9655 ± 0.006652	**0.9396 ± 0.007764**
Trojan	0.9506 ± 0.006956	**0.9328 ± 0.008120**
Virus	**0.9793 ± 0.004567**	**0.9747 ± 0.007739**
Worm	0.9689 ± 0.005599	**0.9192 ± 0.015026**

average which is lower than the AUC on the T_1 for about 0.22. Although the method using IG-A performed terribly on the T_2, it is still better than the random classification. This is because the IG-A consists of the features of both benign programs and malware. The detailed constituent of the IG-A will be described in Section 11.8.

The performance of the method using DFCIG-B on the T_1 is almost as good as the performance of the method using IG-A from Table 11.6. However, when we applied DFCIG-B to detect infected executables, the AUC dropped down sharply to 0.55 on average, which is nearly equivalent to the random classification. The phenomenon is consistent with that in Section 11.6. It is very clear that the DFCIG-B is helpless to classify benign programs and infected executables, although it is effective to classify benign programs and malware loaders. From these results, we believe that the features in the DFCIG-B are the features of benign programs.

The results in Table 11.7 demonstrate that the method using DFCIG-M is able to detect malware loaders and infected executables effectively. The results on the T_2, $AUC = 0.95$ are almost equivalent to the results on the T_1, $AUC = 0.97$, on average. The method using DFCIG-M achieved excellent AUCs on both the T_1 and T_2 because DFCIG-M has the ability to recognize malware. As we know, the malware features are able to recognize malware, including malware loaders and infected executables. They are the effective features to detect malware. The results proved the features in the DFCIG-M are malware features. For the performance reduction on the T_2 compared to the T_1, the reason is likely that the difficulty of detecting infected executables is larger than that of detecting malware loaders. In fact, an infected executable is a latent form of a malware loader that would help itself escape from the anti-malware scanner.

The results of the methods using IG-A, DFCIG-B, and DFCIG-M on the T_1 were basically equivalent to each other, whereas the results on the T_2 were significantly different. On the T_2, the results of the method using IG-A ($AUC = 0.75$ on average) is much better than the results of the method using DFCIG-B ($AUC = 0.55$ on average), but worse than those of the method using DFCIG-M ($AUC = 0.95$ on average) definitely. The reason is the classes of the features in the DFS. The features in the DFCIG-B are the features of benign programs that are helpless to discriminate infected executables from benign programs. The features in the DFCIG-M are malware features, which are able to recognize malware effectively. Because the IG ignored the class information of the features naturally, the features in the IG-A are mixtures of the features of benign programs and malware. Based on this analysis, the features in DFCIG-M are the most suitable and helpful features to detect and recognize malware, regardless of the form of malware. The CIG selected the features with the highest information content for a specific class successfully.

The 95 percent confidence intervals of all the methods were relatively small (see Tables 11.5–11.7). They suggested that the results of these methods were very stable and believable.

11.7.2 Experiments on the Henchiri Dataset

We applied the proposed method to the Henchiri dataset to verify its effectiveness and stability. The experimental results on this dataset positively proved the theory of the CIG and the effectiveness of the proposed method once again.

The Henchiri dataset is mainly composed of computer viruses. The number of the files in other categories of malware in the Henchiri dataset is too small to train and evaluate the proposed method. What we did here was merely mix these files into the computer viruses. In this way, the whole dataset, including 2994 malware, was used in the five-fold cross validation. The same process had been done to the CILPKU08 dataset.

The experimental results of the methods using IG-A, DFCIG-B, and DFCIG-M on the T_1 and T_2 are shown in Fig. 11.11(a) and (b), respectively. Figure 11.11(a) illustrates that all the methods using IG-A, DFCIG-B, and DFCIG-M performed excellently without significant differences on the T_1 of the Henchiri dataset. However, the ROC curves of the methods using IG-A and DFCIG-B both are almost a diagonal shown in Fig. 11.11(b) on the T_2 of Henchiri dataset. That is to say, the methods using IG-A and DFCIG-B are equivalent to random classification for detecting infected executables. Not to our surprise, the performance of the method using DFCIG-M on the T_2 is as good as that on the T_1. The malware features are very stable to detect malware.

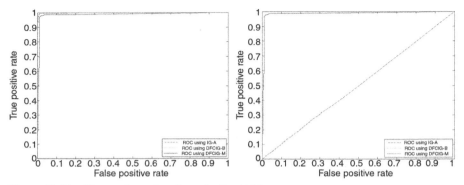

Figure 11.11   The experimental results on the Henchiri dataset.

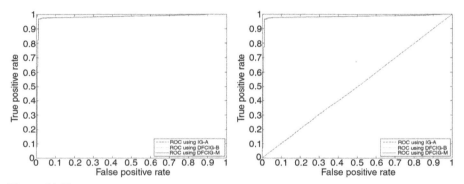

Figure 11.12   The experimental results on the CILPKU08 dataset.

11.7.3   Experiments on the CILPKU08 Dataset

One more experiment was conducted on the CILPKU08 dataset. The experimental results on the T_1 and T_2 of the CILPKU08 dataset are shown in Fig. 11.12(a) and (b), respectively.

The results here on both the T_1 and T_2 are similar to the results on the Henchiri dataset. The methods using IG-A and DFCIG-B performed very well on the T_1 and comparably terrible on the T_2. However, the method using DFCIG-M performed excellently on the T_1 and T_2. From the experimental results on the CILPKU08 dataset, we believe that the CIG has selected the features of benign programs and malware, respectively.

11.8   DISCUSSION

The experimental results suggest that the CIG is able to select the features for a specific class (e.g., DFCIG-M), and the proposed CIG-based malware detection method is an effective and universal way to detect both malware loaders and infected executables. Although the features of benign programs (i.e., DFCIG-B) are able to discriminate benign programs from malware loaders, they are useless in detecting infected executables and recognizing malware.

To obtain malware features (i.e., DFCIG-M), we just need to process the candidate features appearing in malware instead of all the features appearing in the training set. In this way, the memory requirement of the proposed method is brought down dramatically to about 60 percent empirically, comparing to the IG-based methods.

11.8.1   The Relationship Among IG-A, DFCIG-B, and DFCIG-M

Table 11.8 shows the statistics of the relationship among IG-A, DFCIG-B, and DFCIG-M in the experiments discussed in Section 8.3.4. The symbols in Table 11.8 are defined as

$$
\begin{aligned}
R_1 &= \frac{|DFCIG - B \cap IG - A|}{|IG - A|} \\
R_2 &= \frac{|DFCIG - M \cap IG - A|}{|IG - A|} \\
R_3 &= \frac{|DFCIG - B \cap DFCIG - M|}{|IG - A|}
\end{aligned}
\tag{11.5}
$$

The top six lines in the table come from the experiments on the VXHeavens dataset and the last two lines come from the experiments on the Henchiri dataset and CIL-PKU08 dataset, respectively.

Table 11.8 illustrates that the DFCIG-B is completely different from the DFCIG-M. Compared to the experimental results in Section 8.3.4, the AUCs of the method using DFCIG-B are practically equal to 0.5 for detecting infected executables, which means random classification. The results suggest that the features in the DFCIG-B are helpless to detect infected executables. However, the AUCs of the

Table 11.8   The Relationship Among IG-A, DFCIG-B, and DFCIG-M

Data source	R_1	R_2	R_2
Backdoor	93.15%	0.00%	0.00%
Constructor	44.65%	20.85%	0.00%
Miscellaneous	55.80%	34.05%	0.00%
Trojan	54.20%	27.95%	0.00%
Virus	74.00%	16.35%	0.00%
Worm	67.25%	13.85%	0.00%
Henchiri	93.15%	0.00%	0.00%
CILPKU08	95.85%	0.00%	0.00%

method using DFCIG-B are pretty good for detecting malware loaders. The phenomenon proves the features in the DFCIG-B are just the features of benign programs.

From this analysis, we believe that the features in the DFCIG-M are malware features. The experimental results in Section 8.3.4 prove this deduction. The AUCs of the method using DFCIG-M for detecting infected executables do not have the significant differences of those in detecting malware loaders. Furthermore, the experimental results of the method using DFCIG-M are as good as that of the method using IG-A in detecting malware loaders.

From Table 11.8, we can see that the IG-A is a mixture of a part of the DFCIG-B, a part of the DFCIG-M, and other N-Grams. The distribution of the features in the IG-A depends on a specific dataset. In these experiments, more than 44 percent of the features in the IG-A are in the DFCIG-B, which is made up of the features of benign programs, and the percentage of the malware features in the IG-A is less than 35 percent. This result definitely proves the deduction "The features of benign programs usually had larger $IG(f)$" in Section 11.3 and the guess of the discussion by Reddy and Pujari [12]. The malware features in the IG-A are the key to make the AUCs of the method using IG-A get a greater value than 0.5 for detecting infected executables. However, the features of benign programs in the IG-A tend to recognize the infected executables as benign programs and bring down the AUCs on the T_2 dramatically. That is to say, the composition of the IG-A results in the decrease of the AUCs of the method using IG-A on the T_2. The essential reason is that the IG cannot choose malware features, whereas the CIG in this chapter can do it primely.

11.8.2   Space Complexity

From the analysis in Section 11.8.1, it is easy to see that the features in the DFCIG-M are the critical features to detect malware, including malware loaders and infected executables. We believe that the features in the DFCIG-M are malware features, which should appear in malware at least once. Hence we just need to handle the features appearing in malware and ignore the features that merely occur in benign programs in order to select the features in the DFCIG-M. As we know, the memory requirement of this kind of method mainly comes from keeping a huge number of N-Grams in memory. If we only handle the features appearing in malware, the memory utilized by plenty of features that just appear in benign programs could be cut down. The space complexity of the proposed method would drop down sharply. The proportions of 4-Grams in the experiments in Section 8.3.4 are given in Table 11.9. The symbols in Table 11.9 are defined as

$$R_4 = \frac{|N_B|}{|N_B \cup N_M|}$$

$$R_5 = \frac{|N_M|}{|N_B \cup N_M|} \tag{11.6}$$

$$R_6 = \frac{|N_B \cap N_M|}{|N_B \cup N_M|}$$

Table 11.9 The Proportion of 4-Gram in the Experiments

Data source	R_4	R_5	R_6
Backdoor	47.60%	55.65%	3.25%
Constructor	58.37%	44.61%	2.97%
Miscellaneous	50.60%	54.50%	5.10%
Trojan	43.58%	67.76%	11.35%
Virus	73.35%	32.95%	6.30%
Worm	56.61%	47.19%	3.80%
Henchiri	94.20%	6.69%	0.89%
CILPKU08	96.59%	4.07%	0.66%

where N_B and N_M denote the sets of N-Grams appearing in benign programs and malware, respectively. And the $|N_B|$ and $|N_M|$, respectively, are the numbers of N-Grams in the two sets.

From Table 11.9, the proportions of 4-Grams appearing in both benign programs and malware, expressed by R_6, are lower than 12 percent. It means the intersection set of the 4-Grams appearing in benign programs and malware is comparatively small. Based on this fact, we can save lots of memory by processing the features appearing in malware instead of the features in the training set.

Theoretically, if we just consider the N-Grams appearing in malware, $|N_B - N_M|$ N-Grams are not needed to be analyzed anymore. The percentage of the memory saved is $|N_B - N_M|/(|N_B \cup N_M|)$. In this way, the memory requirement of the proposed method is less than that of the IG-based methods by about 60 percent.

11.9 SUMMARY

This chapter proposed the concept of the Class-Wise Information Gain (CIG) which is able to select the features with the highest information content for a specific class. Then a novel CIG-based malware detection method was presented to detect malware loaders and infected executables. Furthermore, it is also obvious that the features of benign programs are helpless to detect infected executable, so they are not suitable to detect malware.

It was demonstrated that the proposed CIG-based malware detection method is an effective and universal way to detect malware loaders and infected executables. Compared to the IG-based methods, the effectiveness of the proposed method has a big increase in detecting infected executables, nearly 20 percent, without a decrease in detecting malware loaders. The memory requirement of the proposed method is just about 60 percent less than that of the IG-based methods.

REFERENCES

1. Wikipedia. URL http://en.wikipedia.org/wiki/Malware.
2. F-Secure Corporation, (2007), F-secure reports amount of malware grew by 100% during 2007, Press release (2007).
3. Forrest, S., Perelson, A., Allen, L., and Cherukuri, R. (1994) Self-nonself discrimination in a computer, in Research in Security and Privacy, 1994. Proceedings., 1994 IEEE Computer Society Symposium on, IEEE, pp. 202–212.
4. Forrest, S., Hofmeyr, S., Somayaji, A., and Longstaff, T. (1996) A sense of self for unix processes, in Security and Privacy, 1996. Proceedings., 1996 IEEE Symposium on, IEEE, pp. 120–128.
5. Yang, Y. and Pedersen, J. (1997) A comparative study on feature selection in text categorization. International conference on machine learning, pp. 412–420.
6. Chang, C.C. and Lin, C.J. (2011) Libsvm: A library for support vector machines. *ACM Transactions on Intelligent Systems and Technology (TIST)*, **2** (3), 27.
7. Henchiri, O. and Japkowicz, N. (2006) A feature selection and evaluation scheme for computer virus detection, in Data Mining, 2006. ICDM'06. Sixth International Conference on, IEEE, pp. 891–895.
8. Wang, W., Zhang, P., Tan, Y., and He, X. (2009) A hierarchical artificial immune model for virus detection, in Computational Intelligence and Security, 2009. CIS'09. International Conference on, IEEE, vol. 1, pp. 1–5.
9. Zhang, P., Wang, W., and Tan, Y. (2010) A malware detection model based on a negative selection algorithm with penalty factor. *Science China Information Sciences*, **53** (12), 2461–2471.
10. Kolter, J.Z. and Maloof, M.A. (2004) Learning to detect malicious executables in the wild, in Proceedings of the Tenth ACM SIGKDD International Conference on Knowledge Discovery and Data Mining, KDD '04, pp. 470–478.
11. Kolter, J. and Maloof, M. (2006) Learning to detect and classify malicious executables in the wild. *Journal of Machine Learning Research*, **7**, 2721–2744.
12. Reddy, D.K.S. and Pujari, A.K. (2006) N-gram analysis for computer virus detection. *Journal in Computer Virology*, **2** (3), 231–239.

Index

adaptive immune system, 2, 136
adaptive immunity, 2, 34
affinity vector, 35, 66–69
AIS, 5–7
anomaly detection, 5, 9, 12, 47, 53
antibody, 5, 6, 9, 12, 47, 66, 68, 137
antigen presenting cell, 12, 14, 138
antigen-nonspecific feature vector, 139
antigen-specific feature vector, 139
antigens, 2, 4–7, 9, 11, 14, 27, 33, 47,
    66–68, 138, 142
anti-malware, 26, 27, 29, 30, 32, 35, 119,
    152, 161, 167
application programming interface, 27, 150
artificial immune network, 7, 11, 14
artificial immune system, 5, 26, 58, 65
assembly codes, 30, 101

backdoors, 27, 98, 106, 122, 131, 143, 150
B cells, 3, 7, 9, 12, 14, 20, 136–138
benign, 51
benign program, 28, 31, 34, 37–40,
    86–95, 98, 104, 112, 120, 125, 131,
    142–144, 150–156, 158, 160–162,
    166, 170
benign program malware-like signature
    library, 87
binary code sequence, 48
biological immune system, 2–5, 14, 27, 57,
    58, 136
BP neural network, 51
byte-level file content, 32, 110

cells, 1–5, 7, 9, 10–12, 14, 15, 20, 39, 47,
    58, 66, 136–138
cellular immunity, 3, 136–138
chemical molecules, 14

CILPKU08 dataset, 40, 41, 93, 97, 122,
    161–162, 168
classification, 32, 38, 40, 53, 76, 80, 87, 117,
    118, 120, 129–132, 140–142, 145, 148,
    150–153
classifiers, 27, 65, 69
class tendency, 102–103
class-wise information gain, 150–171
clonal selection, 66–67
clonal selection algorithm, 9–10
computer security, 6, 7
continuous matching, 78, 79
control engineering, 21
cross validation, 94–96

danger feature, 101–108, 136, 137, 139
danger theory, 11–12, 18, 34
data analysis, 21–22
the data fragment set, 66
detecting feature set, 151
detection time, 108
detector library, 111–112
detector set, 5, 7–9, 58, 65
disassembled code, 31
DNA, 76, 78
dynamic techniques, 27, 30–31

false positive rates, 26, 32
feature, 105
feature extraction, 148
feature selection, 158–160
feature vector, 114–122
frequent patterns, 32

gene, 76
genetic algorithm, 59
growth algorithm, 59

Artificial Immune System: Applications in Computer Security, First Edition. Ying Tan.
© 2016 the IEEE Computer Society. Published 2016 by John Wiley & Sons, Inc.